A Perfect Injustice

A Perfect Injustice

Injustice

Genocide and Theft of Armenian Wealth

Hrayr S. Karagueuzian
and Yair Auron

Routledge
Taylor & Francis Group

LONDON AND NEW YORK

First published 2009 by Transaction Publishers

2 Park Square, Milton Park, Abingdon, Oxfordshire OX14 4RN
711 Third Avenue, New York, NY 10017

Routledge is an imprint of the Taylor & Francis Group, an informa business

First issued in paperback 2017

Library of Congress Catalog Number: 2009018496

Library of Congress Cataloging-in-Publication Data

Karagueuzian, Hrayr S.
   A perfect injustice : genocide and theft of Armenian wealth / Hrayr S.
   Karagueuzian and Yair Auron.
      p. cm.
   Includes bibliographical references and index.
   ISBN 978-1-4128-1001-2 (alk. paper)
      1. Armenian massacres, 1915-1923--Economic aspects. 2. Armenians-
   -Turkey--Claims. 3. Life insurance claims. 4. Life insurance policies. I.
   Auron, Yair. II. Title.

DS195.5.K298 2009
956.6'20154--dc22

                                                                2009018496

ISBN 13: 978-1-4128-1001-2 (hbk)
ISBN 13: 978-1-138-50727-2 (pbk)

Contents

Illustrations appear between pages 72 and 73

Introduction

In November 1916, Aaron Aaronsohn, the leader of the "Nili Group," sent two reports to the British War Office. The Nili Group, a pro-British Jewish spy organization in Palestine composed mostly of young, locally born children of Jewish colonists, which numbered no more than forty active members at any time, operated during the First World War. The group identified empathetically with the then ongoing tragedy of the Armenians, a calamity that influenced their activities. The two documents, both written by Aaronsohn himself, dealt with the massacres of Armenians by the Turks.[1] Aaronsohn's reports, which were transmitted by the British War Office to the Foreign Office and to the British intelligence services, were also sent to the British Military Command in Cairo. They were highly regarded by the British authorities.

According to his diary, Aaronsohn had been asked to write a report to the War Office "about the acts of brutality against the Armenians."[2] He gave the first report the title "Pro-Armenia," which testifies to its character. It is not only a comprehensive intelligence report of twenty pages, which presents facts and details, but also, and perhaps primarily, a personal statement, humane and moral, from the vantage point of a Jewish observer. Aaronsohn's spirit and personality infuse the report.

The second report dealt mainly with two topics: the severe damage to the faltering Ottoman Empire following the Armenian massacre, and the theft of Armenian property by the Turks. The Turks were not well versed in the economic or agriculture management, or in organizing the country's civil service without the Armenians, who had provided the brains and hands for the Turkish government. There was also the organized theft of Armenian property and its distribution to influential Ittihadist Turkish leaders without any compensation to the Armenians. This was termed "internal colonization." According to Aaronsohn, this theft was implemented by the Turks but had first been proposed by the Germans, and it replicated the latter's recent "internal colonization" in Posnan, which was intended to block the Polish advance. Aaronsohn remarks that information about the Turkish actions initially reached the outside world despite censorship of the German press by the German and Turkish authorities, but was later successfully blocked.

Aaronsohn is extremely critical of the Germans, and his comments on the German mentality arouse wonder today: "The Armenian question was a safe question to tackle with official Germans and the writer failed on no occasion to start on it, so he had the opportunity to have the minds of hundred stories [*sic*] proving the cruelty of the Turks, the useless and shameless barbarity, and so on."[3] Aaronsohn was also shocked by the Germans' exploitation of the Armenians' distress:

> Every clean-minded man would shrink at the idea of making any profit from a situation like that the Armenians were in. Not so the Germans. They made bargains. It would be unfair to say they robbed the Armenians, but these poor souls being compelled to consideration – the Germans took advantage of conditions and bought carpets, jewelry, trinkets at a tenth part of their real value. Germany will be the richest country in carpets....
>
> The wholesale massacre of the Jews ordered by the Roman general Titus is the only record in history to be paralleled with the wholesale massacre of the Armenians. And now just as then, here just like there, it was a government scheme....
>
> The full and entire responsibility of the Turkish Government – whatever and whoever it be – in these massacres makes no doubt. The massacres were planned out by the Central Government in Constantinople and it is only for that reason that it was possible to carry them out on such a large scale, with such simultaneousness, perseverance and method....
>
> Even in these days of fierce battles the tremendous numbers of innocent people killed and destroyed call out attention. Morally and economically the Armenian people in Turkey is totally ruined – although a few private fortunes were, by clean or unclean ways, spared destruction. From one of the most thrifty and most industrious elements of the Turkish Empire, if not the most thrifty and most industrious – mind it is a Jew that gives this certificate – the Armenian race is now a race of starving downtrodden beggars, the purity of its family life destroyed, its manhood killed, its children, boys and girls, enslaved in the Turkish private homes for vice and debauchery, that is to what the Armenian race in Turkey has come to. [4]

Aaronsohn sees imperialistic political reasons for the German approach to the Armenian question. The Germans thought that if it was worthwhile to attempt colonization of areas in East Africa and other places, it was criminal to ignore Anatolia, which was so blessed in its geography, climate, agriculture, and natural resources. Seventy-five years earlier, Helmuth von Moltke (chief of the Prussian, and then German, general staff at the end of the nineteenth century) had pointed out that this land was desirable for future colonization by Germans, and now more and more Germans were pointing this out. In his report Aaronsohn sums up:

> Looking at it from this light, would any one who knows something of Germans and the long and sometimes crooked way they can go for the realization of their high ambitions, which are in fact nothing less than divine missions, would any such man hesitate to say that wiping out of those countries the thriftiest element there was, could not have displeased, not even hurt German politics? And would not the Germans themselves, when better fed and in more boisterous spirits than today, said: a crime? That is arguable, but good, farsighted German realpolitik, is it not?

The Armenian massacres are the carefully planned acts of the Turks, and the German will certainly be made forever to share the odium of these acts.[5]

Frank Chalk and Kurt Jonassohn, in their classic *The History and Sociology of Genocide*, propose a typology that classifies genocides according to the motives of the perpetrator: (1) to eliminate a real or potential threat; (2) to spread terror among real or potential enemies; (3) to acquire economic wealth; or (4) to implement a belief, a theory, or an ideology. In any actual case, more than one of these motives will be present. The authors propose to assign each case of genocide to one of these types by deciding which of the four motives was dominant. A number of other dimensions may be considered as bases for constructing a typology. While Chalk and Jonassohn have temporarily rejected them in favor of their simpler typology based only on motives, they consider them to be important dimensions to be explored in future research.[6] Although they also propose delineations between types of society, types of perpetrators, types of victims, types of groups, types of accusations and types of results for the perpetrator society, the division according to the motive of the perpetrator is, in their view, the main one.

Chalk and Jonassohn claim that throughout history most genocides were committed to eliminate a threat, to terrorize an enemy, or to acquire and keep wealth. Another way of putting this is to say that they were carried out in order to build and/or maintain empires. These types of genocides have become rare in the twentieth century. Their fourth type, committed to implement an ideology, has become more frequent and seems to be associated with the rise of new regimes and states. [7] In principal, we accept what Chalk and Jonassohn say about genocide in the twentieth century. We also support the ideas of two other scholars, Helen Fein and Robert F. Melson, who in general support Chalk and Jonassohn's arguments. Their ideas about the Armenian Genocide and the Jewish Holocaust are therefore summarized briefly below.

A Jewish historian, Helen Fein deals with the Holocaust and the victimization that preceded it in her book, *Accounting for Genocide*. [8] The characteristics of the process, according to Fein, were similar in the cases of the Armenians in Turkey and the Jews in Germany. At the same time, Fein indicates the dissimilar political roles of the Armenians, who could challenge the central political regime, and the Jews in Germany, who were most likely to view themselves as "Germans of the Jewish faith." In Fein's view, certain prevailing conditions led to the premeditated genocide of both the Armenians and the Jews:

1. The victims had previously been defined as being outside the universe of obligation of the dominant group: exclusion of the Jews from the Christian world, exclusion of the Armenians from the Islamic world.
2. The rank of the state had been reduced by defeat in war and/or internal strife: in the case of Germany, its defeat in the First World War, in the case of Turkey, the weakening of the Ottoman Empire.
3. The rise to power of an elite that, in order to justify the nation's domination and/or expansion, adopts a new political formula idealizing the singular rights of the dominant group: in the case of the Armenians, the rise of the Young Turks and pan-Turanism; in the case of the Jews, the rise of Nazism.
4. The calculus of the costs of exterminating the victim – a group excluded from the circle circumscribed by the political formula – changes as the perpetrators instigate or join a (temporarily) successful coalition at war against antagonists who have earlier protested and/or might conceivably be expected to protest persecution of the victim: Turkey entered the First World War as an ally of Germany.

According to Fein, there are both differences and parallels in the background and in the prior conditions that led to the genocide of the Armenians and to the Holocaust.

Robert Melson's *Revolution and Genocide* was dedicated to his grandparents, who perished in Treblinka in 1942.[9] Melson concludes that inasmuch as both the genocide of the Armenians and the Holocaust were total domestic genocides of distinctive peoples, they are essentially different from other instances of genocide and mass destruction in the modern era. An analysis of the events, says Melson, indicates that in both cases, that of the Armenian Genocide and the Holocaust, each was:

1. A product of revolutionary transformation in the Ottoman Empire and in imperialistic Germany.
2. The victims were ethno-religious groups with a traditionally low status that had dramatically improved its socioeconomic situation in modern times.
3. Both instances occurred during a world war.

Thus, claims Melson, there is a similar etiology.[10] Nonetheless, he recognizes significant differences between the two genocides, including the status of the Armenians in the Ottoman Empire as compared with the status of the Jews in Europe, and the intentions and methods of the perpetrators. The Jews, historically, were stigmatized pariahs in Europe, and thus different from the status of *dhimmis* ascribed to the Armenians, and messianic German racism and the institution of the death camp were significantly different from Turkish nationalist ideology and the process of massacre and starvation that characterized the Armenian Genocide. Melson points out three other differences. First, because of the differences in the social and territorial status of the Jews and the Armenians, the reactions to the aspirations of the Jews in Germany were different from those of the Armenians in Turkey. An anti-Armenian ideology equivalent to European anti-Semitism never developed in the Ottoman Empire. Second, because the reach of Nazi millenarian racism was broader than the integral nationalism of the Turkish Committee of Union and Progress (CUP, [*Ittihad vé Térakki Jemiyeti*], formed in 1895; its members came to be known as Ittihadists, or Unionists.), the scope of the Holocaust was broader than the Armenian Genocide; the Young Turks, the original founders of the CUP, were motivated by nationalism, not by racism. Third, comparison of the methods of extermination reveals that while the death camps were a successful adaptation to the exigencies of mass murder in the Third Reich, less sophisticated methods, including repeated massacres and mass starvation, can be efficient in implementing total domestic genocide. [11] Melson does not believe, however, that these differences substantially weaken the comparison between the two cases. On the contrary, the differences in etiology and methods of destruction enable us to understand how a total domestic genocide proceeded under specific conditions.

Even though we accept the typology proposed by Chalk and Jonassohn we claim that while acquiring and keeping wealth was not the main motive in either the Armenian Genocide or in the Jewish Holocaust, it became a significant aspect not only during both of these genocides, but also after them. In both cases, the perpetrators, sometimes those who supported them, and also various "third parties," acquired economic wealth by and because of the genocides. The fact that not only the perpetrators enjoyed the economic wealth related to the genocides, during the genocides, and after them, is very significant.

The third or "neutral" parties benefiting from genocide were exposed during an investigation by the U.S. Senate Banking Committee under the chairmanship of Senator Alfonse M. D'Amato, Republican of New York. At the center of these investigations were the Swiss banks that during World War II were charged with having "laundered" looted Nazi gold confiscated from the occupied countries and in particular from communal and private properties of European Jews. The hearings, which started on April 23, 1996 and ended in August 12, 1998, brought together a group of prominent and influential witnesses that included U.S. Under Secretary of Commerce and Presidential Envoy for Property Restitution Stuart Eizenstat, World Jewish Congress President Edgar Bronfman, and Hans Baer, who represented the Swiss Bankers Association (SBA). Gregg J. Rickman, who at the time was the legislative director for Senator D'Amato, and also directed the Senate Banking Committee's "Swiss Bank Inquiry," provided a detailed and meticulous report of the hearings that often took nasty turns, causing a great deal of frustration, pain and anger to surviving heirs and the financial institution alike. In his 1999 book entitled *Swiss Banks and Jewish Souls*, Rickman provided an around-the-clock account of the tortuous hearings that shocked the Swiss people and shattered the prevailing myth of Swiss neutrality.[12] Convening the hearing, D'Amato stated that the issue at hand was about the "systematic victimization of people," and that the victims had placed their trust with the Swiss banks, and that trust "was broken," the irony being that "the very bank secrecy laws enacted in Switzerland to attract Jewish funds, were now being used against the family of the claimants to keep them from their asset." [13] Rickman shows how the Swiss bank executives and Swiss government officials alike made a concerted effort to hide the dormant Jewish assets in Swiss banks and Swiss life insurance companies (assets estimated to total between $7 to $8 billions) but were also engaged in a hateful and nasty attack on the claimants. The statement made by the then president of the Swiss Confederation, Jean Pascal-Delamuraz, equating the Jews and their allies as "blackmailers" and "extortionists" perhaps well characterizes this initial vengeful and bitter Swiss attitude.[14] On January 14, 1997 however, just two days after his infamous statement, Delamuraz put his apology to the Jewish community on paper by stating: "I am very sorry that I offended your feelings…particularly those of the Jewish community at large….The information on which I had based my statement regarding the fund was inaccurate."[15] The debate over the hidden Jewish assets in Swiss banks assumed a new dimension when a caring night watchman of Jewish descent named Christoph Meili discovered, on the night of January 8, 1997, Holocaust-era documents in the shredding room of a Zurich branch of the Union Bank of Switzerland (UBS). When he examined the documents he saw bank ledgers dating back to 1875 from one of Switzerland's formally largest banks, Eidgenossiche Bank, bought after the war by the UBS. Meili eventually took two of the ledgers, hidden under his coat to his home. One of the book contained documents relating to forced property sales by Jews from the 1930-1940 period which Meili turned to Werner Rom, the head of the Israeli Cultural Center in Zurich who then turned over what was saved from certain destruction to the Zurich police.[16] On January 14, 1997 Peter Cossandey, District Attorney for Zurich, announced that not only UBS was being investigated for violating the new law forbidding the destruction of documents, passed only one month before, but that Meili was also under investigation for removing the documents from the bank, a violation of bank secrecy laws.[17] While the Swiss police had announced before Meili's discovery that historical documents were being shredded by the UBS, it was only after Meili's discovery that the president of the UBS, Robert Studer announced on Swiss national television what the world already new, "the UBS had regrettably shredded documents."[18] Senate hearings came to an end on the eve of August 11, 1998 when a settlement over a $1.25 billion to be disbursed over four years was reached.[19] While this sum was only a fraction of the estimated at $8 billion Jewish assets, a measure of justice was at least delivered to the heirs of the victims after fifty years of prevarication.

It is a sad fact that today in both the Armenian Genocide and in the Jewish Holocaust, more than ninety and sixty years after the events, the seized and stolen properties were not restored to the victims or to their heirs, and that the process of restitution for such properties to the survivors of the Jewish Holocaust has been only partial, slow and most often agonizing and painful. The victims and their heirs had to struggle to get their properties back, with the result of only partial restitution in the Jewish case and virtually no restitution at all in the Armenian case.

Two unique characteristics of the Armenian Genocide are the totality of the denial by the perpetrators and their heirs, and the fact that the international community does not recognize the genocide. The Turkish slaughter of the Armenians in 1915-1916 was one of the most horrendous deeds of modern times. In 1918, Henry Morgenthau, Sr., the American ambassador to Turkey from 1913 to 1916, wrote: "I am confident that the whole history of the human race contains no such horrible episodes as this," describing it as "the greatest crime in modern history," and observing that "[a]mong the blackest pages in modern history, this is the blackest of them all."[20] Morgenthau was one of the few people who tried to assist the Armenians, insofar as circumstances allowed, in reducing the extent of their destruction. American Major General James G. Harbord, chief of the American Military Mission to Armenia, who in 1919 was sent to investigate the situation in the areas previously inhabited by the Armenians, wrote, "Mutilation, violation, torture and death have left their haunting memories in a hundred beautiful Armenian valleys. The traveler in this region is only infrequently released from the evidence of the greatest crime of all times."[21]

With the exception of a short period after its defeat at the end of World War I and the ensuing armistice, the Turkish state has denied, and continues to deny to this day, that there was ever a policy of intentional destruction of the Armenians. The Turks have invested considerable effort in erasing the memory of the Armenians and Armenian history in the Ottoman Empire, as though they had never existed, or been part of it. Vast sums of money have been spent and continue to be spent to eradicate all memory of their past crimes and profit from the proceeds and to deny the guilt. Armenian sites, including churches, have been neglected, desecrated, looted, destroyed, or requisitioned for other uses, and Armenian place names have been erased or changed. The 1913-1914 census in Turkey put the number of Armenians living in their historic homeland as close to two millions. At present, there are none and only a few thousands remain in the city Istanbul.

It appears that massive efforts of denial and contemporary political interests are part of the attempt of the Turks and their supporters to undermine the certitude of the claim that there was, indeed, a genocide. These efforts have succeeded in creating disagreement among researchers, seeming historical controversies, and claims of lack of proof. In addition, these efforts created productive uncertainties, intentional neglect and repression of the subject, along with confusion over the events surrounding it. Oblivion and intentional efforts at denial have resulted, several decades later, in questions – most of them tendentious – that did not exist before. Many scholars agree that the denial of its occurrence is the final stage of a genocide. Recognition of the Armenian Genocide on the part of the entire international community, including Turkey – or perhaps, first and foremost by Turkey – is therefore a moral obligation of historical, educational, and political significance of the first order. Recognition of the Armenian Genocide by Israel is crucial in this regard, since the denial of the Armenian Genocide is very similar to the denial of the Holocaust of the Jews. Understanding and remembering the tragic past is an essential condition, even if not sufficient in and of itself, for preventing future crimes against humanity. Recognition of the Armenian Genocide by the international community is also necessary regarding the struggle for recognition of the genocide by Turkey, and for compensation of life insurance benefits from European and American companies and for restitution of the organized theft of Armenian properties, movable and immovable assets, bank deposits of gold, cash and safe boxes containing jewelry and other valuables by the Turks.

In our opinion, without the recognition of the Armenian Genocide it will be very difficult to realize even the "imperfect justice" that was achieved regarding Jewish property during the Holocaust, to cite the book by Stuart E. Eizenstat [22] regarding the Jewish gold, Jewish insurance accounts, and Jewish assets that were looted by the Nazis and by others. Indeed the question of restitution for – and in some cases of – Jewish property is unfinished business regarding the Holocaust and even more so regarding the Armenian Genocide. Both the State of Israel and individual Jews received reparations from Germany, in sharp contrast to the Armenians, who both collectively and individually did not receive any reparations or restitution of property.

The attitudes and the behavior of third parties regarding the victims before during and after the genocide are highly significant. Acts of genocide can be committed only when the balance of power is such that the perpetrators have complete power over the victims. Such a state of affairs is dependent to no small degree on the behavior of "third parties"– those not involved directly – the side that always comprises almost the whole of human society. When genocide is being committed there is always a "third party," which can be divided schematically into three groups:

- Those who assist the murderers for various reasons, including the fact that since the murderers are the "strong ones" it is better to be "on good terms" with them.
- The comparatively few who, for moral, ethical, or compassionate reasons, come to the aid of the victims. (When these are non-Jews who aided Jews in the Holocaust, they are recognized in Israel as "Righteous Gentiles.")
- The bystanders, the vast majority, that remain on the sidelines and do nothing.

A question, whose importance cannot be exaggerated, immediately comes to mind: Don't those who stand by and do nothing share some of the responsibility, and perhaps even some of the guilt, for the crimes committed, which they witnessed but did nothing to prevent? We think that, in practice, the bystanders in effect support the perpetrators, never the victims.

Who are the "third parties" after the genocide? In the case of the Armenian Genocide they are, for example, the American, British, French, German, Swiss, and other European banks and insurance companies that over the course of ninety years, as we will see in this book, refuse to put into practice the basic principal of restitution for looted property and the "dormant" assets of the heirs of the victims. England, France, and the United States were not on the Turkish side during the war and the genocide; they were against Turkey, one of the Central Powers. But as we will see later in this book, because of political and economic concerns both the U.S. and the British governments do not recognize the Armenian Genocide. In practical terms, financial and manufacturing companies in these two and in other countries were, and are, even today, against the interests of Armenian victims and survivors, and their heirs. It has to be noted that restitution for part of the Jewish property was achieved in great measure in the 1990s in the unique international situation that followed the collapse of the Soviet Union and the Eastern Bloc, and with great and direct involvement of the U.S. government and its president.

Ninety years after the Armenian Genocide the situation remains unchanged. While it may be argued that it is easy to understand the immoral and cynical behavior of greedy European and American bankers and insurance companies, such an understanding remains subliminal to the acceptance of these misdeeds. Requests for death certificates from the heirs of the victims and lack of openness about the victims' bank accounts and unclaimed life insurance policy benefits remain a daunting and poignant matter of unfinished business in the case of the Jews and a totally ignored business matter in the case of the Armenians. It is as if Germany would ask for death certificates of the Jews that died or were murdered in the extermination camps. No adequate reparation for the deeds committed against the Armenians and Jews is possible, or indeed, perhaps even conceivable. Resolving various different aspects of the stolen property, however, is a symbolic gesture toward the victims and their heirs. A precondition for a traumatized victim and his often psychologically affected heirs to enter a recovery process depends largely on the recognition by the larger society of the evil committed against him. We have to realize that the recovery of the Armenians from the ongoing trauma of the genocide depends to a great extent upon the world's recognition of the evil that was done. Genocide "refuses to be buried," and denial does not work. The efforts of "third parties," people or groups that were neither among the perpetrators nor the victims, is very significant; their voices and their support can help the victims. But when bystanders are forced to take sides, they unfortunately sometimes side with the perpetrators. In so doing, we claim, they share in the guilt.

*   *   *

This book is written by two people. One of us is an Armenian-American living in the United States and the other is a Jewish Israeli. The former is professor of medicine involved in basic research that aims to elucidate the fundamental mechanisms of cardiac arrhythmias that cause heart attack and the latter is a professor of history working in the fields of contemporary Jewish history and genocide in general. The Armenian-American has devoted many years of study to the memory of his late parents, who had survived the Armenian Genocide. The Jewish Israeli had been struggling for two decades for recognition of the Armenian Genocide by the world,[23] including by his own country, for Israel unfortunately still does not recognize the events as genocide.

We hope that this book will be a modest contribution to the discovery of different aspects of the looted Armenian wealth (life insurance benefits and bank accounts), which are studied scientifically here for the first time. By doing so we hope that a fair and objective debate will be opened about it, at least in democratic countries, and that a long overdue voice against corporate greed and political control of knowledge will be articulated. As Horace Walpole wrote more than two centuries ago, "Justice is rather the activity of truth, than a virtue in itself. Truth tells us what is due to others, and justice renders that due. Injustice is acting a lie."[24]

Notes

1.   Document 242528, December 1, in file 221220, collection F.O. 3712783. The same report appears again as document 253852, F.O. 3712781. Also F.O. 3712783, 221220. It seems that it is to this second document that Aaronsohn refers in his diary on November 21, 1916: "At 5 to Gribbon and he reads me the report which he wrote based on my testimony and notes. He has gathered it all very well into 21 pages." The original manuscripts of those two reports are preserved in the Aaronsohn Archives in Zichron Yaakov, in Israel.

2.   Yaron Efraty (ed.), *Aaronsohn Diaries: 1916-1919* (Tel Aviv: Karni, 1970 [Hebrew]), pp. 130-131 and footnotes; dated November 17, 1916.

3.   Ibid., passim.
4.   Ibid., passim.
5.   Document F.O. 3712783, 221220.
6.   Frank Chalk and Kurt Jonassohn, *The History and Sociology of Genocide*: *Analyses and Case Studies*. (New Haven and London: Yale University Press, 1990).
7.   Ibid., p. 30.
8.   Helen Fein, *Accounting for Genocide: National Responses and Jewish Victimization during the Holocaust* (New York: The Free Press, 1959), pp. 3–18.
9.   Robert F. Melson, *Revolution and Genocide: On the Origins of the Armenian Genocide and the Holocaust* (Chicago and London: University of Chicago Press, 1992).
10. Ibid., p. 256.
11. Ibid., pp. 256–257.
12. Gregg J. Rickman, *Swiss Banks and Jewish Souls,* (New Brunswick, NJ:, Transaction Publishers, 1999).
13. Ibid, p. 51.
14. 14. Ibid, p, 107.
15. 15. Ibid. pp. 108-109.
16. Ibid., p. 121-122.
17. Ibid., pp. 122-123.
18. Ibid., p. 123.
19. Ibid., p. 230.
20. Henry Morgenthau, *Ambassador Morgenthau's Story* (New York: Doubleday and Page, 1918), p. 321.
21. James G. Harbord, "Report to the Secretary of State, October 16, 1919," excerpted from *International Conciliation CIL* (New York: June 1920).
22. E. Stuart Eizenstat, *Imperfect Justice: Looted Assets, Slave Labor, and the Unfinished Business of World War II*, (New York: Public Affairs, 2003). See also Gregg J. Rickman; *Conquest and Redemption: A History of Jewish Assets from the Holocaust* (New Brunswick, NJ Transaction Publishers, 2007).
23. In the last ten years, he has published, among other books, five dealing with genocide: *The Banality of Indifference, The Banality of Denial,* and *The Pain of Knowledge*, (New Brusnwick, NJ: Transaction Publishers, 2000, 2003, 2006, respectively) and, in Hebrew, *Sensitivity to World Suffering* (Tel Aviv: Seminar Hakibbutzim, 1994), and *Forgetting and Denying* (Ra'anana: Open University Press, 2007).
24. Horace Walpole, Horace Walpole's Miscellany 1786-1795, p. 62, ed. Lars E. Troide, Yale University Press (1978), cited in *The Columbia World of Quotations*, 1996 available on line at http://www.bartleby.com/66/86/63186.html.

A Note on the Chapters

There are only few scattered references in the literature alluding to the existence of Armenian life insurance policies at the outbreak of World War I. A concise and documented narrative on the number, fate, and present-day validity of these life policies is still lacking. The former U.S. ambassador to Turkey, Henry Morgenthau, Sr., in his 1919 memoir, briefly mentions Turkish attempts to collect the benefits of life insurance policies of the Armenian victims, but does not dwell on the subject.[1] The late Shavarsh Toriguian, an attorney and an expert on international law, in his 1988 book *The Armenian Question and International Law*, mentions Morgenthau's assertion of the Turkish government's sinister scheme to collect the proceeds of Armenian life insurance policy benefits and briefly alludes to the issue of the stolen five million Turkish gold pounds of Armenian wealth which he erroneously linked to a similar amount of money that was taken over by the victorious allies after the armistice.[2] The Canadian-Armenian jurist, Kévork K. Baghdjian of the University of Concordia in his 1987 book written in French, conservatively estimated that the loot of the Armenian properties (houses, shops, bank deposits, etc.) in different provinces was worth hundreds of millions in Turkish pounds. Part of the fortune was embezzled by individual Ittihadists in the immediate aftermath of the Genocide and the remainder of the riches was misappropriated during the Kemalist government in 1923.[3] The 1915-23 theft of Armenian wealth would amount to trillions in today's U.S. dollars according to Dikran Kouymjian, director of Armenian Studies at California State University.[4] Outside these brief reports there are no other accounts in English or French (save Levon Vartan's *Haygagan Dasnehinke Yev Hayerou Lekyal Kouykere* [Beirut, 1970, in Armenian]) regarding the subject of the looting of Armenian wealth in the post-Genocide era. The absence of such information stems perhaps from the fact that much data about pre-Genocide era life insurance policies had remained classified for over seventy-five years. The declassification in the late 1980s of State Department documents related to the Armenian Genocide, while by no means complete, has made, at least in part, the construction of the mechanisms of the theft possible and, moreover, has also helped greatly to bolster the recent successful claims against two large life insurance companies in Los Angeles, California.

Chapter 1 presents a brief overview of the history and conditions under which the Armenians lived on their historic homeland in Ottoman Turkey. The repeated requests made by the Ottoman Armenians for reforms, equal rights, and relief from heavy government taxation led the Turkish authorities to use lethal force as the ultimate arbiter of any such requests. Intermittent and incremental violence, starting in 1862 and ending only in 1923 witnessed the first major instance of large-scale massacre: the 1915 genocide that claimed the lives of more than one million Armenians. During the years following the end of World War I (1918–1923), the Kemalist regime "finished" the Ittihadists' genocidal acts, which led to a complete eradication of the Armenian nation in their ancient homeland.

Chapter 2 analyzes U.S. State Department documents, discovered by the authors of this book, and shows that on the eve of the 1915 massacres, Armenians had bought thousands of life insurance policies from various European and American insurers. Given the wartime deaths of the insured, a legal question was raised as to the eligibility of the victims' heirs to the policy benefits (war-related deaths are not covered by the life insurance policies and therefore not eligible for benefits). The insurers, however, found the victims "eligible" for the policy benefits. This is discussed in chapter 3. While the survivors of the insured victims made desperate attempts to collect their policy benefits, the Turkish government, for its part, was actively and officially engaged in efforts to collect the benefits for itself. This sinister scheme is discussed in chapter 4. The documents analyzed in this book further demonstrate the "illegal" nature of the mass murders of the Armenians and demonstrate their non-relatedness to war efforts or "due judicial process." However, the large and increasing number of insured victims had meanwhile created a business dilemma for the insurers. Refusal to pay would create a public relations nightmare. At the same time, however, the sudden increase in the number of policy claims could undoubtedly inflict heavy losses on the insurers. These considerations led the insurers to hold Turkey liable. This is discussed in chapter 5. Did the insurers have a legal basis to hold the perpetrators liable? The murderous sinking of the British civilian liner *Lusitania* by a German submarine in 1915 is a case in point. Eleven of the 128 American victims held life insurance policies with American insurers who held

Germany liable on charges of "act of murder," reminiscent of the Turkish "illegal killings" of the Armenians. This legal "mini-precedent" is discussed in chapter 6.

In an effort to avoid making payments, the insurers requested that their respective governments craft or amend specific articles of the 1920 Sèvres Treaty that would explicitly recognize the Armenian life insurance policies as a Turkish liability. Such articles would have then relieved the insurers of their obligations to their insured and held Turkey liable. These behind-the-scenes political maneuvers that led to the infamous Lausanne Treaty are discussed in chapter 7. Are the unclaimed policies recoverable today after many decades of dormancy? This important issue is detailed in chapter 8 in light of several recent successful, although symbolic, settlements and is compared to Holocaust-era Jewish life insurance policy claims.

While the Turkish government failed to collect the life insurance policy benefits from the foreign insurers, who kept the proceeds for themselves, the situation with respect to Armenian assets and wealth deposited in Ottoman Imperial Bank branches was different. Safe deposit boxes and bank accounts had been accessed and confiscated in direct violation of all applicable Ottoman laws. When pressed by branch bank directors on the illegality of such patent breaches of Ottoman laws, receipts of the confiscated riches were issued to the executives of the Ottoman Imperial Bank branches and the actions justified by invoking the "Abandoned Properties Act." The 1915-16 theft of the bank assets of the Armenians produced five-million Turkish gold pounds (the 1915 equivalent of $22 million dollars), most of which was deposited in 1916 in a Berlin bank in the personal accounts of top Ittihadist leaders. While the victorious Allies in the aftermath of the war confiscated an equivalent sum from Berlin banks (chapter 9), these monies had nothing to do with the looted money, which till now remains unaccounted for and is discussed in chapter 10.

Authors' Note

The authors of this book are not connected in any way with the lawsuits brought against two insurance companies in Los Angeles, California. Upon a request made by one of us (HSK), the New York Life Insurance Company had sent us, from its archives, a few and selected internal documents that were never processed or reported previously in any form; these internal documents were received in May 1996, before a claim was filed against the New York Life Insurance Company in 1998.

On the Use of the Terms "Ottoman" and "Genocide"

It is necessary to address the alternating use in this book of the words "Ottoman," "Ottoman Empire," "Turkey," and "Turkish Empire." The words Ottoman and Turkey were used interchangeably in the American and French documents analyzed in this book. From the insurers' perspective the words "Ottoman" and "Turkey" were synonymous and had no political significance. It seems that such alternate use of the two words was a common practice in German and Austrian literature as alluded to by Dadrian:

> …the words "Ottoman" and "Turk" have been used alternately – in keeping with the prevalent contemporary practice among many historians and diplomats, including those from Germany and Austro-Hungary, Ottoman Empire's wartime allies. A separation of the meaning of these two terms for the present purposes is considered to be more of an etymological rather than a historical issue. The countless quotations originating from these authors [sources] do require the adoption of this method of alternation.[5]

The noted British historian Martin Gilbert also makes no distinction between the words "Ottoman" and "Turkey." The caption of a map used in his monograph, for example, reads "The Turkish or Ottoman borders."[6]

It must also be emphasized that the word "genocide" was coined only in 1944 by Rafael Lemkin, a Polish Jew. Moved by the extermination of the Armenians and the Jews, Lemkin described the Nazi annihilation of the Jews as "genocide," a word comprised of the Greek derivative *genos* meaning "race" or "tribe," and the Latin derivative *cide*, from *caedere*, meaning killing.[7] The word genocide, extensively used in this book, is defined in Articles 1 and 2 of the United Nations Convention of the Prevention and Punishment of the Crime of Genocide" (UNGC), which describes the scope and the categories of ill-treatments of victim groups that fulfill the definition of "genocide":

Article 1

Contracting Parties confirm that genocide, whether committed in time of peace or in time of war, is a crime under international law which they undertake to prevent and to punish.

Article 2

In the present Convention, genocide means any of the following acts committed with intent to destroy, in whole or in part, a national, ethnical, racial or religious group, as such:

1. Killing members of the group;
2. Causing serious bodily or mental harm to members of the group;
3. Deliberately inflicting on the group conditions of life calculated to bring about its physical destruction in whole or in part;
4. Imposing measures intended to prevent births within the group;
5. Forcibly transferring children of the group to another group.[8]

As will be seen later in this book, the mass murder of the Armenians from 1915 to1923, while at the time described as "massacres," "illegal killings," "fatal exposure," or "forced deportation," all fall within the U.N. definition of the word "genocide."

Notes

1. Henry Morgenthau, *Ambassador Morgenthau's Story: The Documented Account of the Armenian Genocide First of the Century Reported by America's Ambassador to Turkey* (Plandome, NY: New Age Publisher (reprinted edition; originally published in 1919 by Doubleday Page & Co.) p. 222.
2. Shavarsh Toriguian, "Letters Concerning Armenian Insurance Policies," in The *Armenian Question and the International Law* (La Verne, CA: University of La Verne Press (2nd edition), 1988), pp 144-156.
3. Kévork K. Baghdjian, *La Confiscation, Par le Gouvernement Turc, Des Biens Dits Abandonnés*, (Montreal, 1987).
4. Dikran Kouymjian, "Confiscation and Destruction: A manifestation of the Genocide process," *Armenian Forum*, 1:3, Autumn 1998, pp. 1-12.
5. Vahakn N. Dadrian, *Warrant for Genocide: Key Elements of Turko-Armenian Conflict* (New Brunswick, NJ: Transaction Publishers, 1999), p. 3.
6. Martin Gilbert, *A History of the Twentieth Century*. Volume One: 1900-1933 (New York: Avon Books, 1997), section "MAPS," map no. 14.
7. Samantha Power, *A Problem from Hell: America and the Age of Genocide* (New York: Basic Books, 2002), pp. 17, 42.
8. Resolution 260 (III) A, adopted unanimously by United Nations General Assembly on December 9, 1948; http://www.hrweb.org/legal/genocide.html

1

Ottoman Armenians: From Reform to Genocide

A Brief History of Armenia

Armenia is an ancient nation that once stretched from Transcaucasia in the east to the Anatolian plateau in the west, and from the Black Sea in the north to Mesopotamia and Syria in the south. Situated at one of the principal junctions between Europe and Asia, this mountainous country has been the site of repeated conquests for over two thousand years from the east, west, north, and south. Whether during the eastern advances of Westerners (Greeks, Romans, Byzantines, Crusaders) or the advances westward of Easterners (Persians, Arabs, Mongols, Turks, Russians), the route these invading forces used was almost always through Armenia. Located between the Persian and the Roman empires during antiquity, and later between the Islamic and the Christian Byzantium empires, Armenia was alternately the prey of the East and of the West. Its mountainous configuration allowed however, for only partial occupation during periods of foreign domination by an empire or a powerful neighbor.[1]

In the 1860s Armenia was divided between Ottoman Turkey (i.e., Turkish or Western Armenia) and tsarist Russia (i.e., Russian or Eastern Armenia), a status that persisted until the collapse of Soviet rule. With the demise of the Soviet system, Russian Armenia gained its independence in 1991 while Turkish Armenia, forcibly depopulated of its Armenian population, became an integral part of present-day Turkey. Depopulation was materialized by a series of intermittent and incremental massacres and deportations, and by forced conversion to Islam.

The Armenian People

In 1867, the Ottoman Empire appointed Salaheddin Bey to determine the number of Armenians living in the Ottoman Empire. This Turkish official put their total at 2,400,000.[2] Half of the Armenians lived in the six Armenian provinces, called *vilayets,* (Erzerum, Van, Bitlis, Kharpout, Sivas, and Diarbekir) in eastern Turkey, where they constituted either the absolute majority of the population (in Van and in Bitlis) or a relative majority (in Erzerum, Kharpout [Harput], Sivas and Diarbekir). Relative majority meant that the Armenians were the largest single ethnic group compared either to the Turks or to the Kurds, counted separately.[3] The reported population of 2.4 million is higher by a half-million than that of the Armenian Patriarchate's 1913-14 census that put the number of the Armenians in Turkey at 1.91 million.[4] Taking into account the lives lost during the 1867–1914 massacres,[5] the numbers reported by the two different sources are reasonably close to each other and have a strong measure of credibility. The Armenian population of the present independent Republic of Armenia and the surrounding former Soviet republics is about four million; there are an additional four million Armenians spread all over the world (the Armenian diaspora), with about one million of them in the United States.

Language and Religion

With its distinct language, religion, and art, the Armenians are a member of a group in the Indo-European-speaking family.[6] In 301 AD St. Gregory the Illuminator, the first Armenian Patriarch, converted King Tiridate III of Armenia to Christianity, and Armenia adopted Christianity as a state religion in that same year, a decade earlier than the conversion of the Roman Emperor Constantine.[7] As Yehuda Bauer, the noted Israeli historian who defined the causes of the Jewish Holocaust using the comparative method, observed: "The Armenian Christian civilization competed with Turkish civilization, which it had preceded on what later became Turkish territory by many centuries."[8] In fact, as we shall see, in addition to the issue of competing civilizations, in the late nineteenth and early twentieth centuries the economic ascendancy of the Armenian minority in Turkey was perceived by the Young Turks as a threat to the country's security requiring a radical solution.

Economic Wealth and Genocide

Despite their minority status, Armenians in Ottoman Turkey owned many businesses and properties, assumed high governmental positions, and played a prominent role in the state's local and international economy.[9] In touch with industrial developments in the West, the Armenians introduced various technical innovations such as steam engines, mechanical weaving machines, and iron and steel mills. Most of the tobacco, textile industries (wool, linen, and silk) and naval manufacturing were largely in the hands of Armenians. Active in finance and trade, Armenians played an important role in international commerce. With the financial modernization of the Ottoman Empire in the mid-1800s, Armenians assumed high-ranking positions in the government, including ministerial and provincial leadership positions.[10] The relative economic prosperity of Armenians was perhaps one reason why the Young Turk Ittihadist regime considered the Armenians a "threat" to Turkish national independence, triggering an intense dual hate-fear syndrome against this non-Muslim minority group and leading to intermittent and incremental massacres during 1909, and 1915-23.[11]

Two-thirds of the income of the Armenians was collected as taxes, levied at three times the amount charged to non-Armenians.[12] The relative economic prosperity of the Armenians in the midst of a less than friendly atmosphere led many of the well-to-do to buy life insurance policies as a measure of security for their loved ones.

In 1915, the Turkish government began the implementation of the "evacuation order"– in essence the expulsion and murder of the Armenians. This was assigned to the police and units of the Ch'ette, the Special Organization established by the Ministries of the Police and the Interior. The Ch'ette was a paramilitary unit, manned by criminals and convicts who were released from prison, created especially for this purpose. The evacuation was announced in public places in the Armenian villages and towns. The population was given only few short days to prepare for the evacuation, which was ostensibly for military reasons. The evacuees were permitted to take their personal effects with them and were given a promise that their homes and property would be protected until their return. They were then gathered in convoys and ordered to march south towards the Syrian Desert.

The evacuation and expulsion of the Armenian population was an important prelude to the process of the genocide and looting that followed, which usually comprised several stages. At first, after leaving their villages or cities, males over the age of fifteen were separated from the rest of the group (it should be remembered that the men between the ages of twenty-five and forty-five, who had been serving in the Ottoman army, were murdered by military squads), taken to a spot not far away, and executed by shooting or by more primitive methods. Women, children, and the elderly were forced to march hundreds of miles and thus sentenced to a slower, more drawn-out death. The convoys traveled through the most difficult terrain, under harsh climatic conditions, and were frequently subjected to attacks by units of the Special Organization, the gendarmes, and the local population, particularly the Kurds. Women and children were raped, and those who managed to survive the journey were kidnapped and handed over to Turkish families as servants (as slaves, in fact); many were sold in slave markets. Throughout the long and arduous march, the refugees were given only minute quantities of food and water. Starvation and thirst, intense cold or enervating heat, and epidemics that broke out due to the thousands of unburied bodies, all increased the number of fatalities. In some cases, entire families committed suicide; in others, mothers were forced to leave their dying children behind and to continue on.

The intended direction of the journey was the region around the city of Aleppo in northern Syria. From there, the few who had survived were transported to the desert regions of Iraq and Syria. Out in the desert, near Deir al-Zor, many of the survivors were executed. Very few of those who had begun the journey lived to see its end. Estimates place the number of survivors at 10 percent, and in certain convoys even fewer. (The report of the American Consul in Aleppo to the American Secretary of State on October 16, 1915, detailed the tribulations of one of the convoys in which only 150 women and children, out of 18,000 deportees who began the march, reached Aleppo seventy days later.) It appears that by July of 1915 the Armenians had been expelled from the six Armenian provinces, and most of them had already been murdered. During the latter half of 1915 the deportations were carried out in the Armenian areas of Cilicia.

Insurance and Genocide

While it is not the objective of this book to study and document the Armenian Genocide, in the context of life insurance policies examined in this book it is necessary to reassert that the mass destruction of the Armenians during World War I was a "genocide" according to the definition adopted by the United Nations and was totally unrelated to acts of war.[13] This is important from the insurers' point of view because for a life policy to be eligible for benefit collection, death must not result from "acts of war," or from "judicial condemnation" due to "treason" or "acts of spying." Specific articles in life insurance policies, at least those sold in Turkey during the pre-genocide era, authorized the insurers to lapse the policies and regard them as "null and void" in cases of deaths resulting from "judicial condemnation" or "acts of war or treason." The insurers thus had at their disposal the necessary mechanisms to deny payments in cases of loss of life resulting from acts of war. On the other hand, the insurers considered the deaths of those insured resulting from "forced deportations," "massacres," "illegal killings," "fatal exposure," "wanton killings," (i.e., indiscriminate killings of unarmed civilians), as legitimate causes for claims by the beneficiaries. The largest destruction of Armenians that conforms to the United Nation's definition of "genocide," occurred in 1915-16 and was "finished" by the Kemalists during 1921-23.[14] Today, there are fewer than 50,000 Armenians living in Turkey, most of them in Istanbul, the former capital city Constantinople.[15] A recent study estimated that the Armenian wealth (in terms of estates, properties, and bank assets) illegally confiscated by the Turkish governments in the aftermath of the 1915-1923 massacres would amount to trillions in today's dollars![16]

In the following section, compelling evidence drawn from published evidentiary materials that attest to the genocidal nature of the war-time mass destruction of the Armenians is presented. This theme will also be discussed in chapter 5 in conjunction with the insurers' claims that the Turkish government should be "held accountable" for the payments of the life policy benefits because of its direct responsibility in the "premeditation, planning and implementation" of the genocidal killings.

"The Murder of a Nation"

The genocidal nature of the 1915 massacre of more than one million Armenians has not only been documented in American and European official state documents, but also by the proceedings of the 1918-1919 Turkish Military Tribunals held in Constantinople in the immediate aftermath of World War I. The proceedings of these postwar trials of the ruling Ittihadist party leaders, who were qualified in the court proceedings as members of a "criminal organization," were published in the official gazette of the Ottoman government supplement, *Takvimi Vekâyi*. They represent not only a milestone in the history of war crimes tribunals, but also a bone fide confession by Turks of crimes against humanity committed by their fellow Turks. The proceedings that began on December 28, 1918 came to an abrupt end on May 13, 1919, thanks to the rising nationalist forces led by Mustapha Kemal (Kemal Atatürk). The abridged and forceful termination of these trials was unmistakably designed to save the mounting incriminating evidence against all responsible military leaders in exile who were steadily joining the Turkish army under Kemal's leadership. Nevertheless, the evidence gathered during this truncated trial was sufficient to convict in absentia the top Ittihadist leaders, including the masterminds of the genocide, the "triumvirate," Talât, Enver, and Djemal, and to sentence them to death for "planning and implementing" a "premeditated" mass murder of unarmed civilians. These murders, in the opinion of the court, amounted to no more than "common crimes" (*ceraimi adiye*) unrelated to war or acts of treason.[17] Historians and social scholars grasped this unprecedented opportunity to dub the trials "The Nuremberg that failed."[18]

The European and American insurers alike declared to their respective governments that the killings were unrelated to acts of war and that the deaths did not result from due process (judicial condemnation); they put the blame plainly on the Turkish government. Their revelations provide yet another level of primary source material that independently asserts the state sponsored wartime destruction of the Armenians. The decision to rid Turkey of its Christian Armenian subjects appears, however, to have been conceived long before the war. In an August 6, 1910 secret meeting outside the purview of the formal sessions of the annual convention of the Ittihad Party (Committee of Union and Progress, or CUP), and attended exclusively by the top Ittihad leaders, the then Interior Minister Mehmet Talât, – one of the masterminds of the Genocide, who later became Grand Vizier (prime minister) – delivered a speech in which he emphatically stated that "[T]he principal of equality is no longer applicable for the subject non-Muslim minorities of the Ottoman Empire, declaring it anathema to Islam."[19] The postwar discovery of a secret operational blueprint for the destruction of the Christian minority in Turkey, which attests to the premeditation of the sinister plan, was made by the British intelligence. The English translators dubbed the blueprint "The Ten Commandments," as it specifies ten steps and actions to be taken in order most effectively implement the carnage. The document, which is dated December 1914–January 1915, is headed: "Documents Relating to Comite [*sic*] Union and Progress Organization in the Armenian Massacre"; the subtitle is "The 10 commandments of the Comite [*sic*] Union and Progress." It enumerates in detail the administrative measures, types of lethal violence, and incitement of Muslim masses against the Armenians, as well as other measures necessary for deception and secrecy. The actions included the closure of all Armenian societies, schools and churches, deportation, arrests of any who worked against the government, murder of all males and forced Islamization of girls and children. Article 142 of the Sevres Treaty signed in 1920 to which Turkey was a signatory explicitly repelled the forced Islamization imposed by the "terrorist" regime that was in place at the outbreak of the war. As the issue of forced Islamization still remains a taboo in present-day Turkey we provide the full text of the article:

> Whereas, in view of the terrorist regime which has existed in Turkey since November 1, 1914, conversions to Islam could not take place under normal conditions, no conversions since that date are recognized and all persons who were non-Moslems before November 1, 1914, will be considered as still remaining such, unless, after regaining their liberty, they voluntarily perform the necessary formalities for embracing the Islamic faith. In order to repair so far as possible the wrongs inflicted on individuals in the course of the massacres perpetrated in Turkey during the war, the Turkish Government undertakes to afford all the assistance in its power or in that of the Turkish authorities in the search for and deliverance of all persons, of whatever race or religion, who have disappeared, been carried off, interned or placed in captivity since November 1, 1914. The Turkish Government undertakes to facilitate the operations of mixed commissions appointed by the Council of the League of Nations to receive the complaints of the victims themselves, their families or their relations, to make the necessary enquiries, and to order the liberation of the persons in question. The Turkish Government undertakes to ensure the execution of the decisions of these commissions, and to assure the security and the liberty of the persons thus restored to the full enjoyment of their rights.[20]

The total banishment of Armenians from their historic homeland is perhaps the strongest present-day evidence of the Ittihadist leaders' sinister scheme. Arnold Toynbee, who collected massive documents on the Armenian genocide, dismissed the Turkish charges of treason and rebellion against the Armenians as fabrications that would "not bear examination" and concluded that "it is evident that the war was merely an opportunity and not a cause."[21]

Henry Morgenthau, Sr., the American ambassador to Turkey during this period (1913-1916), left no doubt in his memoir regarding the entrenched determination of the Ittihadists to exterminate the entire "Armenian race." Technically speaking, Morgenthau had no right to intervene on behalf of the Armenians, as the United States was not at war against Turkey and the treatment of the Turkish subjects by the Turkish government was purely an "internal" affair. However, deeply moved by the enormity of the tragedy, the intrepid Columbia University law-graduate-turned-diplomat went beyond and above the usual diplomatic protocol and directly requested from the all too powerful Interior Minister Talât Pasha to spare what was left of a "murdered race." "Americans," stressed Ambassador Morgenthau, "are outraged by your persecution of the Armenians. You must base your principles on humanitarianism not racial discrimination, or the United States will not regard you as a friend and an equal."[22]

Talât, who considered the ambassador a person from whom he could benefit economically and financially because of America's neutrality in the war, snapped:

> Why are you interested in the Armenians anyway? You are a Jew; these people are Christians. The Mohammedans and the Jews always get on harmoniously. We are treating the Jews here all right. What have you to complain of? Why can't you let us do with these Christians as we please?"[23]

On another occasion, when the genocide was already in full swing (August 1915), Talât asked Morgenthau to not bring his own interpreter with him and said that he would provide an interpreter. The member of the U.S. Embassy staff who did the interpreting for Morgenthau was an Armenian, (Arshag Shmavonian) and Talât seemed to be uncomfortable with laying his plans before the American ambassador in the presence of an Armenian. In this meeting the Ittihad party boss and the mastermind of the genocide spelled out the motives for the extermination of the Armenian race:

> I have asked you to come today, so that I can explain our position on the whole subject. We base our objections to the Armenians on three distinct grounds. In the first place, they have enriched themselves at the expense of the Turks. In the second place, they are determined to domineer over us to establish a separate state. In the third place, they have openly encouraged our enemies. They have assisted the Russians in the Caucasus and our failure there is largely explained by their action. We have therefore come to the irrevocable decision that we shall make them powerless before this war ends....We have already disposed of three quarters of the Armenians; there are none at all left in Bitlis, Van and Erzerum. The hatred between the Turks and the Armenians is now so intense that we have got to finish with them. If we don't, they will plan their revenge. I have asked you to come here so as to let you know that our Armenian policy is absolutely fixed and that nothing can change it. We will not have the Armenians anywhere in Anatolia. They can live in the desert but nowhere else. No Armenian can be our friend after what we have done to them.[24]

It is all too remarkable that three years after Talât's confessions of the reasons for slaughtering the Armenians and robbing their wealth, Adolf Hitler explained his first anti-Semitic motivations and agenda for slaughtering and robbing the Jews as a "national necessity" that mirrored well the Turkish agenda. Hitler in his September 16, 1919 letter to Reichswehr News and Enlightenment Department in Munich, a time during which Talât was in exile in Berlin under an assumed name before he was assassinated by the son of a victimized family in 1921, wrote:

> The value of the individual is no longer decided by his character or by the significance of his achievements for the totality but exclusively by the size of his fortune, by his money. The loftiness of a nation is no longer to be measured by the sum of its moral and spiritual powers, but rather by the wealth of its material possessions. This thinking and striving after money and power, and the feelings that go along with it, serve the purposes of the Jew who is unscrupulous in the choice of methods and pitiless in their employment. In autocratically ruled states he whines for the favor of "His Majesty" and misuses it like a leech fastened upon the nations. In democracies he vies for the favor of the masses, cringes before the "majesty of the people," and recognizes only the majesty of money.... The deduction from all this is the following:

an antisemitism based on purely emotional grounds will find its ultimate expression in the form of the pogrom. An antisemitism based on reason, however, must lead to systematic legal combating and elimination of the privileges of the Jews, that which distinguishes the Jews from the other aliens who live among us (an Aliens Law). The ultimate objective [of such legislation] must, however, be the irrevocable removal of the Jews in general. For both these ends a government of national strength, not of national weakness, is necessary.[25]

Twenty-four years later in October 1943, Heinrich Himmler, speaking to SS officers in Posen declared plainly, "We have taken away the riches that they had…"[26]

The Armenians put the number of their victims at one and one half million, a figure that matches well the "three quarters of the Armenians," killed admitted by Talât. This figure is also consistent with the pre-genocide Armenian Patriarchate census of 1.92 million.[27] The ever hopeful Ambassador Morgenthau continued his plea with the mastermind of the genocide in order to sway his mind: "Suppose a few Armenians did betray you. Is that a reason for destroying a whole race? Is that an excuse for making innocent women and children suffer?" Talât, unshaken by the ambassador's remark, snapped back: "We have been reproached for making no distinction between the innocent Armenians and the guilty; but that was utterly impossible, in view of the fact that those who were innocent today might be guilty tomorrow!"[28]

Gerald D. Feldman, professor of history at the University of California, Berkeley, in his comprehensive study of the Berlin-based Deutsche Bank that financed the Baghdad Railway, highlighted remarkable records of eyewitness accounts of the murder of the Armenians that he had discovered in the archives of the influential German bank. In Feldman's estimation the treatment of the Armenians by the Turkish authorities amounted to genocide: "The Baghdad Railway had become a nightmare in every sense – especially those involved became direct witnesses to the genocidal policies pursued against the Armenians."[29] The vice president of the railway company in Constantinople, Franz Günter, described the Turkish atrocities in his August 17, 1915 letter to the managing board member of the Deutsche Bank in Berlin, Arthur von Gwinner as follows:

One has to go back into the history of humanity to find something comparable in its bestial horribleness as in the extermination of the Armenians in today's Turkey. The pogroms against the Jews in Russia, which I know, are child's play, and one has to go back to the expulsion of the Moors from Spain and the persecution of the Christians by Rome to find an analogy to what is taking place here. It appears that the government wants to eradicate the entire tribe, root and branch, for this is the only thing that can result from their behavior, and if things go on this way, they may only too well succeed....The fact in any case is that the eastern provinces [historic Armenia] have become freed of all Armenians.[30]

The World Reaction

The Armenian genocide was, without question, committed with the knowledge and in the presence of the diplomatic representatives of Turkey's allies, the German Empire and the Austro-Hungarian Empire. They were to be found in the capital as well as in other cities throughout the Ottoman Empire. German military representatives were also stationed throughout the Empire. Germany was Turkey's military ally, equipping the Turkish army, and involved at the highest levels in training and commanding Turkish troops. German military commanders and soldiers undoubtedly saw and knew and, it is alleged, participated – at least indirectly – in the genocide. American diplomats, too, were stationed in various parts of the empire until April 1917, when the United States abandoned its position of neutrality and joined the war against Germany.

Furthermore, throughout the Ottoman Empire there were American, German, and other missionaries, as well as teachers, tourists, and travelers who reported what they saw, and journalists reported the events as well. As early as the spring of 1915, reports of the killing of large numbers of Armenians reached the outside world, and details of the atrocities were featured prominently and frequently in the European and American press. On May 24, 1915, France, England, and Russia issued a joint protest and warning against the acts of murder.

Germany was perhaps the only country that could have changed the Turkish policy of genocide at that time. American Ambassador Henry Morgenthau wrote to the U.S. secretary of state on June 10, 1915 that the German embassy would make do with "giving advice and a formal protest for the record, in order to absolve themselves of responsibility in the future." The letter was one of many that Morgenthau sent.

Documents that appeared in the West during the war revealed terrible events. Of particular interest are the U.S. State Department documents compiled in "The Blue Book" by Toynbee and Bryce (compiled during the war and later made public), and the publications of the German missionary, Dr. Johannes Lepsius, some of which appeared during the war and others only after the war ended. Each of these publications contains hundreds of documents. Additionally, there were publications by private persons. A German teacher in Aleppo, Dr. Martin Niepage, documented what he and others had seen in *The Horrors of Aleppo* (published in English in 1917). Dr. Armin T. Wegner, a German medical officer, published photographs and reports of what he had seen. Wegner worked to oppose the Nazis in the 1930s and was accorded the title of "Righteous Gentile" by the Yad Vashem Holocaust Memorial Museum in Jerusalem. By December 1915, more than a hundred articles and items about the Armenian genocide had appeared in the first six pages of the *New York Times* alone. So the world did know, and it knew in real time. In spite of all these reports, during the entire course of the war Turkey consistently denied all accusations of planned mass deportations and murder. In fact, after 1916 the attempts of protest and condemnation became, for all practical purposes, meaningless: by that time most of the Armenian population of the Anatolian Plateau and Cilicia had been exterminated.

In the framework of this short survey of political and diplomatic developments up to the end of the war and during the peace agreements that followed, it is important to note, however briefly, the humanitarian efforts that were made. Beginning in April 1915, the American consular corps and American missionaries attempted, to the best of their limited abilities, to aid the survivors. Despite the repeated attempts by the authorities to prevent any assistance to the victims, they supplied food, water, and sometimes refuge in monasteries. In September 1915, Ambassador Morgenthau, stationed in Constantinople, requested emergency aid from his government, and in the same year the American Committee for Armenian and Syrian Relief (ACASR) was established. In 1916, assistance efforts, under the auspices of the American congress, were reorganized as the "Near East Relief" (NER). The organization collected substantial sums of money from foundations, private donors, and the government. During the advanced stage of the expulsions, when the deportees who survived the march arrived in Aleppo, workers of the organization, assisted by missionaries, provided first aid, water, food, and clothing. Representatives of the American consulate took part in the assistance efforts. Later on, refugee camps were organized in various places in the Middle East for the survivors; schools were organized and orphanages were established for children. Some of the Armenian children who were found in the homes of Turkish families were returned and rehabilitated. There is no doubt that tens, perhaps hundreds of thousands, of Armenians were saved due to these humanitarian efforts. The survivors began their long and arduous efforts to rebuild their lives.

Epilogue

There is no doubt, based on different and varied sources from the period, that the comprehensive mass extermination of the civilian population in various regions of Turkey (and certainly not just in the battle zones) was carried out at the indisputable order of Turkish authorities in Constantinople. While certain facts and details can be legitimately debated, and some of the Armenian claims about the genocide can be questioned, the historical sources create an unequivocal and unshakable picture. The term "genocide" did not exist, as mentioned, at the time the atrocities were committed against the Armenians, but what the Young Turks did to the Armenians was indeed genocide. Again, one can argue with some of the facts, details, or circumstances, but there can be no doubt about the fact of the genocide itself. In this sense, the denial of the Armenian genocide is very similar to the denial of the Holocaust of the Jews. And yet, Talât Pasha is viewed in Turkey today as a national hero. His bones were repatriated to Turkey by Nazi Germany in 1943 and are interred in a national mausoleum in Constantinople. With the exception of a short period immediately after the end of the war the Turkish government denied – and continues to deny to this day – that there was ever a policy of wholesale destruction of the Armenians.

The Armenians talk of the "forgotten genocide," which took place under three regimes – The Sultanate, the Young Turks, and the forces of Mustapha Kemal. The Turks, on the other hand, talk about the "alleged genocide" and charge the Armenians with treachery and subversion. It appears that massive efforts of denial and contemporary political interests are part of the attempt to undermine the certainty of the claim that there was, indeed, a genocide. These efforts have succeeded in creating disagreements among researchers, seeming historical controversies, and claims of lack of proof. The result of Turkish efforts has been intentional neglect and repression of the subject and the creation of confusion over the events surrounding it.

The Western world, slightly embarrassed by its abandonment of the Armenians, preferred to ignore their fate, and within the international *realpolitik* the Armenians were utterly powerless. The 1920s and 1930s were also decades of struggle against totalitarian and fascist regimes. After the Second World War, the world was stunned and absorbed by horrors of the Holocaust. There are Armenians who assert that interest in the Holocaust was at the expanse of the Armenian tragedy, which became "the forgotten genocide." It should be remembered that at the same time the Turks destroyed the Armenians, they wiped out other minority populations, albeit considerably smaller in size, like the Assyrians. They have been even more forgotten by the world, and their destruction has become "the obliterated genocide."

Since the 1960s and 1970s some changes have begun in the public awareness of the Armenian Genocide. In the 1970s and early 1980s Armenian organizations committed terrorist acts against Turkish institutions and diplomats in various parts of the world. The acts of terror, aimed at arousing world opinion, resulted in raising the Armenian issue, and it was during those years that important scientific research on the subject of the Armenian Genocide began. The fruits of this research have had some effect, and scholars, intellectuals, educators, and human rights activists have begun to reexamine the issue. The growing awareness of the Holocaust may also have sparked new interest in the Armenian Genocide, and the multi-generational Armenian trauma has become a subject of greater understanding and response. In January 1984, President Francois Mitterrand of France gave public recognition to the historical fact of the Armenian genocide; and in 1985, the United Nations, through its Sub-Commission on Human Rights, recognized the atrocities committed against the Armenians as genocide, recognition that was denied in 1973 due to pressure by the Turkish government. In 1987, the European Parliament in Strasbourg declared that Turkey could not join the European Community unless, among other things, it recognized its responsibility for the genocide. In contrast, in 1989 and then again in 2000, 2004 and 2007, a motion for the recognition of the Armenian Genocide was defeated in the American Congress, although it was supported at one stage by a majority of the members; the motion would have declared April 24 as the official day of the Armenian Genocide. However, although on October 12, 2007 the U.S. House Foreign Affairs Committee passed the Armenian Genocide resolution, intense White House pressure prevented the resolution from reaching the floor of the House.

The debate over recognition of the Armenian Genocide did enter the parliaments of some countries. Affirmation of the Armenian Genocide is mentioned in resolutions of the Uruguayan Senate and House of Representatives (April 20, 1965), the Cypriot House of Representatives (April 20, 1982), the Argentinian Senate (May 5, 1993), the Russian Duma (April 14, 1995), the Hellenic [Greek] Parliament (April 25, 1996), the Lebanese Chamber of Deputies (April 3, 1997), and the Swedish Parliament (March 29, 2000), in a Lebanese Parliament resolution (May 11, 2000), and by Italy (November 10, 2000). It is also mentioned in a declaration of Vatican City (November 10, 2000) and by France (January 18, 2001). Furthermore, it was mentioned, affirmed, and recognized in one way or another (the differences are sometimes very significant) in official reports of the U.N. by the European Parliament (July 18, 1987 and again November 15, 2000), by heads of states, U.S. presidential statements, twenty-five U.S. states, several provincial governments of Canada, municipal governments across Europe and North America, international organizations, and in public petitions. The struggle for recognition of the Armenian Genocide by specific states gained momentum as recently as 2000-2001. For example, two-and-a-half years after the French Senate refused to consider a bill that would debate official French recognition of the Armenian Genocide – as the French Lower House of Parliament, the Chamber of Deputies (l'Asemblée), had done in a unanimous vote on May 29, 1998 – and after a long debate and struggle, the final steps of French recognition were taken in 2000–2001: on November 9, 2000, the French Senate formally recognized the Armenian Genocide, and on January 18, 2001, the Chamber of Deputies recognized it and it became French law.

At around the same time, on March 29, 2000, the Swedish Parliament passed a formal resolution recognizing the Armenian Genocide, this after a Swedish parliamentary report asserted that "An official statement and recognition of the genocide of the Armenian is important and necessary." Sweden urged Turkey to do so as well. Canada also recognized the genocide. (The Italian and Austrian parliaments as well as the Swiss and the German parliaments recognized and debated this issue of the Armenian Genocide without a conclusion.)

The Czech writer, Milan Kundera wrote that man's struggle against power is the struggle of memory against oblivion. In this sense, all of the reasons that justify remembrance of the Holocaust are valid for the Armenian genocide as well. Furthermore, the Turkish governments that have ruled after the crimes were committed deny they ever took place. The Turks have escaped judgment for their crimes and, with the direct politically-motivated assistance of some of the world's powers, have been partially successful in their denials. Nevertheless, Turkey is a country that within living memory committed terrible crimes of murder – and continues to deny what it did. It is as if Germany had denied its crimes in the Second World War.

Motivated by economic and political expediencies, the denial of the Armenian Genocide evolved over time to impunity. "After all," the noted genocide scholar, Israel Charney, argued, "It was with the same purpose, fervor, and gratification that the Nazis committed their genocidal acts as their once close military ally, Turkey." The Armenian Genocide, asserted Charney, "was a dress rehearsal for the Holocaust."[31] The question-statement "After all, who speaks now of the extermination of the Armenians?"

was reportedly uttered by Hitler in a speech he gave to his top military aids on the eve of his scheme to exterminate the Jews of Poland.[32]

Taken collectively, the wealth of evidence (official state documents, eyewitness accounts, diplomatic corps correspondence and material evidence), point to the genocidal nature of the war-time mass destruction of the Armenians in Turkey. It is ironic that the Berlin Treaty of July 13, 1878, notably article 61, which stipulated the introduction of "improvements and reforms" into the Armenian provinces and the protection of the Armenian minority, became the Turkish preamble of the "Armenian Question" requiring a radical solution. This preamble led Turkey to intermittently and incrementally employ the use of lethal force as the ultimate arbiter for the resolution of the Armenian Question.[33] To this day not a single word of condemnation – or a single dime in restitution – has been paid for the blood of the victims. A recent study estimated the assets and properties stolen by the Turkish Government from the victims to be valued in trillions of dollars in present terms.[34] More importantly, international jurists found "valid legal grounds" in the articles of the Lausanne Treaty that entitled the victims and their heirs to indemnities and claims of all illegally seized assets and properties. Four prominent experts in international law have unanimously reached the conclusion that the wartime confiscations of the Armenian properties and assets were illegal.[35] These arguments were not only valid in the immediate aftermath of the war but were also found to have valid legal ground according to the articles stipulated by the Lausanne Treaty of July 24, 1923. Article 1 of the Lausanne Peace Treaty (Annex) and entitled "Life Assurance," contains five paragraphs that recognize the validity of life insurance contracts entered between an insurer and a person of an "enemy" country. The irony is that the British insurance company Star of London rejected life policy claims by the heirs of the Armenian victims on the basis that the claimants were subject of an "enemy" country. Given the validity of these policies according to the Lausanne Treaty we provide the text of these five paragraphs (articles) that appear in the Annex under the title Life Assurance:

Paragraph 1

Life assurance contracts entered into between an insurer and a person who subsequently became an enemy shall not be deemed to have been dissolved by the outbreak of war or by the fact of the person becoming an enemy. Every sum which, during the war, became due upon a contract deemed not to have been dissolved in accordance with the preceding paragraph shall be recoverable after the war. This sum shall be increased by interest at 5 per cent per annum from the date of its becoming due up to the day of payment.

If the contract has lapsed during the war, owing to non-payment of premiums or has become void from breach of the conditions of the contract, the assured, or his representatives, or the persons entitled, shall have the right at any moment within twelve months from the coming into force of the present Treaty to claim from the insurer the surrender value of the policy at the date of its lapse or annulation, [sic] together with interest at 5 per cent per annum. Turkish nationals whose life insurance contracts entered into before the 29th October, 1914, have been cancelled or reduced before the Treaty for non-payment of premiums in accordance with the provisions of the said contracts, shall have the right, within three months from the coming into force of the present Treaty, if they are still alive, to restore their policies for the whole of the amount assured. For this purpose they must, after having undergone a medical examination by the doctor of the company, the result of which the company considers satisfactory, pay the premiums in arrear with compound interest at 5 per cent.

Paragraph 2

It is understood that life assurance contracts in money other than the Turkish pound, entered into before the 29th October, 1914, between companies possessing the nationality of an Allied Power and Turkish nationals, in respect of which the premiums have been paid before and after the 18th November, 1915, or even only before that date, shall be regulated, first, by determining the rights of the assured in accordance with the general conditions of the policy for the period before the 18th November, 1915, in the currency stipulated in the contract at the current rate in its country of origin (for example, every amount stipulated in francs, in gold francs, or in "francs effectifs" [sic] will be paid in French francs), secondly, for the period after the 18th November, 1915, in Turkish pounds paper–the Turkish pound being taken at the pre-war par value. If Turkish nationals whose contracts were entered into in currency other than Turkish currency show that they have continued to pay their premiums since the 18th November, 1915, in the currency stipulated in the contracts, the said contracts shall be settled in the same currency at the current rate in its country of origin, even for the period after the 18th November, 1915. Turkish nationals whose contracts, entered into before the 29th October, 1914, in currency other than Turkish currency with companies possessing the nationality of an Allied Power are, owing to payment of premiums, still in force, shall have the right within three months after the coming into force of the present Treaty to restore their policies for the full amount, in the currency stipulated in their contract, at the current rate in its country of origin. For this purpose they must pay in this currency the premiums which have become due since the 18th November, 1915. On the other hand, the premiums actually paid by them in Turkish pounds paper since that date will be repaid to them in the same currency.

Paragraph 3

As regards insurances in Turkish pounds, settlement shall be made in Turkish pounds paper.

Paragraph 4

The provisions of paragraphs 2 and 3 do not apply to policy holders who, by an express agreement, have already settled with the insurance companies the fixation of the value of their policies and the method of payment of their premiums, nor to those whose policies shall have been finally settled at the date of the coming into force of the present Treaty.

Paragraph 5

For the purposes of the preceding paragraphs, insurance contracts shall be human life, combined with the rate of interest, for the calculation of the reciprocal engagement between the two parties.[36]

The insurers knew and admitted that the deaths of their policy holders were unrelated to war and were perpetrated by illegal means, and that their clients were not guilty of any wrongdoing. The insurers were also well aware that the carnage was executed with the full acquiescence of the Turkish government. This evidence compelled the insurers to consider the claims which resulted for a very few payments to the miraculously surviving heirs. However, when the claims passed a quarter of a million dollars, the insurers switched their policy and denied the claims. They pursued the policy of denial of the payments by requesting non-existent death certificates, by invoking lapses in premium payments, and by considering the policy holder as an "enemy" subject. While the denial of life insurance policy benefits was the game of the insurance companies, the state-sponsored systematic and institutionalized looting of the bank accounts and the properties of the Armenian was the goal of the Ittihadist leaders which they successfully implemented.

Notes

1. Herand Pastermadjian, in *Histoire de L'Arménie* (Paris: Librairie Oriental, H. Samuelian, 1971), pp. 11-20.
2. Salaheddin Bey, *La Turquie a L'Exposition Universel de 1867* (Paris, 1867), pp. 216-217. Cited by Herand Pastermadjian, ibid., p. 338. According to Pastermadjian, the French foreign minister, Gabriel Hanotaux, and his Russian counterpart, Lobanof, relied on this figure.
3. Ibid., p. 338.
4. Raymond Kévorkian and Paul Paboudjian, *Les Arméniens dans l'Empire Ottoman a la Veille du Génocide* (Paris: Arhis, 1992), pp. 55-60. This monumental book provides a meticulous analysis of the census that was conducted between February 1913 and August 1914 and details the economic wealth of the Armenians in the pre-Genocide era. It is necessary to dwell in some detail on this census as Turkey continues, at the time of writing, to distort the number of Armenians murdered during the 1915-16 genocide. The Patriarchate estimated the number of Armenians living exclusively in the Armenian provinces (*vilayets*) of Van, Erzerum, Bitilis, Mamurat-el-Aziz, and Dyarbekir to be around 804,500. Realizing the inadequacy of such a partial census, the Patriarchate then embarked on a more ambitious and systematic effort to count Armenians living in all of the Ottoman Turkey. Starting on February 20, 1913, a circular letter and questionnaires were sent to all Armenian dioceses in Turkey. The parishioners of each diocese were instructed to prepare the lists of all Armenians living in their administrative districts and send

them to Constantinople, the capital of Turkey, for final tabulation. The census was completed in the summer of 1914, one year later than the originally anticipated date of May 1913. The census, compiled according to 17 administrative units, put the total number of Armenians at 1,914,620. The West had a vested interest in the census as it was considering the introduction of administrative reforms in the Armenian provinces. To this end two European delegates were at hand to monitor the results of the census. Because of some difficulties of access to certain hostile regions controlled by armed Kurdish bands, the census could actually have been an underestimation. According to Kévorkian and Paboudjian, the Armenians owned a total of 2,538 churches, 451 monasteries, and 1996 schools attended by 173,022 students in a total of 2,925 towns and villages. Nearly 800,000 Armenians lived in the eastern Armenian provinces, with 90 percent of them engaged in agriculture. In the west (Constantinople, Smyrna, and Thrace) there were some 215,131 Armenians, while in the south (Cilicia and Adana) about 175,000 lived, also mostly engaged in agriculture. The gross annual productivity in the Armenian provinces during the 1913-14 period reached about 6.6 million dollars per year (1.3 million Turkish pounds). The urbanized Armenians were engaged in various crafts, such as weaving, carpentry, jewelry, ceramics and stone carving, and in inter-regional trade. No less important were tissue printing, processing and dyeing of wool, silk and leather. In the coastal areas, fishing and maritime transport were quite important. In Constantinople, no fewer than 1,500 shops, out of a total of 5,000, were in the hands of Armenians; 35,979 professional workers and about 15,000 craftsmen were employed in them.

5.   Vahakn N. Dadrian, *The History of Armenian Genocide: Ethnic Conflict from the Balkans to Anatolia to Caucausus* (Rhode Island: Bergham Books, 1995).

6.   J.P. Mallory, *Search of the Indo-Europeans* (London: Thames and Hudson Ltd., 1989), pp. 33-35.

7.   Gérard Dedeyan, ed., *Histoire des Arméniens* (Toulouse: Privat, 1982), pp. 141-184; The New York Times, June 30, 1999, p. A19. See also Dadrian, *The History of Armenian Genocide* (note 5).

8.   Yehuda Bauer, *Rethinking the Holocaust* (New Haven, CT: Yale University Press, 2001), pp. 45-46. Bauer also observes that "Apart from Armenian peasants, there was the Armenian middle class in the Turkish towns and cities, which had an important commercial, cultural, and intellectual influence."

9.   Kévorkian and Paboudjian, op. cit., (note 4), pp. 55-60.

10.   Vahakn N. Dadrian, *Warrant for Genocide: Key Elements of Turko-Armenian Conflict* (New Brunswick, NJ: Transaction Publishers, 1999), pp. 1-2. See also Vahakn N. Dadrian, "Genocide as a problem of national and international law: The World War I Armenian case and its contemporary legal ramification," *Yale Journal of International Law*, 14:2, 1989, pp. 221-334.

11.   Vahakn N. Dadrian, "Genocide as a problem of national and international law: The World War I Armenian case and its contemporary legal ramifications," *Yale Journal of International Law*, 14:2, 1989. Vahakn N. Dadrian, The Secret Young-Turk Ittihadist Conference and the Decision for the World War I Genocide of the Armenians. *Holocaust and Genocide Studies*, 7 (2) Fall 1993, pp173-201. Given its unique importance, the English translation of this secret document is provided in full:

1)   Profiting by Arts: 3 and 4 of Committee of Union and Progress, close all Armenian Societies, and arrest all who worked against Government at any time among them and send them into the provinces such as Baghdad or Mosul, and wipe them out either on the road or there.

2) Collect arms.

3) Excite Moslem opinion by suitable and special means, in places as Van, Erzerum, Adana, where as point of fact the Armenians have already won the hatred of the Moslems, provoke organized massacres as the Russians did in Baku.

4) Leave all executive to the people in the provinces such as Erzerum, Van, Mamuret ul Aziz, and Bitlis, and use Military disciplinary forces (i.e., Gendarmerie) ostensibly to stop massacres, while on the contrary in places as Adana, Sica, Broussa, Ismidt and Smyrna actively help the Moslems with military force.

5) Apply measures to exterminate all males under 50, priest and teachers, leave girls and children to be Islamized.

6) Carry away the families of all who succeed in escaping and apply measures to cut them off from all connection with their native place.

7) On the ground that Armenian officials may be spies, expel and drive them out absolutely from every Government department or post.

8) Kill off in an appropriate manner all Armenians in the Army, this is to be left to the military to do.

9) All action to begin everywhere simultaneously, and thus leave no time for preparation of defensive measures.

10) Pay attention to the strictly confidential nature of these instructions, which may not go beyond two or three persons.

12. Vahakn N. Dadrian, *The History of Armenian Genocide: Ethnic Conflict from the Balkans to Anatolia to Caucasus* (Rhode Island: Bergham Books, 1995).

13. Vahakn N. Dadrian, "The historical and legal interconnection between the Armenian genocide and the Jewish Holocaust: From impunity to retributive justice," *Yale Journal of International Law*, 23:2, Summer 1998, p. 545.

14. Lévon Marashlian, "Finishing the genocide: Cleansing Turkey of Armenian survivors, 1920-1923," in R.G. Hovannisian (ed.), *Remembrance and Denial: The Case of the Armenian Genocide* (Detroit, MI: Wayne State University Press, 1998), pp. 113-145.

15. The Armenian National Institute: http://www.armenian–genocide.org

16. Dikran Kouymjian, "Confiscation and Destruction: A manifestation of the Genocide process," *Armenian Forum*, 1:3, Autumn 1998, pp. 1–12.

17. Dadrian, supra 11, pp. 302-303.

18. Gary J. Bass, *Stay the Hand of Vengeance: The Politics of War Crimes Tribunals* (Princeton, NJ: Princeton University Press, 2000), pp. 106-146.

19. Dadrian, op. cit. (note 11), pp. 301 303.

20. Fred L. Israel, ed., *Major Peace Treaties of Modern History,* Volume IV (New York: Chelsea House Publishers and McGraw Hill Book Co, 1967).

21. Dadrian, op. cit. (n. 13), pp. 508–509. The issue of the loyalty of Armenian soldiers to the Ottoman army and soldiers needs to be emphasized because the revisionists have variably qualified the Armenian soldiers as "traitors" and/or "spies" siding with the Russians against Turkey. The Minister of War and de facto commander-in-chief of the Ottoman Armed Forces, Enver Pasha, praised the outstanding combative courage and skills of Armenian soldiers in the large Turkish attacks against the Russians during the winter of 1914-1915. He went on record to praise, in writing, to the Armenian primate in Konya, Karékin Khatchadourian, the Armenian acts of bravery during the war, which he "personally had observed." On another occasion, Enver told the Armenian patriarch in Constantinople that a swift and a tactical move by an Armenian lieutenant, Hovannes Aginian, a veteran of

the Balkan war, saved his life during a surprise Russian attack. Enver promoted Aginian to the rank of captain and sent a certificate of congratulations and thanks to his family. The twofold irony of this, however, is that after his promotion the soldier was killed on the battlefield, and his parents could not receive the certificate as they had been deported from Sivas to Surudjand and were killed en route by the death squads. See also Vahakn N. Dadrian, *Warrant for Genocide,* op. cit. (note 9), p. 114.

22. Henry Morgenthau, *"Ambassador Morgenthau's Story: The Documented Account of the Armenian Genocide First of the Century Reported by America's Ambassador to Turkey* (Plandome, NY: New Age Publishers, reprinted edition, 1965, originally published in 1919 by Doubleday Page & Co.), p. 222.

23. Ibid., p. 223.

24. Ibid., pp. 224–225.

25. *Adolf Hitler's First Antisemitic Writing, September 16, 1919,* translated by Richard S. Levy, available online at http://www.h-net.org/~german/gtext/kaiserreich/hitler2.html.

26. "Himmler's October 4, 1943 Posen Speech, 'Extermination,'" Nizkor Project, translated by the Nizkor Project, cited by Gregg J. Rickman, *Conquest and Redemption: A History of Jewish Assets from the Holocaust* (New Brunswick, NJ: Transaction Publishers, 2007), p. 9.

27. Kévorkian and Paboudjian, op. cit. (note 4). In his recent book, "The Remaining Documents of Talât Pasha," Murat Bardakci analyzed Talât's own handwritten documents given to him by Talât's widow, Hayriye, before she died in 1983. According to Talât's long-hidden secret documents, 972,000 Ottoman Armenians disappeared from official population records from 1915 through 1916. (See article by Sabrina Tavernise, New York Times, March 9, 2009).

28. Morgenthau, ibid., (n. 22) , p. 223.

29. Lethar Gall, Gerald D. Feldman, Harold James, Carl-Ludwig Holtfrerich, Hans E. Büschgen, *The Deutsche Bank: 1870–1995* (London: Weidenfeld & Nicolson, 1995), p. 142.

30. Franz Günter to Arthur von Gwinner, 17 August 1915, HADB, OR1704, in *Historisches Archiv der Deutschen Bank,* cited by Feldman, in ibid. For German complicity see: Vahakn N. Dadrian, *German Responsibility in the Armenian Genocide* (Watertown, MA: Blue Crane Books, 1996); and Ulrich Trumpener, *Germany and the Ottoman Empire 1914–1918* (New York: Caravan Books, Delmar, 1989).

31. Israel W. Charney, "Introduction," p. ix, in a monograph by Vahakn N. Dadrian, "Documentation of the Armenian Genocide in German and Austrian Sources," reprinted from *The Widening Circle of Genocide. Genocide: A Critical Biographic Review,* vol. 3, Israel C.W. (ed.), (New Brunswick, NJ: Transaction Publishers, 1994.) See also, Robert F. Melson, *Revolution and Genocide: On the Origins of the Armenian Genocide and the Holocaust* (Chicago: University of Chicago Press, Chicago, 1992). Melson conceptualizes the processes of genocide by the comparative method and draws parallels between the Armenian and the Jewish genocides. He argues that both genocides evolved around "a revolution contingent upon a set of factors, including twisted ideologies and ill-considered fantasies rotating around a murderous hinge and targeting a highly vulnerable population, while taking advantage of the opportunities afforded by the war."

32. Kévork B. Bardakjian, *Hitler and the Armenian Genocide* (Cambridge, MA: Zoryan Institute, 1985). The remark attributed to Hitler appears in a summary of Hitler's speech to his generals, on August 22, 1939, about his plans to wage a war against Poland. Within days, Louis P. Lochner of the Associated Press in

Berlin received from an "informant" a copy of the speech, which was based on notes taken by Admiral Wilhelm Canaris, head of Hitler's military intelligence. See also, Vahakn N. Dadrian, "The historical and legal interconnections between the Armenian Genocide and the Jewish Holocaust: From impunity to retributive justice," *Yale Journal of International Law*, 23:2, Summer 1998, p. 535; Martin Gilbert, *The First World War: A Complete History* (New York: Henry Holt & Co., An Owl Book, 1994), p. 143; and Vahakn N. Dadrian, *German Responsibility in the Armenian Genocide* (Watertown, MA: Blue Crane Books, 1996).

33.   Vahakn N. Dadrian, *"The History of Armenian Genocide: Ethnic Conflict from the Balkans to Anatolia to Caucasus* (Watertown, MA: Blue Crane Books, 1995), p. xviii. The mistreatment of the Armenians in their historic homeland mobilized the public conscience in the West as intellectuals, writers, and political activists rose in protest and called for the protection of the Armenians. The public concern however, did not run in tandem with the political expediency of the European states. While the European Powers promised to implement reforms in the Armenian provinces, they failed to honor their promise. Political expediency and conflicts of interests prevented the Great Powers from implementing reforms in the Armenian provinces as stipulated by articles of the Berlin Treaty of July 13, 1878.

34.   Kouymjian, ibid. (note 16), pp. 1-12.

35.   *Confiscation des Biens des Refugiés Arméniens par the Gouvernement Turc* (Confiscation of the Properties of the Armenian Refugees by the Turkish Government) Consultation of M.M. Gilbert Gidel, Albert De Lapradelle, Louis Le Fur, André N. Mandelstam (Paris: Imprimerie, Massis, 1929).

36.   Fred L. Israel, ed., *Major Peace Treaties of Modern History,* Volume IV (New York: Chelsea House Publishers and McGraw Hill Book Co, 1967), pp. 2341-2342.

2

Thousands of Armenian Life Insurance Policies

By the time World War I began, the New York Life Insurance Company and the Paris-based Union-Vie had each sold thousands of policies to Armenians. A third insurer, the Equitable Life Assurance Society of New York (Equitable), was also active; it had sold a large, but smaller number of life policies to Armenians. While documentary evidence will be presented on these three insurance companies, it is necessary to mention that many other European companies, British, Austrian, Swiss, Italian, German and Spanish, were also active in the life insurance business in Turkey prior to the start of World War I. No quantitative or detailed information is yet available on these insurers, largely because it remains concealed and outside the public domain. However, U.S. State Department documents show that two particular companies, Star of London and the Swiss firm La Fédèrale, were very active.[1]

New York Life and Armenian Insurance Policies

New York Life maintained one of the largest business operations in Turkey. Established in 1845 and known to insiders as "The Company," in the vision of its founders and directors New York Life was and was perceived – and revered – as a missionary movement.[2] The first definite allusion to New York Life's appetite for foreign expansion appears in a declaration made by the company's president, on January 28, 1863, in his annual report to the Board of Trustees: "We shall press forward in the prosecution of our work until the blessings of life insurance shall be widely disseminated not only throughout our land but…from sea to sea and…to ends of the earth."[3] Its field of operations extended from Russia in the north to South Africa in the south and from England in the west to China and Japan in the east, and it was also well established in the islands of the Caribbean and in South America. It has been said that the employees of New York Life stationed in distant parts of the world conducted their affairs "like the proconsuls of the ancient Roman empire, separated from home but devoting them with loyalty to the great organization of which they were a component part."[4] The Company continued its business in Turkey until the outbreak of the war in 1914.

New York Life found a fertile business milieu amongst the well-to-do and family-oriented Armenians in Turkey. According to a State Department document, the total amount of life insurance contracts that New York Life held in Turkey on the eve of World War I exceeded ten million dollars. This document, a letter written by New York Life's general counsel and addressed to the U.S. Secretary of State William Jennings Bryan, is dated March 20, 1915, only five months after Turkey entered the war (on October 18, 1914). The letter expresses concern over potential war-related financial losses by the New York Life and lays its decision to stop new business transactions in Turkey and to quickly liquidate all its outstanding accounts in Turkey:

> New York Life Insurance Company, a corporation of and domiciled in New York, has been transacting the business of life insurance in the Turkish Empire for some twenty years past, so that it now has outstanding contracts of insurance with subjects of that Empire aggregating in the neighborhood of $10,281,134. After breaking out of the European War, and in August last, the Company discontinued making new contracts of insurance in the Turkish Empire, and pursuant to this determination there and then duly cancelled its contract with all soliciting agents in the Empire.[5]

An appreciation of the relative value of ten million dollars relative to New York Life's assets, holdings and collaterals in 1915 may be found in an appraisal made by the New York's Life's Board member, Lawrence F. Abbott:

> It is, therefore, all the more to the credit of the executives in charge of the New York Life that they proceeded on the assumption that sooner or later the entire civilized world might be involved [in the war]. The Company began immediately to husband its resources. It sold securities and even borrowed money on collateral, thus accumulating the unusual sum of $13,697,000 of cash in bank, at the close of 1914.[6]

It is clear from this report that The Company's outstanding balance in Turkey was only $3 million short of all securities, collaterals and holdings that were available to the Company. In this letter to the U.S. Secretary of State, the New York Life executive requested that the U.S. ambassador in Constantinople, Henry Morgenthau, Sr., help set up a "liquidation office" in Constantinople to settle all its outstanding accounts, "without inconvenience to the policyholders and as rapidly as possible." Furthermore, in an attempt to evade the payment of war taxes imposed by Turkey on foreign firms doing business in Turkey, New York Life's vice president requested from the secretary of state to instruct his ambassador in Turkey to persuade Turkish authorities to exempt New York Life from the new tax law:

> The Turkish Empire passed a law imposing such exacting conditions for the right of foreign insurance companies to do business in Turkey.... Among the conditions imposed by this law is the requirement to deposit in a bank designated by the Minister of Commerce a cash caution of from 5,000 £ to 15,000 £ [i.e., Turkish pounds].... Therefore, may we not ask for the good offices on our behalf of the American Ambassador to the Ottoman Empire to the end that the company may obtain permission to maintain a local office or offices in the Turkish Empire for the liquidation of outstanding contracts with its Turkish insured, without subjecting itself to the new Turkish insurance law? [7]

Secretary of State Bryan complied with New York Life's request by immediately instructing Ambassador Morgenthau to use his authority to help the company liquidate its outstanding accounts in Turkey.[8] Morgenthau responded that the embassy was complying with the secretary's instructions by "according all possible assistance…in the settlement of Company's affairs."[9]

Although the letter from New York Life indicated the total amount of the company's business transactions in Turkey, neither the number nor the identities of the policyholders were disclosed. However, another letter, a document dated November 20, 1922, reveals for the first time that the majority of the people in Turkey who had bought life insurance policies from New York Life were of Armenian origin. This letter was sent by the New York Life vice-president Thomas A. Buckner to the United States secretary of state Charles Evans Hughes and reads in part: "Much of this insurance…was written upon the lives of subject peoples, such as the Armenians and others who have, during the years since the outbreak of the European War, been subjected to massacre and illegal killing and fatal exposure."[10] Indeed, the large number of Armenians holding life policies must have captured Ambassador Morgenthau's attention, as he mentions in his lucid and authoritative memoir: "The extent to which this people [Armenians] insured their lives was merely another indication of their thrifty habits."[11]

Reverend Stapleton, and Armenian Life Policies

Some of the policies that the Armenians had purchased from foreign insurers were left behind on the eve of their forced deportations from their homes. The terror-stricken Armenians turned to foreigners, such as

American missionaries, for help and shelter. A few were able to leave their valuables, including insurance policies, with the American missionaries in the towns from which the Armenians were forcefully deported.[12] One such recipient of Armenian life policies was Reverend Robert Stapleton of the American Mission in Erzerum, a city that witnessed the deportation of tens of thousands of Armenians. Reverend Stapleton, the director of the missionary schools in Erzerum, provided a concise account of the life policies left behind by the deported Armenians. He asked Oscar S. Heizer, the American consul stationed in the nearby port city of Trebizond, to visit him for advice and guidance on the eve of the massive forced deportations of the Armenians from the city. Ambassador Morgenthau approved the visit of Consul Heizer to Erzerum. Upon the completion of his visit, on September 25, 1915, Heizer sent the following report to Ambassador Morgenthau, which reads in part:

> Arrangements were immediately made and I left Trebizond August 12th on horseback accompanied by *cavass* (team leader) Ahmed and a *caterdji* (horse-man) with my traveling outfit, also two mounted gendarmes furnished by Governor General. I reached Erzerum about midnight August 17th and was allowed to enter the city gate only after communicating with the Commandant. I found the two American families well. Rev. Robert S. Stapleton, who is director of the American schools and Treasurer of the Mission Station, is living with his wife and two daughters in the upper story of the Boy's School building. Dr. Case and wife and two small children were living in the upper part of the Hospital building, the lower part being used as a Red Crescent Hospital....Over 900 bales of goods of various kinds were deposited by 150 Armenians in Rev. Stapleton's house for safekeeping. There are also about 500 bales in Dr. Case's house and stable. The value of the bales is estimated by Mr. Stapleton at from Ltq. 10,000 to Ltq. 15,000 [equivalent of $50,000 to $75,000].... Many policies of insurance in the New York Life Ins. Co. were found in these packages....[13]

Reverend Stapleton gave Heizer a list of the names of seventeen Armenians in Trebizond who held nineteen life insurance policies with New York Life, each of which was valued at $500 to $2,000. An unspecified number of premium receipts were also handed over to Heizer. On October 12, 1915 Heizer forwarded the receipts of the premiums and the list of the insured Armenians to Ambassador Morgenthau with the following cover letter:

> Referring to a report from this office dated September 25th concerning affairs in Erzerum. I now have the honor to enclose herewith a list of life insurance policies issued by the New York Life Ins. Co. of which J. W. Whittall & Co. are the agents for Turkey, which are in Mr. Stapleton's hands, having been left with him by the owners before being deported. In some cases loans have been obtained upon the policies and in those cases, only the receipts for premiums were found, the policy being with the Company.... It is probable that many if not all of the above mentioned persons have perished. Possibly the above information would be of some value to the Agents of the

New York Life Ins. Co. In addition to the above there were a number of life policies in French, German, and Austrian Companies.[14]

Morgenthau then swiftly forwarded the policies sent by Heizer to New York Life's agents in Constantinople for consideration.[15] The State Department then sent a copy of the list of the insured Armenians presumed dead to New York Life's home office in New York City.[16] The home office, in a letter to the United States Assistant Secretary of State Alvey Adee, and the latter duly acknowledged receipt of the list:

> Permit me to acknowledge and thank you for your esteemed favor of the 22nd inst. Enclosing a copy of a communication received from the Consul Heizer giving a list of policies which have been issued by this company on the lives of Armenians, deposited at the Consulate at Trebizond. If you should receive any further advices [sic] indicating the fate of the persons insured under these contracts it would be appreciated as a further favor if you could advise us.[17]

In response, Assistant Secretary Adee indicated his willingness to comply with New York Life's desire to receive updates on the fate of the deported Armenians who held life insurance policies with New York Life with the hope of benefit payments to the victims' heirs.[18]

Archives of New York Life

The existence of a large number of insured Armenians is further confirmed by documents derived directly from the archives of New York Life. An undated internal memo, entitled "Turkey & Egypt," indicates that the large number of Armenians insured with New York Life necessitated the creation of a separate and new folder made of several files and labeled "Supplementary Accounts." This internal memo, most probably written by an experienced claims officer, provides a detailed account of the location of the files and the methods of handling Armenian claims resulting from the massacres. A section of the memo reads as follows:

> The Supplementary Accounts (of which there are about 20 because of Armenian death losses) are in the same places as for other countries. The correspondence file covering the Agreement and policies will be found in the 'Turkey & Egypt" drawer of the foreign files. In addition to the aforementioned Supplementary Accounts there is also a bound book containing the Supplementary Accounts 1 to 4, inclusive. This book which is in the same place as the other Supplementary Accounts, contains much information about Turkish death losses which resulted from Armenian massacres during World War I.[19]

Attempts by one of us (HSK) to secure from New York Life the names of the insured Armenians were unsuccessful. A written correspondence from Mrs. Tracy Ramos, a current New York Life Archivist, stated that she has "not come across the Supplementary Accounts." Based on these accounts, it was anticipated that the list of all Armenians insured in Turkey with the New York Life could have been found in the "bound book" containing the "Supplementary Accounts."

Equitable Life Assurance Society and the Armenian Life Policies

In a letter dated August 9, 1916, and addressed to the United States Embassy in Constantinople, Mr. Henry L. Rosenfeld, the fourth vice-president of Equitable, appraises the budgetary and financial status of Equitable in Turkey at the outbreak of the World War I as follows:

> On January 1, 1916 the Society had outstanding in Turkey 371 policies for $689,883 of insurance. The collection of premiums and payment of claims under old policies outstanding at the time the Society ceased the transaction of new business in Turkey in 1912. Prior to the present war the Turkish business was administered through Paris. Since the entrance of Turkey into the war the Society has for the convenience of its policyholders collected premiums, made loans, paid claims, etc in three Turkish cities, namely: Constantinople through Mr. Mitrani, Jerusalem through Levin and in Smyrna through L. and L Varbetian.... [20]

The timing of this letter, just a few months after Equitable's Constantinople agent was served with a Turkish government memo requesting the names of all of its insured Armenians (as was the case with the New York Life), suggests that a large number of its insured were of Armenian origin. The agent, perplexed by such an unusual request, informed the American Chargé d'Affaires in Constantinople, Hoffaman Philip Esq., that he must "communicate with the home office before he could comply with the request made by the Turkish Government."[21]

The Union-Vie and Armenian Life Policies

The French Union-Vie, part of the Compagnie de l'Union (currently part of AXA S.A.), was also very active in Turkey. According to the Director of Union-Vie, a great number of life policies had been sold to Armenians. This information comes from a letter sent by the director of Union-Vie to the French foreign ministry. This highly revealing and insightful letter was discovered as an enclosure in New York Life Vice President Buckner's letter addressed to the U. S. secretary of state, discussed above. Union-Vie's letter, translated into English by New York Life officials, indicated that the majority of the Union-Vie life policies in Turkey were sold to Armenians. The letter, dated April 11, 1922, reads in part:

> Our Constantinople Agency, already long-established, has assumed considerable development. The amount of risks insured by the "Union-Vie" in the Ottoman Empire

reaches on the 31st of December, 1914, Fr. 42,335,000, and the whole of these risks was spread over 10,899 contracts. We are thus placed in the first rank among the French and foreign companies which operate in that country. As regards the Armenian Massacres, the situation is as follows: The greater number of our contracts are on the lives of Armenians, in the first place, because these clients had been particularly canvassed by our representant [sic] at Constantinople, who belonged himself to the Armenian race and further because the Catholics [meaning Christians] constitute above all the insurable element, life insurance being speculative contract which may appear contrary to Koranic principles.[22]

An analysis of the documents derived from the three insurance companies (New York Life, Union-Vie and Equitable) shows that in the pre-genocide era tens of thousands of Armenians held life insurance policies with American and European companies. While quantitative data were obtained only from these three insurers, there were more than a dozen other insurers who transacted life insurance business in Turkey, Swiss La Fédèrale and the British Star being amongst the most active ones. Thus one is led to conclude that the number of Armenians insured during the pre-genocide era in Turkey must have been even larger than the numbers noted above. The insurers further maintained that "Armenians and the Christians constituted all the insurable elements," perhaps because buying life insurance was perceived as being against Koranic principles.[23] It therefore also comes as no surprise to discover that all the major insurers in Turkey had hired agents and representatives who were of Armenian origin. For example, Equitable's Smyrna representative's name was Varbetian; New York Life's Constantinople agent, Han Kenadjian; the executive officer of the Swiss life insurance company La Fédèrale, Carnig Asdzvadour [24]; and the agents of North British and Mercantile, Carnick Seropian and Son.[25] The insurers undoubtedly reasoned that since the Armenians constituted the highest insurable element in Turkey, it made perfect business sense to hire agents that speak Armenian in order to facilitate the task of enticing them to buy life insurance policies.

Notes

1. Shavarsh Toriguian, "Letters Concerning Armenian Insurance Policies," in *The Armenian Question and the International Law* (2nd edition) (La Verne, CA: University of La Verne Press, 1988), pp. 144–156.
2. Lawrence Fraser Abbott, *The Story of NYLIC: A History of the Origin and Development of the New York Life Insurance Company from 1845–1929* (Newark, NJ: A.S. Browne Inc., 1930), p. 113. According to Abbot, New York Life Insurance Company, had commissioned this book in the introduction to which he states that "... special acknowledgment must be made…and above all, to President Kingsley and Vice President Thomas A. Buckner for their conception of the idea of this book, their specific aid in the biographical and legislative portions of the work

and their general encouragement and editorial supervision." It must be noted that Abbott himself was a member of the Board of Directors of the New York Life.

3.   Ibid., p. 117.
4.   Ibid., p. 130.
5.   McIntosh to Secretary of State Bryan, March 20, 1915, U.S. National Archives, RG 59. File 867.5064/3. In this letter it can be seen that the words "Ottoman" and "Turkey" as well as "Ottoman Empire" and Turkish Empire," are used alternately. Such alternate use of the terms was a common practice amongst the diplomats of the day, but represented no historical slant.
6.   Lawrence Fraser Abbott, op. cit., note 2, p. 204
7.   McIntosh, op. cit., note 5, p.2.
8.   Secretary of State Bryan to Ambassador Morgenthau, March 23, 1915, U.S. National Archives, RG 84, File 850.6.
9.   Ambassador Morgenthau to U.S. Secretary of State, April 26, 1915, U.S. National Archives, RG 59, File 867.5064/3.
10.   Buckner to U.S. Secretary State Lansing, November 20, 1922, U.S. National Archives, RG 59, 367.115N483/3.
11.   Henry Morgenthau. *"Ambassador Morgenthau's Story: The Documented Account of the Armenian Genocide, First of the Century, Reported by America's Ambassador to Turkey"* (Plandome, NY: New Age Publisher, 1965), reprinted edition (originally published in 1919 by Doubleday Page & Co.), p. 339. Morgenthau's personal account strongly corroborates the information presented in the present book. Morgenthau was directly involved in assisting communications between insurance companies' representatives in Turkey and their European and American Home Offices and Headquarters.
12.   Compiled by James L. Barton. Ara Sarafian (ed.), *Turkish Atrocities: Statements of American Missionaries on the Destruction of Christian Communities in Ottoman Turkey, 1915-1917* (Edison, NJ: Gomidas Institute, 1998).
13.   Compiled and Introduced by Ara Sarafian, *United States Official Documents on the Armenian Genocide. Volume II: The Peripheries* (Watertown, MA: Armenian Review, 1994), pp. 43–46.
14.   Heizer to Morgenthau, October 12, 1915, U.S. National Archives, RG 59. File 867.5064/6.
15.   Morgenthau to Agent of New York Life in Constantinople, November 1, 1915, U.S. National Archives, Records, RG 84, File, 850.6.
16.   Secretary of State to New York Life in New York City, December 22, 1915, U.S. National Archives, RG 59. File 867.5064/6.
17.   New York Life Secretary Raymond M. Ballard to U.S. Assistant Secretary of State Adee, December 29, 1915, U.S. National Archives, RG 59. File 867.5064/7.
18.   U.S. Assistant Secretary of State Adee to New York Life in New York City, January 10, 1916, U.S. National Archives, RG 59. File 867.5064/7.
19.   New York Life Insurance Company Archives, "Facts on New York Life's Foreign Business," *Turkey & Egypt* (Binder). This undated 2-page memo along with a cover letter was sent, upon request, to us in 1996.
20.   Vice President of Equitable Life Assurance Society to U.S. Ambassador to Turkey, August 9, 1916, U.S. National Archives, RG 84, File, 850.6.
21.   U.S. Embassy in Turkey to Henry L. Rosenfeld, Equitable Life Assurance Society, September 21, 1916, U.S. National Archives RG 84, File, 850.6.
22.   Buckner to U.S. Secretary of State, November 20, 1922, U.S. National Archives. RG 59, 367.115N483/3 (enclosure). A copy of the communication addressed by Union-Vie, to the French Minister of Foreign Affaires, dated April 11, 1922.

23. Ibid., p. 2.
24. La Fédèrale Council Moustafa in Constantinople to Carnik Asfazadour, La Fédèrale, Zurich, March 10, 1916, U.S. National Archives, RG 84, File, 850.6.
25. Carnick Seropian and Son to U.S. Consul in Constantinople, June 12, 1916, U.S. National Archives, RG 84, File, 850.6.

3

Genocide and the Validity of the Victims' Life Insurance Policies

Given the war conditions under which some of the claims for life policy benefits were made, a question arises as to whether the life policy benefits of the Armenian victims were payable at all. The question arises because specific clauses of life insurance contracts allow payment denials due to "war-related acts." In order to ascertain the validity of the claims and to demonstrate eligibility for collection in this class of claims, it would be useful to produce evidence of actual payments made on behalf of such victims on two different levels. First, it must be shown that the insurance companies admit liability to the survivors of the victims. Such an admission should preferably be made by no less than a senior insurance executive in non-ambiguous terms. Second, eligibility becomes a matter of fact if it can be shown that at least some of the victim's heirs in this class of claims have actually collected policy benefits. The coexistence of internal evidentiary documents (of the insurers) and external ones (of the victims' heirs) would provide compelling evidence that the life insurance policies in this class of claims are indeed valid, and payments are due. The documents discussed in this chapter are examples of exactly these kinds of evidence, indicating proven eligibility.

Internal insurance company documents show that only very few claims were actually filed. The very limited number of claims could have resulted from two impediments. First, the filing of a claim was a very difficult, and at times an impossible process. The claimants no longer possessed a "legal residence" and had no means of producing multilayered evidentiary legal and other documents. Secondly, many of the victims' immediate heirs also perished during the forced deportations, leaving no progeny or other inheritors to claim the policy benefits. In the case of policies purchased from the British insurers, for example, the claims were rejected outright because the British government banned "payment of a policy on the life of an enemy during the war."

The documents detailed below show how difficult the claim process was and how crucial and decisive was the role played by the United States diplomatic corps and American missionaries in assisting the victims' heirs to collect the benefits. The paper trails of two victims, Vartivar Kassardjian, who was insured with New York Life, and Ovakim Kevork Massatian, who was insured with Equitable and Star Assurance of London, show that without the support of the members of the diplomatic corps, and U.S. Ambassador Morgenthau specifically, not a single claim could have been processed, let alone paid.

Payments of Claims by New York Life

New York Life accepted a small number of claims made by the heirs of the deported Armenians. In a letter of November 20, 1922 to U.S. secretary of state, New York Life Vice President Buckner detailed the amounts involved in claims made against New York Life on the lives of its insured Armenians:

> Insofar as records are now available, and these are but partial, this Company has actually paid out, or had claims filed against it, as insurance on the lives of persons killed within the Ottoman Empire by massacre or in consequence of deportation, substantially the following sums:
>
> On French franc policies, frs. 1,772,338
>
> On sterling policies,   £ 45,214
>
> On dollar polices, $ 7,938
>
> After deducting the reserves against these polices, there remains:
>
> | | |
> |---|---|
> | Francs, | 1,348,775 |
> | Pounds, | 26,873 |
> | Dollars, | 6,141 |
>
> These sums, at current rates of exchange, amount to approximately $230,000, and measure the loss so far suffered by this Company, for which we believe the Turkish Government is, and should be held, responsible.... Much of this insurance was written upon the lives of subject peoples, such as Armenians and others who have, during the years since the outbreak of the European War, been subjected to massacres and illegal killings.... The ultimate loss will doubtless prove to be greater than has been developed by the claims so far filed.[1]

It was not clear, however, from this letter-document how much of the money was actually paid out and how much of it remained as unpaid claims. The documents detailed below show how difficult the claim process was and how crucial and decisive was the role played by the United States diplomatic corps and American missionaries in assisting the victims' heirs to collect the benefits.

The Case of Vartivar Kassardjian

Few Armenians survived the death marches in the Syrian deserts and were able to reach the northern Syrian town of Aleppo. Some of the survivors later went further south to the Syrian capital city, Damascus. American consulates were present in these two cities in order to protect the interests of the United States Government and the American companies doing business in the region. On December 16, 1915, Mrs. Kassardjian and her two children, Papken and Santouhi, filed a claim against New York Life on behalf of her husband and their father, Vartivar Kassardjian, who had been forcefully deported in the summer of 1915 and was presumed dead. With the help of the American consuls in Aleppo and Damascus and Ambassador Morgenthau in Constantinople, the three survivors of the deceased Vartivar Kassardjian were finally able to receive the life policy benefit in the amount of about $600. The trail of this single policy claim shows that the process of the successful claim involved at least seven pieces of correspondence and, most importantly, the compassionate plea of three high-ranking American officials, in Constantinople, Aleppo, and Damascus. This paper trail is highlighted by five State Department documents cited in the references 2 to 6.

On December 16, 1915, New York Life's agent in Constantinople received the claim on behalf of the deceased Vartivar Kassardjian through the United States Embassy in Constantinople. Upon receipt of the claim, the agent sent the policy documents back to the United Sates Embassy in Constantinople, requesting the certified signatures of the policy's heirs for the purpose of verifying their identity. On December 20 Ambassador Morgenthau forwarded New York Life's request to Jesse B. Jackson, the United States consul in Aleppo, where the deported heirs of the insured victim were last heard from.[2] On January 20, 1916, Jackson acknowledged receipt of Morgenthau's letter and informed him that the heirs were no longer residing in Aleppo but were now in Damascus.[3] In a letter dated February 17, addressed to the United States Embassy in Constantinople, the American consular agent in Damascus acknowledged receipt of Jackson's letter and informed Morgenthau of his meeting with the heirs of the victims. He noted that "Owing [to] the miserable circumstances they were unable to pay the regular consular fee for certification, so I accordingly certified their signatures as a witness."[4] The Damascus-based American consular agent then transmitted the desire of the heirs that the claim be paid through the American consular agency in Damascus. On March 15, the United States Embassy in Constantinople acknowledged the receipt of the sum of 117.05 Turkish Pounds (equivalent to 2,692.40 French francs, about $600.[5] On that same day, March 15, the United States Embassy in Constantinople collected the money, and the American consular agent in Damascus was informed that the sum of 117.06 Turkish pounds, less expenses, was sent to Damascus through the Ottoman Régie as life policy benefits to the heirs of Vartivar Kassardjian.[6]

New York Life's Archives

As of December 31, 1921, New York Life's business in Turkey was reinsured with the Paris-based Union-Vie. The few archival materials that this author obtained from New York Life show that Union-Vie processed some of the claims filed by the heirs of insured Armenians against New York Life. These documents show that the Paris Loss Committee, after approval of the claims, forwarded the claims back to New York Life's headquarters in New York City for final approval and authorization of payments. The process of approval entailed following strict rules, including confirmation of timely premium payments, provision of death certificates, and absence of lapses. The seeming presence of lapses was carefully analyzed and discussed by the committee members to establish if such "lapses" were the result of forced deportations and deaths or caused by willful neglect and/or abandonment of the policy. The Paris Loss Committee's careful analyses of the few claims filed against the New York Life were found to be "valid and in full force" at the time the insured were forcefully deported and subsequently presumed dead.

Between December 23, 1919, and February 17, 1921, twelve such claims were recommended for payment by the Paris Loss Committee and sent to New York Life's headquarters in New York for final disposition. These twelve claims are listed below with the text of the recommendations submitted by the Paris Sub-Office Committee. (Note: the numbers 1-12 were added by the author and do not appear in the original text prepared by the committee.)

1. (Sec. 7) Death-Claim Policy 1,523,711 – Der Sarkissian, Turkey.
This policy, which was payable in Francs in Paris, was settled by payment of Turkish £ at parity rate. The beneficiary, insured's widow, addressed a letter to the Home Office, protesting against the settlement at parity rate, and the matter was referred by the Division of Policy Claims at the Home Office to the Paris Office for the necessary attention. In view of the fact that all the premiums had been received by the Company in Francs, it was voted to readjust the settlement by paying the beneficiary the difference, amounting to Turkish £31.46, between the parity rate and the current rate on the date of settlement, with interest at 4%.[7]

2. (Sec. 5) Death-Claim Policy 1,099,444 – Topalian, Turkey.
Premiums on this policy were paid up to 26 May 1915. It has now been ascertained that the insured, an Armenian, was deported in May 1915, and died in exile shortly afterwards. It was voted to approve the recommendation of the Paris Sub-Loss committee to consider the policy as having been in force at the time of death, the non-payment of the premium of May 1915 being due to "force majeure." The foreclosure entries to be revised and proofs of death to be called for.[8]

3. (Sec. 14) Death-Claim Policy 1- 44,832 – Lusararian, Turkey.
Premiums of this policy were paid up until 6th July, 1915. It has now been ascertained that the insured, an Armenian, was deported in April 1915 and died in exile. It was voted to approve the recommendation of the Paris Sub-Loss Committee to consider the policy as having been in force at the time of death; the non-payment of premiums since July 1915 being due to "force majeure." The entries in connection with the foreclosure of the policy to be reversed and proofs of death to be called for. (Filed jointly with Topalian's claim mentioned above.)

4. (Sec. 11) Death-Claim Policy 2,502,865 – Zortian, Turkey.
The premiums on this policy were paid up to the 19th August 1915, and the insured died on the 19th March 1916. It has now been ascertained that the insured was deported on the 10th August 1915 and died in exile. It was voted to approve the recommendation of the Paris Sub-Loss Committee to consider the policy as having been in force at the time of death; the non-payment of the premiums since August 1915 being due to "force majeure."[9]

5. (Sec. 9) Death-Claim Policy 1,043,890 – Salian, Turkey.
The premiums on this policy were paid to 23rd December, 1914. In order to cover the premium due on date, the insured applied for a loan, which proposition the Company accepted. In June 1915, before the loan transaction could be completed, the insured was deported, and he died soon afterwards. It was voted to approve the recommendation of the Paris Sub-Loss Committee to consider the policy as having been in force, the settlement of the loan having been prevented by "force majeure." [10]

6. (Sec. 6) Lost Policy 4,638,614 – Sakeagulian, Turkey.
In 1917 we were informed by the Department of State in Washington that this policy had been seized by the Turkish Government authorities. It was voted to accept the declaration of the insured as to the loss of his policy and to waive the customary guarantor's indemnity, in issuing a duplicate policy.[11]

7. (Sec. 8) Death-Claim Policy 1,047,723 – Krikorian, Turkey.
This policy lapsed on account of non-payment of the premium and loan interest due 7th September 1915. The insured was deported to Sivas in May 1915, and died in exile on the 11th June 1916. It was voted to approve recommendation of the Paris Sub-Loss Committee to consider the policy as having been in force at the time of

death; the non-payments of the premium due September 1915, while the insured was in exile, been due [to] "force majeure."[12]

8. (Sec. 9). Death-Claim Policy 1,075,877 – Martayan, Turkey.
This policy lapsed on account of non-payment of the premium and loan interest due [not legible] January 1915. In February 1915 insured applied for a loan; loan papers were prepared and the insured paid, in June 1915, the balance of Fr. 49,95 called for thereunder, but the loan agreement was never received, insured's letter having been retained by the postal authorities. Insured died in 1915. In view of the fact that the insured had compiled with the Company's requirements for loan, it was voted to approve recommendation of the Paris Sub-Loss Committee to consider the policy as having been in force at the time of death.[12] (Filed jointly with Martayan's claim mentioned above.)

9. (Sec.13) Death-Claim Policy 1,074,200 – Amadian, Turkey.
Memorandum of the Paris Sub-Loss Committee, dated 18th November hereto annexed, was submitted, and it was voted to approve the recommendation to consider this policy as having been in force at the time of the insured's death.[13]

10. (Sec. 7) Death-Claim Policy 1,527,155 – Thomassian, Turkey
Memorandum of the Paris Sub-Loss Committee, dated 9th December, hereto annexed, was submitted, and it was voted to approve the recommendation to consider this policy as having been in force at the time of the insured's death.[14]

11. (Sec. 7). Death-Claim Policy 1,538,506 – Gatenian, Turkey.
Memorandum of the Paris Sub-Loss Committee, dated 20th December, hereto annexed, was submitted, and it was voted to approve the recommendation to consider this policy as having been in force at the time of the insured's death, the non-payment of premiums having been due to "force majeure."[15]

12. (Sec. 3). Death-Claim Policy 4,674,534 – Kirkorian, Turkey.
This policy lapsed owing to non-payment of the premium due 4th August 1915. The insured died in October 1918. It has now been ascertained that the insured, who was an Armenian, was deported in May 1915. It was voted to approve the recommendation of the Paris Sub-Loss Committee to consider the policy as having been in force at the time of death, the non-payment of the premium having been due to "force majeure."[16]

It was not clear from these reports, however, if the "favorable recommendations" voted in the minutes of the Paris Sub-Loss Committee ultimately led to payments to the victims' beneficiaries. Nevertheless, at the time the claims were presented the committee members found that the policies were valid and payable, and that the seemingly lapsed premium payments were the direct result of forced deportation ("force majeure") and subsequent death of the insured. Nevertheless, in many of the cases New York Life insisted on obtaining proof of death of the deportees before it would honor the claims. It can therefore be inferred from the request for non-existent death certificates that New York Life did not make payments of policy benefit claims as recommended by the Paris Sub-Loss Committee (see for example claim No. 2, Topalian and claim

No. 3, Lusararian, above). As will be shown below, it was not Turkish policy to issue death certificates on behalf of deported Armenians that were massacred or died in the Syrian deserts, and the request for such certificates was therefore no more than a euphemism for denial.

In assessing the post-war financial status of the company, New York Life Board member, L.F. Abbott, noted in glowing terms that

> At the end of 1919, when actual material effects of the war could be measured, it was found that the Company was in a more prosperous condition than ever. That year was for the New York Life in many respects the greatest of its history up to that time. Its new business for 1919 ($531,000,000) exceeded the new business written in any previous year by nearly $2,000,000.[17]

Abbott legitimized the excessive gains realized by New York Life by asserting that "[I]t is testimony to the financial stability of the New York Life that not one of these events imposed any excessive strain upon the Company in successfully meeting each one of its obligation."[18]

Payments Made by Union-Vie

Like New York Life, Union-Vie had also made a handful of payments to the beneficiaries of the survivors, as the enclosure of New York Life's letter to the State Department shows. Here is part of the French company's description of the amount of policy benefit claims:

> The number of our Armenian insured who met their death as a result of deportation and massacres amounts to 327, according to the declarations which have reached us up to this date. The sums insured which we have to pay out on this account amount to ONE MILLION FOUR HUNDRED AND SIXTY THREE THOUSAND ONE HUNDRED FRANCS Fr.1,463,100 [about $290,000]. The mathematical reserves relating to these contracts, that is to say the sums acquired to meet the payments of such insured capital, amount to THREE HUNDRED AND FORTY SIX THOU-SANDS SIX HUNDRED and SIXTY FRANCS Fr. 346,660. The difference is thus ONE MILLION ONE HUNDRED AND SIXTEEN THOUSAND FOUR HUNDRED FRANCS Fr. 1,116,400. This last sum represents the loss to us at present known, [sic] resulting from the death of our insured. Deaths undoubtedly caused through the Turk's fault [sic], and not through the free actions or the normal laws of mortality. [Upper case letters in the original].[19]

Both New York Life and Union-Vie stressed that the claims so far filed were only partial, considering the huge number of insured Armenians who in the estimation of the insurers were likely to have met their deaths. The insurers were clearly concerned that the ultimate numbers of the claims would mount considerably and cause immense losses to them. This concern was clearly spelled out in Union-Vie's letter to the French Foreign Ministry:

We must add that this list is by no means yet closed, and that every day brings us the notification of the death of Armenian insured which for different reasons, it had not been possible to bring to our notice. In such a way, the definite figure of our losses is destined to noticeably exceed the above mentioned sum. The sums which we have actually paid out to Armenian victims of the massacres amounts to FIVE HUNDRED AND SEVENTY THREE THOUSAND, FIVE HUNDRED AND TWENTY FRANCS [or FF 573,520 equivalent of $114,000]. [Upper case letters in the original].[20]

Although France was at war with Turkey, the French government (unlike the British) did not consider payments of life policy benefits to Armenians as payments made to an "enemy." Furthermore, the French insurer did not insist on death certificates, as did New York Life and Equitable. In a dramatically antithetical policy to that of the latter two companies, Union-Vie felt that denial of payments to the heirs of the victims would constitute a shameful debacle strongly detrimental and prejudicial to the "prestige and renown" of France, and "would be unworthy of a great company, contrary to equity and strongly prejudicial to the prestige and renown of our country, to refuse the payments."[21]

The Case of Ovakim Kevork Massatian

The strategy adopted by Equitable and Star of London for the life policy benefit payments to the heirs of the victims will be probed by examining the claims filed on behalf of Ovakim Kevork Massatian's two surviving children. Massatian held two life policies, one from the Equitable Life Assurance Society (Policy No. 1626139 in the amount of 6,000 French francs) and the second from the Star Assurance Company of London (Policy No. 114645, in the amount of 3,000 French francs).

The Claim Against Equitable

In a letter dated October 31, 1916, and addressed to Equitable's executive, the newly appointed U.S. ambassador in Constantinople, Abram I. Elkus, informed the insurance executive in New York that he had received a policy claim made by the two surviving children of Ovakim Massatian. The father of the orphans was forcefully deported and was presumed dead, as was the case with the other deportees. In his letter, Ambassador Elkus makes it clear that it was impossible for this class of claimants to produce legal proof (i.e., a death certificate) that the deported was dead. Cognizant of the fact that no legal document could ever be produced, the ever-receptive and intrepid American diplomat went out of his routine business-as-usual diplomacy by making the following plea:

Gentlemen:

The Embassy has been requested by the American Consular Agent at Samsun, Turkey, to ascertain whether it would not be possible for the children of Ovakim Kevork Massatian holder of policy No. 1626139 for Fcs. 6000, to obtain the amount due to them under this policy, in view of the fact that Mr. Massatian was among the deported Armenians and presumably dead. As the Embassy has learned of many similar cases it would appreciate an expression of the views of your Company as to the method to be adopted by the heirs of the deported Armenians concerning whose death no absolute proof can be furnished for the present. The embassy would also like to know what steps, if any, the immediate members of the families of those deported persons, who are usually in the most destitute circumstances, could take towards obtaining loans from your Company.[22]

Elkus's strong and compassionate letter did not appear to strike a cord of sympathy in Equitable. In his January 3, 1917 reply to Ambassador Elkus, the president of Equitable invoked two insurance clauses that made the collection of Massatian's life policy benefit an impossible task. First, the company's chief executive officer stated that the victim's policy had expired as of December 14, 1916, because "the insured had failed to pay his premiums." The second clause was that Equitable would need an official "certificate of death." These two seemingly valid excuses could not, however, survive scrutiny. In the first place, Equitable's stated date of lapse of premium payment was eighteen months *after* the victim's forced deportation from Samsun, which took place in the summer of 1915. The irony here is that Equitable's letter had indicated that at the time of the deportation, Massatian's policy was in "full force." In the second place, Equitable's first letter had also recognized that it was impossible to secure death certificates in this class of deaths as the Turkish authorities were not in the business of issuing official proof of death on behalf of their victims. Here is the full text of the infamous letter by the president of Equitable:

My Dear Mr. Elkus:

Your letter of October 31th, referring particularly to policy No. 1626,139, Ovakim Kevork Massatian, and generally to the question of furnishing adequate proofs of death in connection with the claims arising upon the lives of deported Armenians and to policy loans under policies issued upon the lives of such persons, has been brought to my personal attention.

As to the specific case about which you inquire I can only say that the contract in question is a Paid-up Term policy of Fcs. 6,000, which term expired as of December 14th 1916. The policy becomes Term contract when the premium due on December 14th, 1916, was not paid. If, therefore, it can be shown that the insured died prior to December 14th 1916, there is due the legal representatives of his estate as a death claim the sum of Fcs. 6,000, but if death occurred after December 14th, 1916, nothing whatever is due under the policy. You will, therefore, see in this particular instance how necessary it is that the date of the insured's death shall be fixed.

Referring to your general inquiries, I would say that the evidence of death ordinarily required by the Society in connection with death claims such as those described by you, is an official certificate of death issued by the civil authorities of the place in which the insured died. I realize, of course, that this cannot always be obtained, for the time being at least, in connection with death claims in this general class of cases, and I am of the opinion that it will be necessary for the parties at interest to wait until the termination of the present war before sufficient evidence will be obtainable to enable the Society to deal with these claims. As you will readily appreciate, we are not free to deal with matters of this kind as our inclination might dictate, but are obliged to have due regard to the liability of the Society to its policyholders generally in making payment of claims.

As to the making of policy loans on policies upon the lives of deported persons, I am glad to be able to inform you that we have inaugurated a temporary system, effective during the continence [*sic*] of the war, which will enable us to grant loan upon the security for such policies upon the strength of a supplementary loan agreement executed by the beneficiaries under the policy, such loan, however, not to exceed an amount sufficient to pay necessary premiums or overdue loan interest in order to maintain the policy in force. No cash loan, however, can be granted upon such arrangement. As you will realize, if we were to advance money without adequate security, we would subject ourselves to severe criticism from the supervisory insurance officials of the various States.

Regretting that I cannot be more helpful in enabling you to meet the situation described, but assuring you that I shall be ready at any time to give prompt consideration to the merits of any specific case you may desire to bring to our attention.

I am truly yours,

(signed) W.A Day, President. [23]

Not surprisingly, Equitable's response infuriated Ambassador Elkus, who in his abrasive reply made it abundantly clear that the insurer's position in this class of deaths was outright denial.

Dear Judge Day:
I have received your letter of January 3, 1917, referring to policy No.1626139 Ovakim Kevork Massatian. I am sending copy of the same to our Consular Agent in Samsoun. I appreciate your considering the matter personally. Our Consular Agent [in Samsoun] writing on the 14th of October 1916 expressed the opinion that the insured could not have been alive at that date [December 14th, 1916] because he was "deported" as early as the summer of 1915. For these deported people it is impossible to obtain an official certificate of death issued by the civil authorities of the place in which the insured died. I am gratified to note that while having due regard to the liability of the Society to its policy holders generally, you take into consideration the exceptional circumstances connected with the case of the insured of this category and I trust you will be able to save some of their surviving heirs from starvation or undue hardship. This would be but just.[24]

The Case of Star and Other British Life Insurance Companies

As mentioned above, Massatian had a second life policy with the Star Assurance Company of London, in the amount of 3,000 French francs.

Here again the American diplomats in Turkey intervened on behalf of Massatian's two surviving children in an attempt to secure the victim's policy benefits. As a first step, Ambassador Elkus, through the U.S. Embassy in London, made a written inquiry, on October 31, 1916, to determine if it would be possible to collect the life policy benefits of Massatian's two children from the Star of London:

> The American Embassy in Constantinople has the honor to transmit herewith, for such action as it may be plausible to take through the proper channels, copies of a letter from the American Consular Agent at Samsun, dated October 14, 1916, relative to a life insurance policy No. 114545, for Fcs. 3000 with the Star Assurance Company, London, in the name of Ovakim Massatian.
>
> The American Consular Agent states that the insured was deported and is presumably dead. As two of his children are at Samsun in a destitute condition, he asks whether it would be possible to obtain payment of the amount of the policy. Inasmuch as the Embassy has heard of many similar cases, it may perhaps be possible to obtain an expression of the views of an English Life Insurance Company, as to the method to be pursued in the case of deported Armenians concerning whose death no absolute proof can be produced at the present time. In this case the Embassy believes that a small loan would already help much toward the support of the children.[25]

Six weeks later the British Foreign Office replied:

> I did not fail to refer to the competent department of His Majesty's Government the memorandum (No.1144) which Your Excellency was good enough to communicate to me on the 18th ultimo, inquiring whether the Star Assurance Company of London will be prepared to pay a life assurance policy of three thousand francs issued by them in the name of Ovakim Kevork Massatian, who is presumed to be dead, and what attitude is adopted by British Insurance Companies generally in the case of deported Armenians concerning whose death no absolute proof can be produced in present circumstances.
>
> In reply I have the honour to state that no payment of a policy on the life of an enemy during the war is allowed except possibly to a person in this country, i.e., where the beneficiary is permanently resident here or the policy has been assigned before the war to a person living here. No payment would therefore to be made to Massatian's children by an Insurance Company even if the Company concerned were willing to assume death.[26]

Two days later, the United States ambassador in London forwarded the British Foreign Office note to Ambassador Elkus in Constantinople.[27] On January 10, 1917, Elkus informed the American Consular Agent in Samson, W. Peter, of the denial of Massatian's claim: "… concerning the life insurance policy of Ovakim K. Massatian who was deported and is presumed to be dead…the insurance company cannot make a payment to Massatian's children. You are instructed to communicate this information to the latter."[28]

Notes

1.   Buckner to U.S. Secretary of State, November 20, 1922, U.S. National Archives, RG 59, File 367.115N483/3.

2.   Morgenthau to Consul Jesse B. Jackson, Aleppo, Syria, December 20, 1915, U.S. National Archives, RG 84, file 850.6.
3.   U.S. Consul in Aleppo, Syria to Ambassador Henry Morgenthau, Constantinople, January 20, 1916, U.S. National Archives RG 84, File, 850.6.
4.   American Consular Agent in Damascus, Syria, to Hoffman Philip, American Chargé d'Affaires,
5.   U.S. Chargé d'Affaires to Han Kenadjian, New York Life Insurance Company, Stamboul (Constantinople) March, 15, 1916, U.S. National Archives RG 84, File, 850.6.
6.   U.S. Chargé d'Affaires to Samuel Edelman, American Consular Agent in Damascus Syria, March 15, 1916, U.S. National Archives RG 84, File 850.6.
7.   Archives of the New York Life Insurance Company. Minutes of Paris Sub-Office Committee Meeting Paris, December 23, 1919 (Der Sarkissian's claim). (See Documents 12-14 in the [MISSING TEXT]
8.   Archives of the New York Life Insurance Company. Minutes of Paris Sub-Office Committee Meeting . Paris, January 15, 1920 (Topalian's and Lusararian's claims).
9.   Archives of the New York Life Insurance Company. Minutes of Paris Sub-Office Committee Meeting. Paris, July 22, 1920 (Zortian's claim).
10.   Archives of the New York Life Insurance Company. Minutes of Paris Sub-Office Committee Meeting. Paris, July 29, 1920 (Salian's claim).
11.   Archives of the New York Life Insurance Company. Minutes of Paris Sub-Office Committee Meeting . Paris, September 2, 1920 (Sakeagulian's claim).
12.   Archives of the New York Life Insurance Company. Minutes of Paris Sub-Office Committee Meeting. Paris, October 21, 1920. [Krikorian's and Martayan's claims].
13.   Archives of the New York Life Insurance Company. Minutes of Paris Sub-Office Committee Meeting . Paris, November 18, 1920 (Amadian's claim).
14.   Archives of the New York Life Insurance Company. Minutes of Paris Sub-Office Committee Meeting . Paris, December 9, 1920 (Thomassian's claim).
15.   Archives of the New York Life Insurance Company. Minutes of Paris Sub-Office Committee Meeting . Paris, December 23, 1920 (Gatenian's claim).
16.   Archives of the New York Life Insurance Company. Minutes of Paris Sub-Office Committee Meeting. Paris, February 17, 1921 (Kirkorian's claim).
17.   Lawrence Abbott Fraser, *The Story of New York Life: A History of the Origin and Development of the New York Life Insurance Company From 1845–1929* (Newark, NJ: A.S. Browne Inc., 1930), pp. 212–213.
18.   Ibid., p. 212.
19.   Buckner to U.S. Secretary of State, November 20, 1922, U.S. National Archives, RG 59, File 367.115N483/3 (enclosure). A copy of a communication addressed by the French Insurance Company, La Compagnie de l'Union, to the French Minister of Foreign Affairs, dated April 11, 1922. (See Document No. 16 p. 2.)
20.   Supra 1, pp. 2-3 of the twelve-page enclosure of Buckner's letter.
21.   Ibid., p 3
22.   U.S. Ambassador Abram I. Elkus to the Equitable Life Insurance Company, October 31, 1916, U.S. National Archives RG 84, 850.6.
23.   W.A. Day, President, Equitable Life Insurance Society to U.S. Ambassador Abram I. Elkus January 3, 1917, U.S. National Archives RG 84, File, 850.6.
24.   U.S. Ambassador Abram I. Elkus to W.A. Day, Equitable Life Insurance Society, April 7, 1917, U.S. National Archives RG 84, File 850.6.
25.   U.S. Embassy in Constantinople to U.S Embassy in London, October 31, 1916, U.S. National Archives RG 84, File, 850.6.

26. Victor Wellesley to U.S. Embassy in London, December 13, 1916, U.S. National Archives RG 84, File, 850.6.
27. U.S. Embassy, London to U.S. Embassy in Constantinople, December 15, 1916, U.S. National Archives RG 84, File, 850.6.
28. Abram I. Elkus to American consular Agent in Samsoun, W. Peter, January 10, 1917, U.S. National Archives RG 84, File, 850.6.

4

The Perpetrators' Claim:
"The Policy Benefits Belong to Us"

Ambassador Henry Morgenthau was perhaps the first to record the determined efforts of the Turkish government to collect for itself the benefits of the policies on the lives of the Armenians who had perished during the deportations and massacres. In his memoir, published in 1918, Morgenthau described the following conversation held during one of his many private meetings with the powerful Interior Minister, Talât Pasha, boss of the ruling Ittihad Party:

> One day Talât made what was perhaps the most astonishing request I had ever heard. The New York Life Insurance Company and the Equitable Life of New York had for years done considerable business among the Armenians. The extent to which this people insured their lives was merely another indication of their thrifty habits. "I wish," Talât now said, "that you would get the American life insurance companies to send us a complete list of their Armenian policy holders. They are practically all dead now and have left no heirs to collect the money. It of course all escheats to the State. The Government is the beneficiary now. Will you do so?" This was almost too much, and I lost my temper. "You will get no such list from me," I said. I got up and I left him.[1]

The Turkish strategy for capital collections involved a two-step process. First, official ministerial memos were distributed to all European and American insurance companies requesting the names of all Armenians insured with them. Second, by order of the Interior Ministry, special "Liquidation Commissions" (*Tasfiyé Komisyonu*) were to be set up in various provinces and cities of Turkey for the submission of the names of the insured Armenians.

The Turks' reasoning behind the collection of life policy proceeds was based on the certain and largely unmistaken understanding that the insured and their heirs were all dead, leaving no one to collect, and therefore the benefits now belonged to the State Treasury. Such an assertion, coming soon after the forced deportations, and from no lesser an authority than

Talât himself, counters all allegations by past and present Turkish governments that the purpose of the deportation was "relocation." As part of this vicious policy of collecting victims' policy benefits, in January 1916 (eight months after the start of the onslaught) the Turkish Ministry of Commerce and Agriculture, by order of Interior Minister Talât, sent circular notes to all insurance companies doing business in Turkey to submit the names of the Armenians insured with them. One such memo was sent to the Constantinople agent of the Swiss insurance company, La Fédèrale, who, worried by such an unusual request, immediately forwarded this report to his company's headquarters:

> We have learned by chance that the Ottoman Government has published a circular, a copy of which is enclosed for your information. The circular is issued by the Ottoman Ministry of Commerce to all insurance companies operating in Turkey and concerns all current accounts held by Armenians deported elsewhere. By an order from the Ministry of Interior, you are requested to transmit to us a list of all deposits, credits and all accounts payable by your company belonging to the Armenians in the following provinces Rodosto, Adana, Djebel Berekel [Bereket], Kozan, Jozgad [Yozgad], Angora, Erzerum, Bitlis, Haleb, Antalia, Guemleik (Guemlik), Biledjik, Sivas, Mergoufour (Marzifon), Tokat, Samsoun, Ardou, (Ordou), Trebizonde, Konia, Mamuret-el-Azise, Ismidt, (Izmid) Adapazar, Sivri-Hissar, Egkoschehir (Eski-Shehir), Cesares, Develi, Nigde, Afion-Karahissar, and Ourfa. These lists must be handed over by your agents in the specified localities to the liquidation commissions, in case of absence of these commissions, the lists must be submitted to civil authorities. In the provinces where you do not have agents, the lists must be transmitted directly to our Ministry by you. In the name of the Ministry of Commerce and Agriculture,

> The Counselor,

> [signed] Moustafa [2]

New York Life and the Equitable were also served with similar notes requesting the submission of the names of all Armenians insured with them.

The Case of New York Life

On January 11, 1916, New York Life's representative in Constantinople received a memo in which the Turkish Ministry of Agriculture and Commerce conveyed the orders of the Turkish Interior Ministry to submit the names of all Armenians insured by that company. The memo, written in French, had in its heading the caption: "On the subject of preparation of the lists of Armenian accounts." Here is the translation of that memo:

> The Ministry of Interior [Talât] having communicated to us the necessity to establish and submit to 'Tasfie Commissionou' (Commissions to settle the accounts) located in

the following towns: Rodosto, Adana, Djebel Bereket, Kozan, Yozgad, Angora, Erzerum, Bitlis, Alep, Marash, Antioche, Brousse, Guemlek, Biledjik, Sivas, Marzifoun, Tokat, Samsoun, Ordou, Trebizond, Konya, Mamouret-el-Azzi, [sic] (Aziz), Ismidt, Adapazar, Eski-Shehir, Sivri-Hissar, Cesaree, Develou, Nigde, Afion-Karahissar, and Ourfa, the lists of accounts receivable and deposits of Armenians in the evacuated localities and who had insured their lives in your Company, and communicate to all your agents in the above localities, if you do have such agents in the said localities, to deliver these lists to high civil employees of these localities to be transmitted to the said Commissions. For the localities where you do not have Company agents you ought to submit these lists of the accounts receivable and deposits of the Armenians directly to the Honorable Ministry.[3]

Baffled by such an unusual request, New York Life's agent in Constantinople immediately responded to the Turkish ministry's note by writing:

In response to your honorable letter of January 11, 1916, N0.39655/34 in which you conveyed us the order to prepare and to submit to you the accounts of the Armenians insured in our Company, as we had already let you know verbally that the requested items are in the files of the General Direction [Head Office For Europe in Paris], and that we communicated to them the necessity to furnish the lists to us, we inform you with this letter that we have already written to our Headquarter Office [Paris] and that we will submit these lists to you as soon as we receive them.[4]

This memo troubled the financial director of New York Life's European Head Office in Paris, P. Duncanson. For him, it was clear that compliance with the Turkish request could potentially inflict heavy losses to his company. Given the potentially high number of insured deportees and their certain deaths, the stakes for the insurers and the Turkish government, while running in opposite directions, were considerably high. For Turkey, an opportunity was suddenly created to "inherit" enormous wealth resulting from the policy benefits left by their victims. At the same time, however, disbursement of large sums of money could seriously erode, if not deplete, New York Life's reserves. Consequently, New York Life's chief European executive resorted to what might be called an instinctive corporate strategy to deal with this worrisome turn of events. This corporate strategy involved a two-level action. First was the strategy of buying time with the hope that the requests might dissolve into oblivion. Second was the strategy of recruiting the respected and well-connected American Ambassador Morgenthau to directly deal with the Turkish government's request on behalf of the company's interest. In this regard, the New York Life official asked Ambassador Morgenthau to inform the Turks that their request was "being considered," but that it was not possible to accommodate the Turkish request because "it was impossible to determine the nationality of the insured" and, therefore, impossible to prepare a "list of insured Armenians." This excuse contradicted an earlier assertion made by New York Life's Constantinople agent, who in his response to the Turkish request for the list had indicated that the actual names of "the Armenians insured with our company...were in the General Direction in Paris." Furthermore, New York Life also requested from the ambassador to inform the Turks that "their request was being communicated to New York Life's Home Office in New York" for "review," which would necessarily cause "some delay." On February 18, 1916, just five weeks after the issuance of the Turkish order, Duncanson, sent the following letter to U.S. Ambassador Morgenthau:

> I enclose herewith copy of communication addressed to our Constantinople Office by the Ministry of Commerce, requesting to be furnished with a list of the names of the Armenians resident in certain Turkish towns insured with this Company. I also enclose copy of the reply given thereto by our Constantinople Office.
> It is very difficult for this Company to comply with the request made by the Ministry of Commerce as we have no means of deciding the nationality of our insured. Furthermore, it is, of course, a very delicate matter for an insurance Company to furnish a list of the names and addresses of its insured and give details of the transactions made between them.
> We are however, communicating with our Home Office in New York on the matter and as this will occasion some delay. I shall be obliged if you will kindly intercede on our behalf, should the authorities take any action on account of the required information not being promptly furnished.
> Owing to present restrictions regarding correspondence, we are unable to write to our Constantinople Office in this matter very fully, and I would, therefore, ask you to be good enough to instruct them to inform you should any difficulty arise with the Authorities.[5]

It is clear from this letter that New York Life was conveniently taking the matter out of the hands of its vulnerable Constantinople agent and entrusting the handling of this sensitive matter to the politically more powerful American ambassador, Morgenthau, in the hope that it would lapse into oblivion. New York Life's letter was forwarded to Ambassador Morgenthau through the U.S. ambassador to Paris, W.G. Sharp, with the following cover letter:

> I beg to enclose herewith a communication addressed to Mr. Morgenthau, which the Financial Director of the Paris Branch of the New York Life Insurance Company has requested me to forward to Constantinople, which I am glad to do for this American Company in submitting it to your consideration as to whether it is possible for your Embassy to comply with the request it contains relative to informing the Constantinople office of the Company with regard to the desire to obtain the names of Armenians insured with the New York Life Co.[6]

Piecing together the documents from the United States National Archives and from New York Life's archives shows that New York Life successfully defied the Turkish request to supply the names of its insured Armenians in Turkey. The letter written by New York Life's vice president to the U.S. secretary of state on November 20, 1922, some seven years after the issuance of the infamous Turkish request of the list of insured Armenians, attests to New York Life's successful defiance of the Turkish demand:

> We may also point out that we have been advised that the Turkish Government proposes, or is considering, the confiscation of claims for the insurance upon the lives of those Armenians and others who have been massacred, with a view to collect itself the insurance upon the lives of its victims.[7]

Turkish attempts to collect the Armenian policy benefits from New York Life remained unsuccessful. An internal memo discovered in New York Life's archives, dated June 7, 1930, shows that the company had actually recorded a net gain of $258,569 in Turkey at the end of the war.[8] These gains appear to have been solidified in the aftermath of the 1923 Amity and Peace Treaty between the Unite States and Turkey in Lausanne, Switzerland, which completely ignored the rights and the plights of the Armenians.

The Case of Equitable

Equitable Life Assurance was yet another life insurance company served with an official Turkish request to submit the names of all its insured Armenians. Equitable's Constantinople agent, Mr. Mitrani, worried about the adverse consequences of submitting the names of its Armenian policyholders, also resorted to delay tactics. He informed the Turkish authorities that he was obliged first to communicate the message to the home office to obtain "authorization" before complying with the Turkish request. Worried by the consequences of such a dramatic turn of events, Mitrani called on the U.S. Embassy in Constantinople for advice and help. He informed U.S. Ambassador Morgenthau that he had notified the Turkish authorities that he first needed to communicate the request to the home office for authorization before complying with the Turkish request. From his presentation it can be inferred without doubt that the list of the insured Armenians was available in the Constantinople office. However, the shrewd and savvy agent stalled in responding to the request by insisting that that approval was needed from the home office before he could comply with it. The chargé d'affaires at the U.S. Embassy in Constantinople assured Equitable's agent that he would be happy to communicate the Turkish request to Equitable's home office in New York. The communication reads, in part:

...Mr. Mitrani told me that he had been asked by the Turkish Government to give them a list of all Armenian policyholders. He is informing them that he must communicate with the home office before he can comply with their request. I told Mr. Mitrani that I should be very glad to do everything I could that would be proper and the Embassy will continue the same arrangement which has been heretofore carried out. If there is anything further that I can do for the Company I shall be very glad to do so.[9]

Equitable, as in the cases of New Your Life and Union-Vie, also escaped the Turkish request and kept the identity of their insured Armenians beyond the reach of the Turkish authorities.

The U.S. State Department documents analyzed in this chapter prove that the Turkish government made a concerted effort to collect for itself the Armenian life insurance policy benefits. These official ministerial efforts were initiated nine months after the start of the forced deportation of the Armenians. It thus becomes clear that the true purpose of the deportation was not "relocation," as alleged by past and present Turkish governments, but extermination. In fact, the purpose of the general mobilization was clearly spelled out in the words of Interior Minister Talât Pasha, discovered in his secret telegrams to provincial governors: "deportation and annihilation" (*tehcir ve imhasi*). [10]

Notes

1.   Henry Morgenthau, *Ambassador Morgenthau's Story: The Documented Account of the Armenian Genocide, First of the Century, Reported by America's Ambassador to Turkey* (Plandome, NY: New Age Publishers, 1965, reprinted edition, originally published in 1918 by Doubleday Page & Co.), p. 339. The personal accounts of Henry Morgenthau, Sr., strongly corroborate all documentary evidence discovered in American, European, and Turkish archives. His memoir constitutes a lucid "documentary" account of the events that took place in Turkey during the years 1913-1916. The late entry of the United States into the war allowed the U.S. ambassador in Constantinople to represent the interests of the Allies, including Britain and France, and to gather much insightful information.
2.   Counselor Moustafa Cheref to La Fédèrale Insurance Company Zurich, March 10, 1916, U.S. National Archives, RG 84, File, 850.6.
3.   Counselor Moustafa Cheref to New York Life Insurance Company, January 11, 1916, U.S. National Archives, RG 84, File, 850.6.
4.   New York Life Insurance Company to Ministry of Commerce and Agriculture, January 1916, U.S. National Archives, RG 84, File, 850.6.
5.   P. Duncanson of New York Life Insurance Company, Paris, to Ambassador Morgenthau, Constantinople, February 18, 1916, U.S. National Archives, RG 84, File, 850.6.
6.   Ambassador Ward to Hoffman Philip, Esq. American Chargé d'Affaires, Constantinople, February 21, 1916, U.S. National Archives, RG 84, File, 850.6.
7.   Buckner to U.S. Secretary of State Lansing, November 20, 1922, U.S. National Archives RG 59 File 367.115N483/3.
8.   New York Life Insurance Company Archives. Historical & Financial Data on All Transfer and Reinsurances of Company's Foreign Business Bank 128A, Drawer

313. This five-page document shows that by 1930 the New York Life Insurance Company had realized a net gain from the reinsurance (transfer) of its foreign businesses.

9.   Philip Hoffman, Esq. American Chargé d'Affaires Constantinople to Henry Rosenfeld, Vice President of Equitable Assurance Company, New York, September 21, 1916, U.S. National Archives, RG 84, File, 850.6.

10.   Vahakn N. Dadrian, "Textual analysis of the key indictment of the Turkish Military Tribunal investigating the Armenian Genocide," *Journal of Political and Military Sociology*, 22:1, Summer 1992, pp. 133-172.

5

The Insurers' Counterclaim: "The Perpetrator is Liable"

The insurers were successful not only in refusing to comply with the Turkish requests to hand over the names of their clients, they also took high-level political actions to hold Turkey directly responsible for the Armenian Genocide. In pursuit of this offensive initiative, both New York Life and Union-Vie, independently, held Turkey directly responsible for the "losses" they had incurred by the few payments already made to the victims' heirs. The two companies went even further and accused the Turkish government of the large number of deaths of their policyholders. In an effort to recover these payments, these two life insurance companies insisted that their governments compel Turkey to go along with their request. New York Life's executive accused the Turkish government as the perpetrator of the Armenian Genocide in the following way:

> Much of this insurance was written upon the lives of subject peoples, such as the Armenians and others who have, during the years since the outbreak of the European War, been subjected to massacre, illegal killings and fatal exposure by or with the acquiescence of the Turkish authorities. In consequence of such illegal action and willful failure of the Turkish Government to protect the lives of those within its jurisdiction, the New York Life Insurance Company has incurred very heavy and extraordinary losses through the lives of its insured [that have] been prematurely terminated by such violent death.[1]

In yet another startling revelation, New York Life spelled out in no uncertain terms the exact dollar amount that Turkey must pay the insurer: "These sums, at current rates of exchange, amount to approximately $230,000, and measure the loss so far suffered by this Company, for which we believe the Turkish Government is, and should be held, responsible."[2] To bolster the legitimacy of its claim, New York Life's vice president indicated to the U.S. secretary of state that his company was not the only insurer involved in such financial "losses" and that many

European insurers were similarly caught. The company's executive, Buckner, reasoned that by uniting the ranks of similarly caught insurers, they could tip the balance to their favor and force Turkey to indemnify the insurance companies for their "losses." To implement this corporate strategy, New York Life's executive laid out the groundwork for Secretary Hughes' immediate consideration and possible action:

> The New York Life Insurance Company is not the only insurance company similarly situated. An important French Insurance Company, known as La Compagnie de l'Union is in a somewhat similar situation. This company has already filed a claim with the French Government [April 11, 1922], a copy of which we enclose herewith, and which deals more fully with some of the technical aspects of the situation. We believe it likely that the French Government will, in connection with the pending negotiation [in Lausanne], seek to have this claim of La Compagnie de l'Union recognized by the Turkish Government, and we respectfully suggest that the similar situation of the New York Life Insurance Company be laid before the appropriate American officials abroad, to the end that they may, if the Department approves, collaborate with the French officials who will be dealing with this problem to the end that the Turkish Government may be brought to recognize in principle their responsibility in this class of cases and recognition of this principle may be subsequently availed of to secure satisfaction of the losses incurred by the New York Life Insurance Company in consequence of the actions of the Turkish Government which are here complained of.[3]

New York Life seems to have been entertaining the notion that payments for deaths not resulting from the natural laws of probability are "losses" warranting actions and measures to avoid payments: "The New York Life Insurance Company has incurred very heavy and extraordinary losses through the lives of its insured having been prematurely terminated by such violent death."[4] The enclosure of New York Life's letter, a translated copy (from French to English) of Union-Vie's claim of April 11, 1922 with the French Foreign Ministry, is a much stronger accusation of the Turkish government in the planning and the execution of the genocide. Union-Vie does not hesitate a moment in holding Turkey directly liable in no uncertain terms for the payments it had made to the victims' heirs:

> We have no need to insist on the character of these massacres. Better than we, you know how they were organized and with what atrocities they were executed; nor are you ignorant of the responsible part which falls upon the Ottoman Government.... Article 6 of the general conditions of our insurance policies stipulates that if a person on whose life the insurance is issued loses his life as a result of a Judicial Condemnation, the insurance is null and void. It adds that, if however, the premiums for the three years, at least, have been paid the Company reimburses to the executors the mathematical reserve of the insured capital in case of death. We thought, and you will certainly agree with us, that in law there had been, in the case of deported and massacred Armenians, no "Judicial Condemnation."[5]

The organized and targeted nature of the mass murders must have been so flagrant that even in the judgment of the insurer it would have been an insensitive, if not outright perversion, to pretend that the deaths of the insured were the result of "judicial condemnation." Despite the fact that such a categorization, which falls within the jurisdiction of Article 6, would have relieved the insurers of heavy liabilities, the French insurer reasoned that refusal of payments by invoking Article 6 might create a public relations nightmare that could backfire and adversely affect the company's business. After all, the French insurer opined, the superiority and trustworthiness of an insurer is judged by honoring legitimate policy claims. This business dilemma was unambiguously articulated by the director of the Union-Vie and laid before the French foreign minister for immediate consideration and government action in favor of Union-Vie:

> Could we have based ourselves on this article [Article 6] and applied the annulments provided for? We thought, and you will certainly agree with us, that in law there had been, in the case of deported and massacred Armenians, no 'Judicial Condemnation'. It would be unworthy of a great Company, contrary to equity and strongly prejudicial to the prestige and renown of our country, to refuse the payments. It would be equally iniquitous that the French life insurance companies should, after mature examination, be the victims of the crimes, excesses and faults committed by the Ottoman dependents with, at least, the complicity of their government. For this reason we ask, in the agreements to be arrived at with the Ottoman government, the principle of its responsibility and of its obligation to repair the damage caused to the French life insurance companies shall be clearly established.[6]

While the largest number of Armenians perished during the 1915 massacres perpetrated by the Ittihadists (Committee of Union and Progress), popularly known as the Young Turks, a new wave of genocidal acts was also carried out during the 1920-1923 period by the nationalist movement headed by Mustafa Kemal (Ataturk). These organized massacres and forced deportations were specifically targeted against the Greeks and the few surviving Armenians in the regions including Smyrna, Bursa, and Konya. (Note: The parents of one of the authors of this book [Hrayr S. Karagueuzuan] were deported in 1921 from Bursa and Konya and survived the horror, safely reaching the city of Varna in Bulgaria, [mother's side] and Damascus, Syria, [father's side]). Many of the life policy benefit claims resulted from deaths that occurred during the Kemalist regime. In their claims with their respective governments, the American and the French insurers insisted that the payments to the victims of the Kemalist regime also be recognized as "losses" and be an integral part of the overall Turkish liability. The insurance executives were well aware that the mass killings by the emerging Kemalist forces in Angora (present day Ankara) had no "legal" character and were executed without "due process." The insurers, however, suspected that the rising Kemalist regime as well could wrap its genocidal acts in a veil of legality and pronounce the killings "capital punishments," a clause that could prevent the insurers from holding Turkey liable.[7] In anticipation of such moves by the Kemalists, the Director of Union-Vie, in its claim with the French Foreign Ministry, insisted that the French government hold Turkey liable for the policy benefit payments during the Kemalist regime:

> There is another category of losses to which we ask permission to draw your attention. Since the signature of the Treaty of Sèvres, during the course of the events which have taken place in Asia Minor, quite a considerable number of our policy-holders, for the most part of Greek origin, were either massacred, or executed after condemnation by the civil or military authorities instituted by the Government of Angora. Up to the present only a dozen of such losses have been brought to our knowledge, representing a capital of about Fr. 160,000; but we fear that a very large number of our policyholders lost their lives under such conditions and without exaggerating it may be assumed that the capital insured by us on their lives would reach, if not even exceed Fr. 500,000.
>
> As stated above, Article 6 of our policies authorizes us to lapse the policy through loss of life due to judicial condemnation. The question arises as to whether the capital punishments resorted by the Kemalists, even by virtue of the judgments rendered by their authorities, constitute "Judicial Condemnations." The point appears doubtful, as, according to our Article 6 what is meant to be conveyed is a regular judicial condemnation, that is to say, pronounced by regular tribunal instituted by a regular government authority. Up to the present, however, neither the French nor the Ottoman Governments have officially recognized the Government of Angora as a legitimate and regular authority. It appears even difficult to admit that at their outset at least when probably the greatest number of deaths took place, the Kemalists were nothing other than revolutionaries or armed bands. We are therefore not certain to gain the lawsuits to which we would be compelled to have recourse in order to ensure application of the terms of Article 6 of our policies. The more so, apart from the irregularity of the authority which pronounced the condemnation, objections may be raised touching even the character of the condemnation, the view being taken that Article 6 only applies to condemnation of an infamous character.[8]

Furthermore, invoking Article 6 to evade payment would in the estimation of Union-Vie portray the company as being engaged in immoral and hostile practices against their own insured:

> But, even in the event of the tribunals or commissions competent to decide as to the application of Article 6, conclusively admitting the lapse and rendering judgment in our favor to the detriment of the beneficiaries of our insurance policies we would nevertheless expose ourselves to grave prejudice. Such prejudice would then be of moral nature and graver perhaps than the first mentioned. Such decision would create a bad effect on the population of this country, cause the discredit of life insurance, if, in such cases, no advantage therefrom would be derived by those who insured as a measure of prudence, and the Company would therefore acquire a bad reputation, which the foreign competition would exploit to their advantage.[9]

The insurers' allegations of state-sponsored massacres of Armenians during the Young Turks and Kemalist regimes are confirmed beyond a shadow of doubt by an enormous corpus of official state documents, not only in American and European archives but also in Turkish national archives. While it is not the purpose or the intent of this book to examine and present documentary evidence that attests to the genocidal intent of the large-scale massacres, some mention of the crimes committed by the Young Turks (Ittihadits) and later by the Kemalists will be briefly highlighted.

The Ittihadist Period

At the urging of Great Britain, on December 28, 1918 a Turkish military court was set up in the capital city of Constantinople (present Istanbul) to try those responsible for the massacres. The tribunals collected and marshaled incriminating evidence to prosecute the Ittihad party leaders and their provincial cohorts on charges of centrally planning massive deportations with the intent of killing, *tehcir* ve *taktil,* that is, deportations *and* killings. On trial were men who had once held such influential titles as minister of interior, minister of war, provincial governor, party secretary general, minister of justice, top religious leader (*shaikh ul–Islam*), and two that of prime minister (grand vizier), one in absentia. As early as May 1915 the Allies had already accused the top Ottoman officials of "crimes against humanity," a categorization that is thought of as having been established only thirty years later in the London Charter for the Nuremberg Trials. The Constantinople tribunal also held trials for the deportation and slaughter of the Armenians from the two towns of Yozgad and Trebizond.

The Constantinople war crimes trials, had they not been prematurely terminated by the Nationalist forces, would have been comparable to the Nuremberg Trials. Gary Bass, in his thorough study of the politics of war crimes tribunals, concluded that "Constantinople was the Nuremberg that failed."[10] Based on documentary evidence authenticated by competent Turkish ministerial officials, the Turkish tribunals found the Ittihadist leaders guilty of mass murders, charged them with conspiracy to commit large-scale premeditated killings, and convicted all three Ittihadist leaders (Talât, Enver, and Djemal) to death in absentia. Transcripts of the proceedings, published in Arabic script in the official gazette of the Ottoman Government, *Takvimi Vekâyi,* provided a detailed account on the control and command system of the mass murders and the intent of the deportations.[11] The later discovery in the British archives of a unique Turkish document, "The Blueprint of the Genocide," provides a vivid description of the roles of the military and the gendarmerie, and the calculated incitement of the masses on religious and nationalistic grounds in the planning and execution of the genocide.[12] With direct German complicity, most of the Turkish officials accused of crimes and theft escaped to Germany before being brought to trial.[13] Many of those convicted later returned to Turkey, however, in order to join the Kemalists and to "finish the genocide." The trials started on December 28, 1918 but were halted on January 13, 1920 by the Kemalist forces, which prohibited their continuation.

The Kemalist Period

The resurgent Nationalist movement in Angora led by Mustafa Kemal not only aborted the Turkish military tribunals but also rejected any compromise with the Armenians. This fiercely nationalistic policy was aimed at destabilizing the 1920 Treaty of Sèvres that had recognized the rights of the Armenians to a free and independent state and had also imposed harsh pecuniary penalties on Turkey for lost lives, properties and assets. The Kemalists even rejected the repatriation of surviving refugees, and their ban against the lifting of the so-called law of "abandoned properties" (*emouali métrouké*) virtually legitimizing all illegally confiscated Armenian properties, estates, assets, and bank accounts.[14] In virtual replication of the genocidal intent and designs set forth by the Ittihadists, a recently discovered ciphered telegram sent by the Kemalist's "Foreign Affairs Minister" to provincial governors attests, in no uncertain terms, to the veracity of the continuation of a genocidal policy:

> By virtue of the provisions of the Sèvres Treaty Armenia will be enabled to cut off Turkey from the East. Together with Greece, she [Armenia] will impede Turkey's general growth. Further, being situated in the midst of a great Islamic periphery, she will never voluntarily relinquish her assigned role of a despotic gendarme, and will never try to integrate her destiny with the general conditions of Turkey and Islam. Consequently, it is indispensable that Armenia be annihilated politically and physically [*ermenistani siyaseten ve maddeten ortdan kaldirmak*].[15]

While military operations, along with deportations, persecutions, and massacres of the surviving Armenians, progressed in the Eastern front, similar operations were under way in the Western part of Turkey, most notably, against the Greeks (particularly in Smyrna).[16] The killings in the Smyrna region by the conscripts of the Kemalist "Death Squads" were aimed at the last remaining Christian elements in Turkey. The brutality with which these acts were committed prompted the British High Commissioner in Constantinople, to include the following in his report:

The Turks have an expression, "*yavash–yavash*," which means to go slowly. That is how clearing Trebizond of its remaining Christian population is being managed.... Now they are going after the little boys. It used to be conscription that was invoked as an excuse to take the men. When they got down to deporting the boys from 15-18, the Turks said it was to give them preliminary training. Now—as I write— they are making a new visitation of the angel of death in Greek homes, and seizing boys from 11 to 14. The poor little kiddies are gathered together like cattle, and driven through the streets to the Government House, where they are put in filthy dungeons half underground. One could not believe this was possible. It would be more merciful for the victims and their mothers to kill them outright. But that is not the way it is done. It would attract attention, and be difficult to deny or explain.... The way it is done is this: the deportees are presumed to have cholera or the plagues, and are made to enter the enclosure. No food is given them.... Then begins the bleeding of the families of the victims. It is intimated that the loved ones will die if food is not brought. A woman has tramped two days over the mountains to bring bread to her husband or son. He is given some to encourage her to return. But a bribe must first be paid, and part of the food is stolen before it reaches the lost soul behind the barbed wire. And it is difficult to get to the Jevisilik camp and back again without being dishonoured—several times a week a Greek girl is shot or stabbed when attempting to escape rape. There is no punishment for this crime. The authorities do not even make an investigation. "The girl got herself into some drunken brawl—a bad lot, these Greeks," you will probably be told if you make an enquiry. The women feel that very soon the experience of the Armenian women of Trebizond will come to them—they will be deported into the interior, and—en route—most of them will be "lost."[17]

Notes

1. Buckner to U.S. Secretary of State, November 20, 1922, U.S. National Archives RG 59, File 367.115N483/3.
2. Ibid., p. 2.
3. Ibid., p. 3.
4. Ibid., p. 2.
5. Ibid., p. 3, enclosure. A copy of the communication addressed by the French Insurance Company, La Compagnie de l'Union, to the French Minister of Foreign Affaires, dated April 11, 1922 (p. 3).
6. Ibid., p 3. Note that in the Sèvres Treaty there was no provision that allowed the life insurance companies to file claims against the perpetrators. However, in the Treaty's "ANNEX," four clauses in section II, entitled "Provisions Relating to Certain Classes of Contracts," under the subheading "Life Insurance," and numbered 9 to 12, the validity of life policy contracts in a former enemy country is stated, as follows:

    Article #9. Contracts of life insurance entered into between an insurer and a person who subsequently became an enemy shall not be deemed to have been dissolved by the outbreak of war or by the fact of the person becoming an enemy. Any sum which during the war became due upon a contract deemed not to have been dissolved under the preceding provision shall be recoverable after the war with the addition of interest at 5 per cent per annum from the date of its becoming due up to the day of payment. Where the contract has lapsed during the war owing to non-payment of premiums, or has become void from breach of the conditions of the contract the assured or his representatives or the persons entitled shall have the right at any time within twelve months of the coming into force of the present

Treaty to claim from the insurer the surrender value of the policy at the date of its lapse or avoidance.

Article # 10. Where contracts of life insurance have been entered into by a local branch of an insurance company established in a country which subsequently became an enemy country, the contract shall, in the absence of any stipulation to the contrary in the contract itself, be governed by the local law, but the insurer shall be entitled to demand from the insured or his representatives the refund of sums paid or claims made or enforced under measures taken during the war, if the making or enforcement of such claims was not in accordance with the terms of the contract itself or was not consistent with the laws or treaties existing at the time when it was entered into.

Article #11. In any case where by the law applicable to the contract the insurer remains bound by the contract, notwithstanding the non-payment of premiums, until notice is given to the insured of the termination of the contract, he shall be entitled where the giving of such notice was prevented by the war to recover the unpaid premiums with interest at 5 per cent per annum from the insured.

Article #12. Insurance contracts shall be considered as contracts of life assurance for the purpose of paragraphs 9 to 11 when they depend on the probabilities of human life combined with the rate of interest for the calculation of the reciprocal engagements between the two parties.

7.   Ibid., pp. 7-9.
8.   Ibid., p. 9.
9.   Ibid., p. 6a-8.
10.   Gary Bass, *Stay the Hand of Vengeance: The Politics of War Crimes Tribunals* (Princeton, NJ: Princeton University Press, 2000), pp. 106-110. It must be noted that Sultan Abdul Hamid, in an apparent signal to European powers not to interfere in Turkey's domestic affairs with their "reform" programs, slaughtered between 100,000 and 200,000 Armenians, through systematic pogroms in virtually every district of Turkish Armenia in the years 1890-1895. Leo Kuper, a noted sociologist and genocide expert, observed that Abdul Hamid's massacres did not appear to have been all that "amateurish and ineffective...they took a somewhat different form from the later genocide in the sense that they were perpetrated on the spot without resort to such devices as the death caravans of the deportation...however, they differed in the immediacy and concentrated nature of their occurrence, [but] they employed many of the same elements as the 1915 genocide, serving somewhat as pilot project for the later genocide." In Leo Kuper, "The Turkish Genocide of Armenians, 1915-1917," in *The Armenian Genocide in Perspective*, Hovannisian, R.G. (ed.), (New Brunswick, NJ: Transaction Publishers, 1991), p. 55.
11.   Vahakn N. Dadrian, "The documentation of the World War I Armenian massacres in the proceedings of the Turkish Military Tribunals," *International Journal of Middle East Studies.*, 23, 1991, pp. 549–576 and Vahakn N. Dadrian, "The Naim–Andonian documents on the World War I destruction of Ottoman Armenians: The anatomy of a genocide," *International Journal of Middle East Studies.*, 18: 1986, pp. 311-360; Vahakn N. Dadrian: "Textual analysis of the key indictment of the Turkish Military Tribunal investigating the Armenian Genocide," *Journal of Political and Military Sociology*, 22 /1, Summer 1992, pp. 133-172. Note: The cipher telegrams sent by Talât to provincial governors clearly instruct and insist that the intent of the deportations *is* destruction. To this end different words were used in these telegrams to describe the intent of the deportations: (1) *tehcir ve imhasi*, literally meaning "deportation and annihilation," and (2) *tehcir ve taktil*, meaning "deportation and killing" (in Dadrian).

12. Vahakn N. Dadrian, "The Secret Young Turk-Ittihadist Conference and the Deci-
     sion for the World War I Genocide of the Armenians," *Holocaust and Genocide
     Studies*, 7/2, Fall 1993, pp. 173-201. See Chapter 1, note 20. Note: For the issue
     of the loyalty of Armenian soldiers to the Ottoman army see Vahakn N. Dadrian,
     Warrant for Genocide: Key Element of Turko-Armenian Conflict (New Brunswick,
     NJ: Transaction Publishers, 1999) p. 114. Dadrian, a renowned genocide scholar,
     pointed out the praise of Minister of War and de facto commander-in-chief of the
     Ottoman Armed Forces, Enver Pasha, for the outstanding combative courage and
     skills of Armenian soldiers in the large Turkish offensive against the Russians
     during the winter of 1914-1915.
13. Vahakn N. Dadrian, *German Responsibility in the Armenian Genocide* (Wa-
     tertown, MA: Blue Crane Books, 1996). German eye-witness accounts of the
     "bestialities" and the "genocidal policies pursued against the Armenians" by
     the Turkish authorities were highlighted by the historian Gerald D. Feldman
     in his studies of the evolution and activities of the Berlin-based influential
     Deutsche Bank, which financed the Baghdad Railway; in Lethar Gall, Gerald
     D. Feldman, Harold James, Carl-Ludwig Holtfrerich, Hans E. Büschgen, *The
     Deutsche Bank: 1870-1995* (London: Weidenfeld & Nicolson, 1995), p. 142.
         While the masterminds of the Armenian Genocide escaped due process, Arme-
     nian gunmen assassinated the major figures of the atrocity, among them Talât. He
     was assassinated in broad daylight on a Berlin street less than two years after his
     death verdict was pronounced at the Constantinople trials. The assassin was tried in
     Berlin and was found not guilty: official Turkish documents produced at the trial,
     and subsequently reproduced in the media, "proved beyond question" that Talât
     and other officials "had ordered the wholesale extermination of the Armenians,
     including the orphan children." A document regarding this appeared in George
     R. Montgomery, "Minster of Interior Talât: Why Talât's Assassin was acquitted,"
     Current History Magazine, July 1921, pp. 551-555. The document included the
     following: "We hear that certain orphanages which have been opened have received
     also the children of the Armenians. Whether this is done through ignorance of our
     real purpose or through contempt of it, the Government will regard the feeding of
     such children or any attempt to prolong their lives an act entirely opposed to its
     purpose since it considers the survival of these children as detrimental."
14. Dikran Kouymjian, "Confiscation and destruction. A manifestation of the genocidal
     process, *Armenian Forum*, 1:3, Autumn 1998, pp. 1–12.
15. Vahakn N. Dadrian, "Genocide as a problem of national and international law:
     The World War I Armenian case and its contemporary legal ramifications," *Yale
     Journal of International Law*, 14:2, 1989, p. 306.
16. Marjorie Housepian Dobkin, *Smyrna 1922: The Destruction of a City,* (New York,
     NY: Newmark Press, 1998 (2nd reprint of the 2nd edition).
17. Lévon Marashlian, "Finishing the genocide: Cleansing Turkey of Armenian survi-
     vors 1920–1923, in R.G. Hovannisian (ed.), *Remembrance and Denial: The Case
     of the Armenian Genocide* (Detroit, MI: Wayne State University Press, 1998), pp.
     135-136.

6

Who is Liable?
The Perpetrators or the Insurers?

The *Lusitania* Case

While the insurers' claims of the Turkish government's direct role in the killings of the Armenians are supported by ample documentary evidence, the question of the liability of the perpetrators for payments of the life policy benefits is a different issue. Does Turkey's murder of the insured Armenians relieve the insurers of their contractual obligations to the insured? Stated otherwise, does Turkey's obligation for compensation for the blood of its victims also encompass material losses suffered by the insurers as a consequence of the premature death of the insured? While there is no exact precedent to the case at hand, the legal liabilities of life policies in the context of crimes against humanity may be compared to other contemporary war crimes involving life insurance. The existence of such a contemporary legal precedent by a primary authority (i.e., a ruling made by a jurist) helps the development of a legal parallel reasoning that justifies emulating a decision adopted by a precedent case. The sinking of the British civilian ship *Lusitania* by a German military torpedo during World War I provides an historic precedent of primary authority that may be used as a precedent of sorts to clarify the issue of liability.

On May 7, 1915, barely two weeks after the beginning of the Armenian Genocide,[1] the British passenger ship *Lusitania* was deliberately hit and sunk by a deadly torpedo launched from a German military submarine, killing 1,198 passengers aboard the ship. Ten of the 128 dead American passengers held eighteen life insurance policies from twelve different companies, including New York Life and Equitable. The twelve life insurance companies were identified as:

- Providence Mutual Life Insurance Company, Docket No. 19;
- New York Life Insurance Company, Docket No. 248;
- Mutual Life Insurance Company, Docket No. 249;
- Penn Mutual Life Insurance Company, Docket No. 250;
- Aetna Life Insurance Company, Docket No. 251;
- State Mutual Life Insurance Company, Docket No. 252;
- Northwestern Mutual Life Assurance Company, Docket No. 253;
- Equitable Life Assurance Society, Docket No. 254;
- Manhattan Life Insurance Company, Docket No. 255,
- Prudential Life Insurance Company, Docket No. 255;
- Metropolitan Life Insurance Company, Docket No. 255;
- Travelers Insurance Company, Docket No. 256.[2]

In the aftermath of World War I, on August 25, 1921, the United States and Germany signed a treaty in Berlin that held Germany liable for losses suffered aboard the *Lusitania*. The United States government, representing the interests of all twelve insurance companies, held Germany liable for general compensation for lost American lives, including payments of life insurance policy benefits, because benefit payments also constituted American "losses." Germany disagreed. Prolonged legal deliberations, lasting until 1924, took place in Washington. The legal dispute was argued by a mixed commission composed of three members: an American, a German and an umpire, Edwin B. Parker (of American origin), who presided over the committee. The committee became known as, the "Mixed Claims Commission." During the deliberations the American side brought into play the 1921 Berlin treaty, with particular emphasis on the following article in the treaty:

> Applying the rules laid down in Administrative decisions Nos. I and II…Germany is financially obligated to pay to the United States all losses suffered by American nationals, stated in terms of dollars, where the claims therefore have continued in American ownership, which losses have resulted from the death or from personal injury or from loss of, damage to, property, sustained in the sinking of the Lusitania.[3]

The American commissioner, Chandler P. Anderson, cited that "in death cases the right of action is for the loss sustained by the claimant, not by the deceased's estate," and that "one of the elements to be estimated in fixing the amount of compensation was the amount which the 'decedent, had he not been killed, would probably have contributed to the claimant.'"[4] Anderson also noted that the "the liability of Germany was not limited to damages for injuries to person or property,"[5] because, it was argued,

> The financial obligations of Germany to the United States arising under the Treaty of Berlin…embrace: A) all losses, damages, or injuries to them, including losses, dam-

ages, or injuries to their property wherever situated, suffered directly or indirectly during the war period, caused by acts of Germany." [6]

The German Commissioner dismissed the American argument asserting that:

> Under the Treaty, Germany is only liable for damages resulting from *injury to a person or property*, and that life-insurance companies have suffered no injury to person or property, because no personal injury was inflicted on the corporate body and the life-insurance policy which was terminated by the death of the deceased did not constitute property in legal contemplation, and the relationship between them and the deceased was not of a character which would justify them in claiming damages for this death. (Emphasis added)[7]

Germany compensated for lost lives aboard the *Lusitania*, but the American commissioner argued that the compensation to American insurance companies was also a German liability thus "justifying" the claims made by insurers.[8] The German Commissioner swiftly dismissed the American argument:

> The contention of the American counsel that through the death of a person insured with an American insurance company such company sustained a loss, and that such fact suffices to make Germany liable makes it necessary to come to a clear and full understanding of the basic principles of the Treaty and, as far as it is governed by international law, to an understanding of the applicable principles of such law. So it is clear that "the loss, damage, or injury must have been done either to a person [i.e., an American national] or to property [i.e., American property].[9]

The German commissioner argued that a life policy did not constitute either a "person" or a "property": "Under international law...the subject of the injury must be a real and existing thing, *id est,* either a person or property."[10] The German counsel stepped up his argument by stressing that the English version of the treaty's text was deliberately misinterpreted by the American Commissioner to suit the purpose of the insurers: "I cannot assume that anybody could contend, on the ground of the punctuation, that "loss" and "damage," being separated through a comma, are meant more generally and that only the word "injury" is confined to their persons or property.[11]

To sort out the punctuation glitch in the English text of the treaty that could conceivably blur the scope of the liabilities, the German jurist relied on the German version of the Berlin Treaty's text, which was equally valid and in as full force as the English version.

> [The German text] has been accepted and signed by the representatives of the United States and has the same controlling influence as the English,... [It]... speaks of their person and their property ('ihrer Person oder ihrem Eigentum') and that no comma separates the words for 'damage' and 'injury'; thus it is absolutely clear that under the

German text the phrase 'Verlust, Nachteil oder Schaden an ihrer Person oder ihrem Eingetum' means 'loss or damage or injury done to the person or the property' of an American national within the meaning of Treaty. My conclusion is therefore that as well under international law as under the Treaty of Berlin it is not sufficient that a national has suffered a *loss*, but the loss – or damage or injury – must have been sustained in the *person* or the *property* of the national.[12]

The German Commissioner further stressed that life policy benefits per se were never mentioned in the Berlin Treaty: "Nowhere in the voluminous Reparation Accounts [of the Berlin Treaty], so far as they are specific, is there any mention of claims for contractual rights and especially for rights of life-insurance companies."[13] And, finally, in his closing statement, the German jurist reiterated:

To avoid misunderstanding I want to make it clear that according to my conception the Treaty does not justify an award for every loss suffered by an *American national* but only for those claims which can be based on provisions of the Treaty, that is for claims for damage done to *persons* or their *property*.

The obligations laid upon Germany under the Treaty go so far beyond what would be justified under international law, and are so heavy, that as already shown, they cannot be enlarged by *ignoring* the rules established under the Treaty. Its wording does not only *fix* Germany's liability but also fixes the *limitations* upon it. Therefore, some American losses are not recoverable under the law of the Treaty, *such law*, and not the interest of the claimant, must prevail....[14] Consequently the logical consequences of a theory differing from the present interpretation would be absurd. (Emphasis added)[15]

Five months after hearing the American and the German arguments, the umpire delivered his twenty-page opinion, part of which said:

The Commission is here dealing with a group of ten typical cases put forward by the United States on behalf of certain American life-insurance companies to recover from Germany alleged losses resulting from their being required to make payments under the terms of eighteen policies issued by them insuring the lives of eleven of the passengers lost on the Lusitania. The American Commissioner and the German Commissioner have certified their disagreement and these cases are before the Umpire for decision. The German Agent, admitting that payments were made by the insurers as claimed, denies that any part of such payments represents losses to them.[16]

The Umpire then pointed out:

It is apparent that in issuing a life-insurance policy without expressly excluding any risk, and in insuring the life of an individual without any restrictions whatsoever, self-protection and sound business policy must have impelled the insurer to take into account every possible risk without limiting itself to those forming the basis of a mortality table used by the insurer compiled more than half a century before the Lusitania was sunk.... One weakness in the Argument of the American Agent is the erroneous assumption of the fact that mortality table absolutely determines the amount of the premium exacted.[17]

The umpire then alluded that the insurers for the sake of their own benefit and to the detriment of their insured could conveniently advocate relief of liability in a series of disasters including natural disasters:

> Deaths from earthquake, fires, and infectious diseases must be within the contemplation of insurers and hence, and even according to the American Agents' argument, paid for.... It is significant that the losses suffered by American insurers in 1918–1919 from the deaths due to influenza – clearly within their contemplation – were greater than their war losses, which the American Agent contends were not within their contemplation.[18]

While the umpire admitted that the insurers suffered losses, he nevertheless based his judgment on the fact that "insurance was a business that guaranteed to cover potential loss of life in return for premiums paid by the insured." The umpire centered his opinion and judgment, first on the contractual obligations that the insurers held to their insured, and second on the articles of the Berlin Treaty that did not stipulate life policies as a German liability:

> The contention of the American agent that the insurers must necessarily have sustained losses where they were compelled to pay for the deaths of their insured, resulting from a war risk not in contemplation and for which no premium was specially exacted to cover such risk is rejected. But it is evident that the acceleration in the time of payments which the insurers had to make resulted in losses to them in the sense that their margins of profit actual or prospective were thereby reduced. For the purpose *of this opinion it will be assumed that in this sense losses were suffered by the insurers...* (Emphasis added][19]

Having recognized the losses claimed by the insurers, the umpire then turned to the Berlin Treaty:

> The question remains, under the Treaty of Berlin is Germany financially obligated to pay losses of this class [i.e., life insurance policy benefits]? The umpire decides that she is not. ... [the] Treaty expressly obligates Germany to make compensation for damages suffered by the American surviving dependents of civilians whose deaths were caused by acts of war occurring at any time during the war period. Nowhere else in Treaty is express reference made to compensation for damages sustained by American nationals through injuries resulting in death. Looking, therefore, to the only provision in the Treaty of Berlin which expressly obligated Germany to make compensation in death cases, we find that such obligation is limited to damage suffered by American surviving dependents resulting from deaths to civilians caused by acts of war. Under familiar rules of construction this express mention of surviving dependents who through their respective governments are entitled to be compensated in death cases excludes all other classes, including insurers of life.[20]

Before pronouncing his final ruling on this class action, the umpire stated that the insurers' strategy of claiming losses had many precedents and all of these had resulted in denials:

On the other hand, there is no reported case, international or municipal, in which a claim of a life insurer has been sustained against an individual, a private corporation, or a nation causing death resulting in loss to such insurer. Such claims have been made but uniformly denied. History records no instance of any payment by one nation to another based on claims of this nature.... The American courts, including the Supreme Court of the United States, have rejected similar claims of insurers as remote consequences of wrongful acts complained of, and hence not cognizable by them, as often as such claims have been presented to them by insurers against American nationals. The United States cannot now be heard to assert such claims on behalf of American insurers against Germany.[21]

In his closing remarks the umpire stated:

...The act of Germany in striking down an individual did not in legal contemplation proximately result in damage to all of those who had contract relations, direct or remote, with that individual, which may have been affected by his death. In this latter class the ten claims here under consideration fall. They are not embraced within the terms of the treaty of Berlin and are therefore ordered dismissed.[22]

The *Lusitania* ruling points to the existence of a dual responsibility for compensation of the victims. The perpetrators of the murder *and* the insurers of the murdered bear separate and independent legal and financial obligations to the heirs of the victim. The insurers, as the *Lusitania* ruling shows, are required to settle the policy claims filed against them in accordance with the terms and provisions stipulated by the contract entered between the insurer and the insured. This was done in the *Lusitania* case, as the heirs of the insured victims collected the benefits of their policies. On the other hand, the perpetrators are responsible for the financial compensation for the blood of their victims, irrespective of the victims' life insurance status. This represents a clear case of the *res inter alios acta* rule. This rule "forbids the use of collateral evidence to the principal matter of dispute."[23] In the *Lusitania* case, life policy claims constituted the principal matter of dispute, while the victimization of the insured aboard the *Lusitania* by a German torpedo constituted collateral evidence, as articulated by the American umpire.

In the case of the Armenian Genocide, Turkey's killings of the insured Armenians, however illegal, constitutes "collateral evidence" relative to the obligations of the insurers to their insured, which as in the *Lusitania*'s case, constitutes "the principal matter of dispute." The illegal acts do not relieve the insurance companies of their primary obligations to their insured. The insurers remain bound to the terms of the contracts entered between them and their insured even in cases involving crimes against humanity.

Notes

1.   Vahakn N. Dadrian, "Genocide as a problem of national and international law, *Yale Journal of International Law*, 14:2, 1989, p. 266.
2.   Mixed Claims Commission. United States and Germany: Opinions and Decision in Life-Insurance Claims. Stanford Law Library, FP, EMS, Gho., 1924, p. 103. The Mixed Claims Commission was established in pursuance of the agreement reached between the United States and Germany on August 10, 1922. The commission members were Edwin B. Parker, Umpire; Chandler P. Anderson, American Commissioner; Wilhelm Kiesselbach, German Commissioner. (More on this subject can be found in "Mixed Claims Commission: United States and Germany Administrative Decisions and Opinions of a General Nature and Opinions in Individual Lusitania Claims and Other Cases to June 30, 1925," Washington: GPO, 1925.)
3.   Ibid., p. 104.
4.   Ibid., ibid.
5.   Ibid., p.109.
6.   Ibid.
7.   Ibid., p. 108.
8.   Ibid., p. 109.
9.   Ibid., p.110.
10.   Ibid., p.111.
11.   Ibid., p.111.
12.   Ibid., pp. 111-112.
13.   Ibid., p.116.
14.   Ibid., pp. 118-119.
15.   Ibid., p. 120.
16.   Ibid., p. 121.
17.   Ibid., pp. 125-126.
18.   Ibid., p. 126.
19.   Ibid., p. 127.
20.   Ibid., 2, p. 132.
21.   Ibid., p. 139.
22.   Ibid., p. 140.
23.   *Black's Law Dictionary*, Black HC, 5th edition, (St. Paul, MN: West Publishing Co, 1979), pp. 1177-1178.

Woodrow Wilson
1913-1921

Warren G.Harding
1921-23

Calvin Coolidge
1923-1929

U.S. Presidents during and in the aftermath of the Genocide

Robert Lansing
(1915-1920)

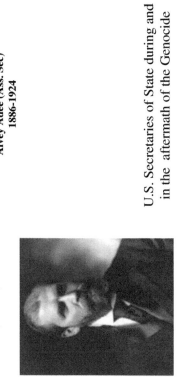

Frank B. Kellogg
(1925-29)

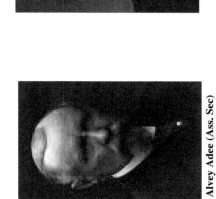

Alvey Adee (Ass. Sec)
1886-1924

U.S. Secretaries of State during and
in the aftermath of the Genocide

William Jennings Bryan
(1913-15)

Charles Evans Hughes
(1921-25)

Henri Morgenthau Sr.
U.S. Ambassador, Constantinople

Oscar Heizer
U.S. Consul Trebizond

James W. Gerard
US Ambassador, Berlin

Jessie Jackson
U.S. Consul, Aleppo

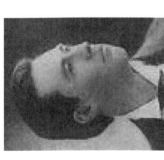

Leslie B Davis
U.S. Consul Erzerum

Ambassador Morgenthau Sr. and his Staff, Constantinople
(Seated first from right is Arshag Shmavonian, Morgenthau's interpreter)

US Embassy, Constantinople

US Mission, Erzerum

Mark L. Bristol
(Rear Adm.)

Gen. James Harbord

Sen. William King

Lloyd George, Clemenceau & Wilson arriving at Versailles for negotiations

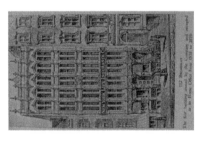

NYLIC from Broadway to Madison Avenue

Thomas Buckner
VP NYLIC

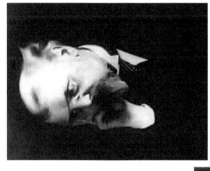

Johannes Lepsius

James Bryce

Arnold Toynbee

Franz Werfel

Rafael Lemkin

Aaron Aaronsohn

Herbert H. Asquith
1908-1916

David Lloyd George
1916-23

Stanley Baldwin
1923-29

**British Prime Ministers during and in the
aftermath of the Genocide**

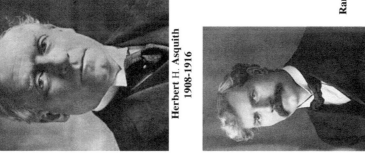

Ramsay MacDonald
1929-35

Talât Pasha

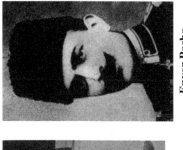

Djemal Pasha

Enver Pasha

Dr. Behaeddin Şhakir

Dr. Mehmet Nazim

Djavid Bey

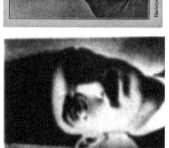

Dr. Tevfik Rüstü Aras, 1882-1972 (disposed the corpses
of the victims in mass graves)

Mustapha Kemal (at atürk)

Ankara,. Kemal with Prince Gustave Adolphe
of Sweden. To the right is Foreign Minister,
Dr. Tevfik Rustu Aras, October 3, 1934

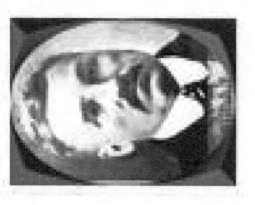

Dr. Nazim, sentenced to death in absentia in 1919; later tried to topple Kemal's regime, convicted to death and hanged in Ankara, on August 26, 1926 (adjoining paper clip) along with other Ittihadists.

İşte Atatürk'ü öldürmek isteyen Fenerli Başkan!

Şaka değil gerçek. Daha önce birkaç kez çeşitli yerlerde yayınlanan bu olay, **Soner Yalçın**'in Efendi isimli kitabıyla yeniden gündeme gelince biz de buradan duyuralım istedik. İttihat ve Terakki Cemiyeti'nin kurucularından **Doktor Nazım Bey, 1916–1918** yıllarında Fenerbahçe'ye başkanlık yapar.

İlerleyen yıllarda siyasetle yakından ilgilenen Nazım Bey, 1926 yılında Atatürk'e suikastten yargılanır ve idam edilir. Ne diyelim, işte G.Saray'ın, Fener'i asla geçemeyeceği bir alan...

Armin Wegner who has taken many photos
of human destruction

"They died all the deaths on the earth, the deaths of all ages." —Armin Wegner

Photos of human destruction

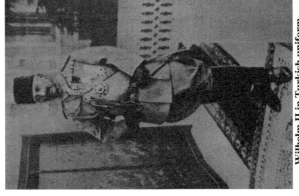

Wilhelm II salutes Grand Mufti. Talât Pasha is directly behind the German Emperor, Envar Pasha is at far left..

Wilhelm II in Turkish uniform

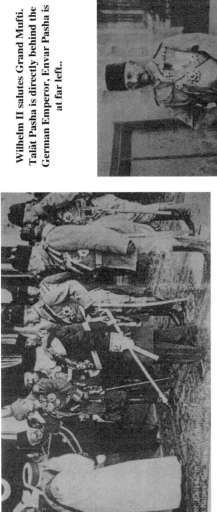

Wilhelm II in German military attire

Deuthsche Bank, Berlin

**Franz Günter
VP Baghdad Railway,
Constantinople**

**Baron von Wangenheim
German Ambassador,
Constantinople**

**Arthur von Gwinner
Director, Deutsche
Bank, Berlin**

Berlin's Reichsbank, 1916

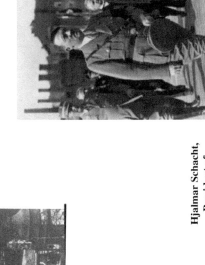

Hjalmar Schacht, President of Reichsbank With Hitler 1931

Ottoman imperial Bank, Constantinople

"All the News That's Fit to Print."

The New York Times

EXTRA
6:30 A. M.

NEW YORK, SATURDAY, MAY 8, 1915—TWENTY-FOUR PAGES.

ONE CENT

LUSITANIA SUNK BY A SUBMARINE, PROBABLY 1,260 DEAD; TWICE TORPEDOED OFF IRISH COAST; SINKS IN 15 MINUTES; CAPT. TURNER SAVED, FROHMAN AND VANDERBILT MISSING; WASHINGTON BELIEVES THAT A GRAVE CRISIS IS AT HAND

The Lost Cunard Steamship Lusitania

SHOCKS THE PRESIDENT

Washington Deeply Stirred by the Loss of American Lives.

SOME DEAD TAKEN ASHORE

Several Hundred Survivors at Queenstown and Kinsale.

STEAMSHIPMEN STUNNED

SHIP LISTS OVER TO PORT

ATTACKED IN BROAD DAY

Only 650 Were Saved, Fear Cable Reports

The sinking of Lusitania in 1915

Soghomon Tehlirian
1896-1964
(Assassinated Talât)

Grynszpan, Herschell
Polish Jew, assassinated
German diplomat Ernst vom Rath
(triggering Kristallnacht)

"Kristallnacht" 1938

7

Dollar Diplomacy and the Extermination of a Race

The timing and the intent of the two letter-documents analyzed in this book (Appendix 2) provide a stunningly remarkable exposition of combined petty corporate greed and self-serving corporate politics. These two letters, dated November 20, 1922 in the case of New York Life[1] and April 11, 1922 in the case of the Union-Vie,[2] coincide in time with the ongoing peace treaty negotiations that the representatives of the United States and the European Allies were conducting with Kemalist Turkey in the Swiss city of Lausanne. The terms of the treaty were purely business-based and were designed to amend most of the articles of the August 10, 1920 Sèvres treaty, which had been signed between the Allies and the defeated Turkey. It was intended to denigrate the suffering of the Armenians and create an "improved" image of Turkey, now a potential lucrative business partner. The earlier Sèvres Treaty had not only recognized the Armenian historic homeland (today's eastern Turkey) as a free and independent state, but also categorized the Ittihadist government as a "terrorist regime." Moreover, specific articles of the Sèvres Treaty held Turkey liable for financial compensation and restitution for the lives, assets, estates, and properties of the victims.[3] The Sèvres treaty did not, however, contain specific legal and financial clauses to indemnify life insurance companies in the countries of the Allies for their "losses" suffered by the few payments made to the heirs of the insured victims. The insurers were becoming increasingly aware that both the articles of the Sèvres Treaty and the ongoing legal battle over the Lusitania could not warrant their claim of perpetrator liability. They thus resorted to a last-ditch attempt to force their governments to introduce new articles in the treaty to be signed in Lausanne that explicitly recognize, in no uncertain terms, the insurers' "losses" as a Turkish liability. Pursuant to this motif, New York Life requested from the State Department:

...that the Turkish Government may be brought to recognize in principle their responsibility in this class of cases and that recognition of this principle may be subsequently availed of to secure satisfaction of the losses incurred by the New York Life Insurance Company in consequence of the actions of the Turkish Government which are here complained of.[4]

The French Union-Vie was much more explicit in its claim filed with the French Foreign Ministry, and demanded "that, in the agreements to be arrived [in Lausanne] with the Ottoman government, the principle of its responsibility and of its obligation to repair the damage caused to the French Life Insurance companies, shall be clearly established."[5] The existing Sèvres treaty did not have specific articles to meet the sensitivity of the insurers. While Articles 142, 144 and 230 recognized the fact of the massacres, and articles 235, 236, and 287 provided financial compensation for the victims' lives, there were no articles that specifically identified the payments made by the insurers as "losses" to the insurers. Here is a portion of Union-Vie's claim with the French Foreign Ministry:

> Did the Treaty of Sèvres signed between the Allied and Associated Powers and Turkey on the 10th of August, 1920, give us full satisfaction on this point? We do not think so. Several articles, notably those numbered 142, 144, 230 recognize the fact of the massacres.... It appears that it is only on Article 235 that we could base the claim with the view to the reparation which we consider we have a right to in view of the massacre of our Armenians insured.[6]

The French insurance company concluded that injury to persons or loss of lives, as in the case of the Lusitania, did not include payments of life policy benefits as "losses." Union-Vie correctly reasoned (as the Lusitania case will show later) that a lawsuit filed against Turkey would not warrant success unless drastic changes were made in the Sèvres Treaty:

> We must expect, in the presence of this text, to see the Ottoman Government oppose to our request arguments drawn from different sources:
> 1. It will contest for a portion of the claims, if not for the whole, that the death of our insured was the consequence of an act or of the negligence of the Ottoman authorities; and the proof would, for us, often be very difficult to establish.
> 2. It will maintain that the expressions "losses or damages experienced in their persons or "their belongings" do not apply to the case in hand, as we have not undergone any loss or damage in our *belongings* in the sense that article 287 appears to attach to this word: and that person of our insured can in no case be considered as constituting for us a *belonging*.
> 3. ...Admitting that the responsibility of the [Turkish] Government be established owing to acts or negligence of its authorities, it could not be held liable to repair any indirect damages, because the fact that the life insurance contract has been entered into between a Company belonging to the Allies Powers [*sic*] and an Armenian subsequently massacred, constitutes in the eyes of the government "*res inter alios acta*" and could not be held to place it in a more unfavorable situation than if the contract never existed. The text of Article 235 therefore does not confer upon us an absolutely indisputable right. It will compel us to submit the lengthy and complicated lawsuits, of which the outcome is not absolutely certain.[7]

Union-Vie also explicitly requested from the French government to call for the recovery of life policy benefit payments it made on the lives of thousands of Greeks massacred during the early Kemalist period.[8]

> There is another category of losses to which we ask permission to draw your attention. Since the signature of the Treaty of Sèvres, during the course of the events which have taken place in Asia Minor, quite a considerable number of our policy-holders, for the most part of Greek origin, were either massacred, or executed after condemnation by the civil or military authorities instituted by the Government of Angora. Up to the present only a dozen of such losses have been brought to our knowledge, representing a capital of about Fr. 160,000; but we fear that a very large number of our policyholders lost their lives under such conditions and without exaggerating it may be assumed that the capital insured by us on their lives would reach, if not even exceed Fr. 500,000.[9]

For the insurance companies it was clear that the acts of killing during the rise of Kemalist nationalist movement, and in particular in Smyrna, which became known as the "final stroke" of all non-Muslim minorities in Turkey, had no legal character and were devoid of due judicial process.[10] The Kemalists, however, showed a degree of sophistication by attaching qualifications to their acts of wanton killings, such as "capital punishments," "punishments rendered by virtue of judgments," etc. These fallacies designed to cover the Nationalist's genocidal campaigns were exposed in no uncertain terms by the Union-Vie:

> Article 6 of our policies authorizes us to lapse the policy through loss of life due to judicial condemnation. The question arises as to whether the capital punishments resorted by the Kemalists, even by virtue of the judgments rendered by their authorities, constitute "Judicial Condemnations." The point appears doubtful, as, according to our Article 6 what is meant to be conveyed is a *regular* judicial condemnation, that is to say, pronounced by *regular* tribunal instituted by a *regular* government authority. Up to the present, however, neither the French nor the Ottoman Governments have officially recognized the Government of Angora as a legitimate and regular authority. It appears even difficult to admit that at their outset, at least when probably the greatest number of deaths took place, the Kemalists were nothing other than revolutionaries or armed bands. We are therefore not certain to gain the lawsuits to which we would be compelled to have recourse in order to ensure application of the terms of Article 6 of our policies.[11]

Invoking Article 6 against the victims could perhaps have provided grounds for denials; Union-Vie, however, had another kind of concern in mind: the moral and ethical consequences of denying payments by invoking Article 6. Bringing into play Article 6 to evade payments for lost lives resulting from wanton killings could bring a public outcry and create a public relations nightmare:

> But even in the event of the tribunals or commissions competent to decide as to the application of Article 6, [by] conclusively admitting the lapse and rendering judgment

in our favor to the detriment of the beneficiaries of our insurance policies we would nevertheless expose ourselves to grave prejudice. Such prejudice would then be of moral nature and graver perhaps than the first mentioned. Such decisions would create a bad effect on the population of this country, cause the discredit of life insurance, if, in such cases, no advantage therefrom would be derived by those who insured as a measure of prudence, and the Company would therefore acquire a bad reputation, which the foreign competition would exploit to their advantage.[12]

In consideration of these concerns, Union-Vie, in its letter filed with the French Foreign Ministry, accused the Kemalists of being the perpetrators and went even further by drafting the language of Article 235 of the Sèvres Treaty:

We are of the opinion that our interest would be safeguarded in regards the Armenian death-losses and those caused by Kemalists, if you could have a clause inserted in the pending new treaty to appear in the first paragraph of article 235. Such clause could be framed in such terms as you think fit to adopt, but we ask to be allowed to submit to you the text already proposed above with reference to the Armenian massacres, with the necessary modifications to cover also losses caused by the Kemalists, so that the clause reads thus: – 'The Ottoman Government will be held liable to repair the prejudice caused to Life Insurance Companies belonging to the Allied or Associated Powers in consequence of death, resulting during the war and until the present treaty enters into effect, of their Turkish policyholders when judging from presumption, such death has been caused by bad treatment inflicted by the Turks, deportation, massacre, Judicial condemnation pronounced by the Ottoman or Kemalist Authorities, and for which the Insurance Companies would not invoke the forfeiture conditions of their policies. Such prejudice (or loss) will be equal to the difference between the guaranteed capital of the insurance policies and the amount of the mathematical reserve of its contracts at the time of Insured's death.'[13]

Finally, under the separate heading of "Loss of Portfolio and Organization," Union-Vie requested that Turkey pay for the "very heavy expenditures involved in the partial reconstruction" of their portfolio and for the "reparation for the prejudice caused to us" by the Ittihadist and Kemalist governments":

(1)   By the massacres of our Armenian policyholders.
(2)   By the capital condemnation pronounced by the Kemalists against our policyholders in Asia Minor.
(3)   By the loss of our portfolio and of the organization of our Constantinople Agency.[14]

The Treaty of Lausanne was finally signed on July 24, 1923. In sharp contrast to the earlier Sèvres Treaty, all allusions to the victimization of the Armenians and pecuniary compensation for the victims were purged from the new treaty.[15] In fact, the words "Armenia" and "Armenian" were conspicuously absent in the new treaty. As the French scholar Yves Ternon observed, "the new treaty was drafted exactly as if the Armenians did not exist."[16] Somewhat vague and nominal allusions were made to non-Muslims, that is, to Christians, using eight articles in a section entitled "Protection of Minorities."[17] Perhaps the non-specification of Armenians served the dual purpose of satisfying both the insurers and the perpetrators. The exclusion of the issue of compensation for war crimes from the new treaty provided the insurance companies an opportunity to let the claims lapse into oblivion. As for the perpetrators of the crimes, the Lausanne Treaty provided successive Turkish governments an "amnesty" to escape their financial and moral responsibilities, and at the same time paved the way for denial, and for characterization of the genocide in non-criminal terms.[18]

The United States did not sign the Lausanne Treaty because technically it was not at war with Turkey. However, on August 6, 1923, two weeks after the signing of the Lausanne Treaty, a thirty-two-page article entitled "Treaty of Commerce and Amity" was signed in Lausanne between the United States and Turkey.[19] This Treaty was strictly a business and a trade deal, and it, too, ignored the rights of victimized Armenians.[20] It was signed when Calvin Coolidge, who became infamous for his perception of business and private moneymaking as a "public virtue" and a "public service," was the president of the United States. Indeed, the treaty's outlook singularly paralleled Coolidge's vision, stated as "The chief business of America is business."[21] This attitude was particularly significant as New York Life considered itself an integral part of the United States "government."[22] It therefore came as no surprise that Coolidge's response to why he chose not to run for a second term as president of the United States was, "because there is no room for advancement."[23] Just three months after the expiration of his term as president of the United States, in May 1929, Coolidge was elected a member to the New York Life Insurance Company's Board of Directors. In his letter of acceptance to New York Life's president Darwin Kingsley, Coolidge expressed his deep conviction that "the people's interest" and the interest of New York Life were one and the same:

> Believing that Life Insurance is the most effective instrumentality for the promotion of industry, saving and character ever devised, that a well managed mutual company is a cooperative society for the advancement of the public welfare, and that, as one of the leaders in this national economic movement, the New York Life Insurance Company may justly be called a Public Service Institution, I accept the nomination you have tendered me to become a member of the Board of Directors of your Company and if elected I shall be glad to participate in its administration.[24]

Coolidge's deep fondness of, and esteem for, New York Life's business and its principles are unambiguously expressed in this letter by his assertion that life insurance is "the most effective instrumentality for the promotion of industry, saving, and character ever devised."[25]

Severe criticism of and opposition to the signing of the Lausanne Treaty were voiced by prominent American university professors, scholars, intellectuals, and politicians.[26] Perhaps the call of the former United States ambassador to Germany, James W. Gerard, in an article entitled "The Senate and the Lausanne Treaty," best describes these feelings of the day:

> The Treaty of Commerce and Amity that the United States, on August 6, 1923, concluded with Turkey at Lausanne, dishonors America.... It ignores the solemn pledges that American statesmen had repeatedly made to the Armenian people; and recognizes by implication calculated murder as policy of government. It is a humiliating treaty.... By signing the Lausanne Treaty, we...fell into the category of petty concession hunters. If we accept, at the hands of the Turks, the counterfeit blood-money that the Lausanne Treaty offers, we shall be humiliated and discredited. The honor of America, no less than every dictate of reason, demands that the Senate rejects the Turkish Treaty.[27]

The sentiment that political and economic deal-making lay at the heart of the treaty was echoed by U.S. Senator William H. King of Utah.

> It would appear that the Chester [oil] concession was the objective of our Government in its participation in the Lausanne conference, and that the price paid for the attainment of that objective was...the betrayal of Armenia and the pursuit of dollar diplomacy.[28]

The Lausanne Treaty effectively removed from the international political scene the moral imperatives and the issue of material compensation to the victims of the Armenian Genocide. Both the insurers and the perpetrators, in a mutually satisfactory and beneficial act of defiance, succeeded in producing a treaty that serviced both corporate material interests and the perpetrators' escape of accountability for crimes against humanity. The dual syndrome of "there is negation in profit and profit in negation" prevailed.[29] The noted scholar on the Armenian Genocide, Dadrian summed up his thoughts of the Lausanne Treaty as follows:

> The Allies abjectly discarded the Sèvres Treaty, which they had signed two years earlier and through which they have set out to prosecute and punish the authors of the Armenian Genocide and at the same time redeem their promises for future Armenia. After expunging all references to Armenian massacres, and to Armenia, from the draft treaty, they put their signatures on the Lausanne Peace Treaty, thereby insidiously helping to codify the condition of impunity by pleading *nolo contendere*, i.e., they would not contest the Turkish insistence to consign to oblivion the episode of the Armenian genocide.[30]

The "down to earth" narrative of a genocide survivor provides a vivid and penetrating view of the sinister motives of the Lausanne Treaty.

> After World War I, in the Treaty of Sèvres President Wilson advocated a strong, free Armenia, which would have included a good portion of our homeland in what is eastern Turkey today – Van, Bitlis, Moush, Erzerum, and some of the Black Sea Coast. That would have made a difference. But that treaty was nullified by the Treaty of Lausanne in 1923, and all was taken back at the request of Ataturk. Had the Treaty of Sèvres passed, it would have said: the civilized world cares about the most ancient Christian nation of the Near-east. It would have said: the martyrdom and suffering of Armenians will not go unheeded. Armenia had built a beautiful civilization for three thousand years and we had to watch it be destroyed. Even [U.S. President] Harding said he would stand behind Wilson's mandate for Armenia. We deserved some justice, and we got nothing. We were left to the perverted barbarism of the Turks, and only Russia came to our aid to help the little bit of Armenia that was left in the Caucasus. And after 1923, no one cared about Armenia. For Armenians it was a pill too bitter to swallow. A pain too bad to feel.[31]

The United States Senate's refusal to ratify the controversial LausanneTreaty eventually led President Franklin D. Roosevelt to withdraw from it on January 12, 1934.[32] Today, the "ghost" of Sèvres has resurfaced again with the mounting European sympathy with the Kurdish movement. Article 62 of the Sèvres Treaty, to which Turkey was a signatory, had stipulated the creation of an autonomous Kurdistan just south of the southern border of the independent Armenia.[33] The Sèvres Treaty, which perhaps constitutes the only diplomatic success garnered at the end of the World War I, is still a burning issue in the Turkish psyche. Turkish historians and sociologists call it "the Sèvres Syndrome," which, according to the Turkish columnist Zulfu Livanelli makes the Turks "afraid of Sèvres."[34] The controversial nature of the Lausanne treaty was felt again in July 1998 when the Swiss government refused to let Turkey celebrate the seventy-fifth anniversary of the treaty in Lausanne and Turkey angrily warned the Swiss government of "bilateral consequences."[35]

Notes

1.   Buckner to Lansing. November 20, 1922, U.S. National Archives RG 59 File 367.115N48/33.
2.   Union-Vie to French Foreign Ministry, April 11, 1922 (enclosure), U.S. National Archives RG 59 File 367.115N48/3.
3.   Fred L. Israel (ed.), *Major Peace Treaties of Modern History: 1648–1967,* Vol. IV (New York: Chelsea House Publishers and McGraw Hill Book Co., 1967), pp. 2055-2213. The Sèvres Treaty perhaps constitutes a short-lived but most successful post-war event in terms of justice and the righting of a wrong. The treaty recognized the establishment of an independent and free Armenian State (Articles 88 to 93 of the Sèvres Treaty). The Treaty categorized the Ittihadists' government that perpetrated the genocide as a "terrorist regime" and imposed harsh financial

obligations for the compensation of the victims' lives and their assets (i.e., Articles, 142, 144, 230, 235, 236 and 287 of the Sèvres Treaty). Support for the establishment of an independent Armenian state was also voiced by William Jennings Bryan, who was U.S. Secretary of State until June 9, 1915. At a meeting organized by the American Committee for an Independence of Armenia, Bryan said, "If any people have earned the right to be free and independent, masters of their own destiny and sovereigns in control of their own government, it is the Armenians. For more than two thousand years they have maintained their existence amidst difficulties and under hardships that would have crushed a weaker people into the dust. They have not only preserved their race, integrity and ideals but they have been "a voice crying in the wilderness" – but their day is here even though that dawn of that day has been reddened by the blood which they have so freely shed. The high character of the Armenians in the United States compels us to respect the country from which they came." In: William Jennings Bryan, "Armenia, the Torch-Bearer of American Ideals," *Armenian Herald*, 1917, 167, 167; cited by Vahakn N. Dadrian in "The historical and legal interconnections between the Armenian Genocide and the Jewish Holocaust: From impunity to retributive justice," *Yale Journal of International Law*, 23:2 (Summer 1998), pp. 515-516.

4.   Buckner to Lansing, op. cit. (note 1).
5.   Union-Vie to French Foreign Ministry, op. cit. (note 2), p. 4
6.   Ibid., p. 4.
7.   Ibid., pp. 6-7.
8.   Lévon Marashlian, "Finishing the Genocide: Cleansing Turkey of Armenian Survivors, 1920-1923," in R.G. Hovannisian (ed.). *Remembrance and Denial: The Case of the Armenian Genocide* (Detroit, MI: Wayne State University Press, 1998), pp. 113-145. See also: Vahakn N. Dadrian, *The History of Armenian Genocide: Ethnic Conflict from the Balkans to Anatolia to Caucasus* (Providence, RI: Berghahn Books, 1995), pp. 356-374.
9.   Union-Vie to French Foreign Ministry, op. cit. (note 2), p. 7.
10. Marashlian, ibid.
11. Union-Vie to French Foreign Ministry, ibid., (note 2), pp. 6-7.
12. Ibid., p. 8.
13. Ibid., p. 9.
14. Ibid., pp. 9-10.
15. Fred F. Israel, ibid., (note 3), pp. 2301–2368. Note: The words "Armenia" and "Armenian" were deleted from the Lausanne Treaty. Only vague mention on the issue of the "Protection of Minorities" is made in Articles, Nos. 37 to 44 of Section III of the Treaty.
16. Gérard Dedeian, "Le Génocide de Turquie et la Guèrre (1914-1923)," in *Histoire des Arméniens* (Toulouse: Privat, 1982), p. 523. Note: As in the Sèvres Treaty, the Lausanne Treaty did not recognize the issue of Armenian life policies. Rather, in the Treaty's Annex, under section "I" entitled "Life Assurance," the treaty stressed, in Paragraphs 1 to 5, the validity of life contracts in a former enemy country.
17. Eight Articles of the Lausanne Treaty, 37 to 44, dealt with the Protection of Minorities' Rights (see Ref. No. 15).
18. Roger W. Smith, Eric Markusen, Robert J. Lifton, "Professional Ethics and the Denial of the Armenian Genocide," *Holocaust and Genocide Studies*, 9:1, Spring 1995, pp. 1-22. See also: Terrence Des Pres, "Introduction: Remembering Armenia," in R.G. Hovannisian (ed.), *The Armenian Genocide in Perspective* (New Brunswick, NJ: Transaction Publishers, 1991), pp. 9-17, and Richard G. Hovannisian, "The Armenian Genocide and Pattern of Denials," in R.G. Hovannisian

(ed.), *Remembrance and Denial: The Case of the Armenian Genocide* (Detroit, MI: Wayne State University Press, 1998), pp.111-133.

19. Dikran H. Boyajian, *Armenia: The Case for a Forgotten Genocide* (Westwood, NJ: Educational Book Crafters, 1972), pp. 268-281.

20. Ibid., ibid.

21. Frank Freidal, *America in the Twentieth Century* (New York: Alfred A. Knopf, 1965), p. 244.

22. Lawrence Fraser Abbott, *The Story of NYLIC: A History of the Origin and Development of the New York Life Insurance Company from 1845-1929* (Newark, NJ: A.S. Browne Inc., 1930), pp. 200–228.

23. Glenn Van Ekeren, *"Speakers Sourcebook, II* (Englewood Cliffs, NJ: Prentice Hall, 1994), p.12.

24. Lawrence Fraser Abbott, op. cit., p. 167.

25. Ibid., p. 117.

26. Dikran H. Boyajian, op. cit., p. 478.

27. "A Resolution and Supporting Speech by Senator William H. King: The Lausanne Treaty and Chester Oil," cited in: Vahakn N. Dadrian, "The historical and legal interconnections between the Armenian Genocide and the Jewish Holocaust: From impunity to retributive justice," *Yale Journal of International Law*, 23:2, Summer 1998, p. 514.

28. Dikran H. Boyajian, op. cit., p. 514.

29. V.J. Vitanza, *Negation, Subjectivity, and the History of Rhetoric* (Albany, NY: SUNY Press, 1996).

30. Vahakn N. Dadrian, *The History of Armenian Genocide: Ethnic Conflict from the Balkans to Anatolia to Caucasus* (Providence, RI: Berghahn Books, 1995), p. 422.

31. Peter Balakian, *Black Dog of Fate: A Memoir* (New York: Basic Books. A Division of HarperCollins Publishers, 1997), p. 207.

32. Vahakn N. Dadrian, "The historical and legal interconnections between the Armenian Genocide and the Jewish Holocaust: From impunity to retributive justice," *Yale Journal of International Law*, 23:2 (Summer 1998), p. 514.

33. Fred L. Israel, op. cit. (supra note 3). Articles 62, 63 and 64 of Section III of the Sevres Treaty dealt with the issue of an autonomous Kurdistan.

34. The New York Times, December 7, 1998, A8.

35. International Herald Tribune, June 23, 1998, p. 5. The refusal of the Swiss Government to celebrate the 75th anniversary of the Lausanne Treaty spurred Turkey's Foreign Minister Ismail Cem to recall Ambassador Taner Baytok from Switzerland. In a stern letter to his Swiss counterpart, Baytok described the refusal as "indignation" and warned the Swiss Government of "the consequences for bilateral ties."

8

Settlements of Claims without
Death Certificates

The archival discoveries presented in this book would be a self-con-
tained academic study specific to the first instance of a major genocide
in the twentieth century if, firstly, the issue of the present-day validity
of Armenian policies in the era of the genocide was not addressed and,
secondly, the question of policy benefits after a long period of dormancy
was not compared to other life policy claims resulting from acts of genocide. In regard to both of these, the case of the Holocaust and the issue of
Jewish life policy benefits will be highlighted. Such a comparative study
could provide a legal precedent and a realistic mechanism by which a fair
and an expedite resolution of this unique class of cases can be pursued.
The *Lusitania* case, for example, made it clear that the insurers have
an unconditional contractual obligation to their insured victims that is
independent of the perpetrator's responsibility: A victim's life policy has
a force and legitimacy of its own irrespective of a third party's actions,
however criminal these actions may be. The terms and benefits of a life
insurance policy are governed and regulated by the contractual obligations entered between the insurer and the insured.

Dual responsibility falling on the shoulders of the perpetrators and
the insurers recently resurfaced in the case of a considerable number
of unpaid Nazi-era life insurance policies of Jewish Holocaust victims.
Beginning in the 1950s, postwar West Germany paid reparations of approximately $70 billion, mostly to the State of Israel, and a small amount
to some of the Jewish victims of Nazi persecution. However, Michael
Bazyler, a prominent legal expert on Jewish restitution, sees this level of
compensation as "small" and coming "nowhere close to compensating
for the suffering endured by the victims or the actual monetary losses
suffered by European Jewry."[1] Thousands of Holocaust victims held life
insurance policies with Swiss, German, Italian, and Austrian insurance

companies. The insurers however, repeatedly, and over a fifty-year period, denied most if not all of the claims made by the heirs of the victims.[2] When the agreement reunifying East and West Germany was reached on September 12, 1990, and the London Debt Agreement's moratorium on Holocaust claims by foreign nationals was lifted, massive class-action law suits against life insurance companies doing business in Germany during the Nazi era poured into United States courts.[3] Holocaust victims who had purchased life insurance policies before the war sued European insurance companies doing business in the United States for failing to honor their claims. These floodgates of litigation have generated so much protest by the defendant companies and their governments that the government of the United States, in order to avoid an international diplomatic debacle, took action to resolve the issue of compensation. However, this remedial action taken by the United States provided considerable leeway and discretion to the insurers that prevented the development of a complete list of all insured Jews in the pre-Holocaust era in Nazi-controlled Europe. The efforts to resolve these claims led to the formation, in October 1998, of an international commission of the National Association of Insurance Commissioners, several European insurance companies, European regulators, representatives of several Jewish organizations, and the State of Israel.

This mixed organization, which became known as the International Commission on Holocaust Era Insurance Claims (ICHEIC)[4] is essentially a voluntary claims settlement organization. It is chaired by Lawrence S. Eagleburger, a former U.S. secretary of state. Eagleburger was charged with establishing a process that would expeditiously address the cases of unpaid insurance policies issued to the victims of Holocaust. In elaborating the mission of the Commission, Eagleburger noted that "[the Commission's] direct responsibility is to pay insurance claims belonging to Holocaust era victims throughout the world. Cooperation among insurance companies, Jewish groups, insurance regulators and government entities has resulted in an unprecedented process to swiftly investigate and pay legitimate claims."[5] Basically, ICHEIC was set up to resolve unpaid life and other insurance claims on policies issued between 1920 and 1945 by preparing a complete list of all insured victims and, using "relaxed standards of proof," ensuring the payment of the benefits. The ICHEIC also agreed to establish an independent auditing process for the review of relevant records and archives.

In addition to providing a streamlined claims process, ICHEIC launched an aggressive, global effort to inform and assist potential claimants. In an effort to locate such claimants, letters were sent to more than 10,000 Jewish survivors of the Holocaust and to organizations in seventy countries, alerting them to the claims process and asking them to help locate and assist any of their constituents who may have unpaid insurance claims. In addition, this outreach program utilized paid advertising in mainstream and Jewish publications, press conferences and various activities of Jewish religious, social, and cultural organizations. ICHEIC also established a three-level mechanism for claim processing. First, claims relating to the five major insurance companies that had joined ICHEIC (i.e., Allianz AG, AXA, Generali, Winterthur Leben, and Zurich Financial Services) and their subsidiaries would be processed directly by the Commission through a centralized processing system. Second, policies issued by insurance companies that are not part of ICHEIC would be forwarded with claims related to their companies for review, with the request and recommendation that they honor these claims in accordance with ICHEIC standards. Third, for policies issued by companies that are no longer in existence, a separate Humanitarian Fund, established by ICHEIC would review the claims.[6]

Some progress, albeit very slow, has been made in the processing and payment of insurance claims against German insurers under the terms of an agreement signed on October 16, 2002. The signatories of this agreement were ICHEIC's chair, Lawrence S. Eagleburger, Dr. Hans Otto Bräutigam of the German "Remembrance, Responsibility, and Future Foundation," and Drs. Bern Michaels and Jörg Freiherr Frank von Fürstenwerth of the German Insurance Association (GDV).[7] The signing of this agreement triggered the release of a total sum of about $275 million, of which 102.26 million Euro (about $110 million) is now being paid to settle valid insurance claims against German companies, and approximately 178.95 million Euro (about $190 million) is being disbursed for humanitarian purposes. In addition, under this agreement former Jewish residents of Germany and their heirs will have access to the most comprehensive listing presently available of insurance policies issued to Jewish residents of Germany during the Nazi era. The original deadline for filing claims, February 15, 2002, was extended to September 30, 2003 in order to provide, according to Lawrence S. Eagleburger, sufficient time to publish additional policyholders' names and thereby enable more individuals to file potential claims.[9] On April 30, 2003, ICHEIC announced the publication of 363,232 names of insurance policyholders on its website, the result of "meticulous investigative" work on a data base involving more than eight million names. This giant investigative work involved a group of archivists and historians who researched German, U.S., and Israeli archives and created a list of the prewar German Jewish population, which was based on names from memorial books and deportation and emigration lists, as well as German registers of Holocaust victims.[10] At the time of writing over 2.5 million entries are being processed to create the most complete list of German Jews ever assembled, a list that had been unavailable for decades. Once completed, the list of Jewish residents of Germany will be made available to various organizations in the United States, Germany, and Israel, and will stand as a lasting memorial to the victims of Nazi oppression.[11] Despite these reported advances, ICHEIC's actual progress toward a successful resolution of the unclaimed and unpaid life insurance policies has been very slow. Only less than 2 percent of the insured Jewish victims of the Holocaust have actually been compensated, and the current five insurance companies that are members of ICHEIC represent only about 35.5 percent of the pre-World War II European insurance market.[12] Evidence submitted in a series of class actions filed against the Italian insurance company Generali, for example, showed that as of November 2001, ICHEIC had resolved only 797 of 77,000 claims, barely over 1 percent.[13] Furthermore, repeated earlier assurances that all non-ICHEIC German and European insurance companies would eventually join the commission failed and it remains unclear whether ICHEIC will ever encompass all Nazi-controlled European insurers.

The voluntary and non-compulsory nature of ICHEIC appeared to have provided the insurers with a convenient and easy way to evade the production of full and complete lists of all victimized policyholders. Cognizant of the potential shortcomings of ICHEIC's voluntary and legally non-binding structure, the State of California enacted its own statute on the Holocaust insurance reporting act, which became known as the California's Holocaust Victims Insurance Relief Act (HVIRA).[14] This 1999 law, passed just one year after the founding of ICHEIC, required any insurer, parent company, or anyone "related" to it, doing business in the State of California to disclose to the State all policies sold in Nazi-controlled Europe between the 1920 to 1945 period. Failure to comply with this law would result in the revocation of insurance licenses of all insurers doing business in the State of California. This legally binding, non-voluntary statute was enacted to ensure two major objectives. First, to secure the list of *all* Jewish policyholders in Nazi-controlled Europe and second, to counter the insurers' intransigence and use of legal loopholes intended to prevaricate the claims.[15] This statute was found necessary because most survivors alive today were too young at the time of the Holocaust to remember or even know of the existence of their parents' life insurance policies, or of the companies that issued the policies to their families. According to HVIRA, insurance companies doing business in California must disclose the list of all those insured and California's Insurance Commissioner must store the information in a public and easily accessible site, that is, the "Holocaust Era Insurance Registry." Furthermore, the Commissioner is empowered to suspend the license of any insurer that fails to disclose the names of the insured. This act, also known as the "disclosure law," entails no obligation to pay on any claim, nor does it authorize litigation of any claim; it only mandates disclosure of information that could reveal the existence of a viable claim to a Holocaust survivor residing in California, which at the discretion of the beneficiary could be pursued for resolution in a variety of forums, including ICHEIC, if so desired. At present there are some 5,600 documented cases of Holocaust survivors residing in California.[16]

The insurance companies bitterly complained that if the California law stands, fifty states could set fifty different requirements for Holocaust-era insurance claims. The insurers have further maintained that some of the required information has been "lost," and that European laws prohibit client information from being given to a third party without the "client's consent." Not unexpectedly, the insurers brought a lawsuit in a California federal district court and defeated HVIRA on three constitutional grounds: (1) interference with the federal government's power over foreign affairs; (2) due process; and (3) the Foreign Commerce Clause.[17] Proponents of the HVIRA appealed, and the Ninth Circuit Court of Appeals reversed and upheld the HVIRA.[18] Both President Clinton and President Bush objected to the HVIRA on the grounds that it interferes with the president's ability to conduct the nation's foreign policy. Both presidents actively rallied to defeat HVIRA in the U.S. Supreme Court. In a November 1999 letter addressed to California Insurance Commissioner and the deputy secretary of state, Stuart Eizenstat argued that "[although] HVIRA reflects a genuine commitment to justice for Holocaust victims and their families, it has the unfortunate effect of damaging the one effective means now at hand to process quickly and completely unpaid insurance claims from the Holocaust period: the ICHEIC."[19]

Five years after the enactment of the California HVIRA, on June 23, 2003, the U.S. Supreme Court struck down California's HVIRA law in a 5 to 4 vote. The High Court argued that HVIRA was "unconstitutional" and that it "interfered with the President's conduct of the Nation's foreign affairs."[20] The Supreme Court's decision triggered angry responses by many survivors of the Holocaust and by congressional leaders. Concerned state insurance regulators and Jewish groups in a friend-of-the-court brief had urged the high court to uphold California's HVIRA, articulating the necessity of its passage by asserting:

> The callous insurance companies that profited from the Holocaust need secrecy not only to keep the properties they stole from corpses, but to continue to do business today with Californians who would be rightly concerned, for both economic and moral reasons, if they learned the truth.[21]

In a written statement, Representative Henry A. Waxman, a Democrat from California, expressed his deep disappointment of HVIRA's reversal by the high court, and vowed to reintroduce a similar bill in the U.S. Congress.[22] While high powered politicians and insurance commissioners strongly argued against the ruling of the Supreme Court, the statements made by William Lowenberg, a Holocaust survivor and a prominent advocate of its documentation, is a vivid reminder of the type of response the surviving victims of the Armenian Genocide received from the insurers more than eighty-five years ago. Lowenberg said:

> Let's face it, the insurance companies are a bunch of *gonaven* [thieves]. It's not millions but billions of dollars they collected through policies. When [survivors] went to collect, they said go get a death certificate. They should be told to go to Hitler to get a death certificate from him. Auschwitz didn't give death certificates.[23]

On March 2007, Chairman Lawrence Eagleburger announced the "successful completion of ICHEIC's claims and appeals processes" and ICHEIC closed its doors shortly thereafter. ICHEIC's website (http://www.icheic.org) however, will be maintained by the United States Holocaust Memorial Museum in recognition of the historical value of ICHEIC's work. It however, remains unclear how truly successful and complete was the claim process, a fact that we may never know.

The origins and the motives for the legal battle by Holocaust victims have many parallels to the Armenian life insurance claims made more than eighty-five years ago. While the Young Turks failed in their demonic attempts to collect their victims' life policy benefits from the insurers, the Nazi government of Germany, in collaboration with the German insurers, confiscated the proceeds of many Jewish life insurance policies issued before and after World War II.[24] The policies that had escaped confiscation were denied payments. As in the Armenian case, the insurers refused to compensate the heirs of the insured Jewish victims by claiming that the policies had lapsed due to unpaid premiums or that the claims could not be honored due to lack of death certificates of the policyholders.[25] The feelings of anguish, anger and devastation experienced by the victims of the Jewish Holocaust are vivid reminders of the same sense of despair and hopelessness experienced earlier by the victims of the Armenian genocide. As in the case of the Jewish victims, the victims of the Armenian Genocide also saw their claims stonewalled and prevaricated by the deliberate and lengthy administrative bureaucracies of the insurance companies. The insurers relied on the absence of formal documentation and other technical lapses, such as the unavailability of death certificates, to turn the claimants away. The genocide survivors were in no position to remedy the insurers' requests. The case of repeated claims made by the surviving children of Massatian in 1915, almost a century ago, is now vividly echoed in San Francisco by the outraged Lowenberg. There are many thousands like Massatian whose names and policy benefits remain concealed in the archives of an untold number of European and American insurance companies, including but not limited to the U.S. Equitable, Star of London, Victoria Insurance Company, and the Swiss La Fédèrale. It would require an "Armenian HVIRA" to compel the insurers to disclose the names of all Armenians who held life policies in the pre-genocide era. Short of obligatory laws, the thousands of legitimate heirs will never know the names of the insurers or the amounts owed to them.

The Holocaust settlement issues clearly and unambiguously point to the present-day validity of life policies held by the Armenians during the pre-Genocide era despite having remained dormant for over ninety years. Indeed, in what might be considered an act of disbelief, a claim filed in 1998 in a California court system by a few heirs of victims of the Armenian Genocide against New York Life finally resulted in a symbolic victory by the claimants after more than eighty-five years of stonewalling. Since this class action lawsuit against New York Life represents the first successful post-Armenian Genocide claim, it sets a precedent for other claims against many other U.S. and European insurers who held thousands life insurance policies on the lives of victimized Armenians. It will therefore be described in some detail.

An Armenian Genocide-Era Claim against New York Life

A claim against the New York Life Insurance Company for a life policy benefit emanating from the Armenian Genocide was made on October 8, 1998, in a district court in Los Angeles, California. The claim had previously been stonewalled on multiple occasions over an eighty-year-long period with no tangible results. Despite the present day availability of effective pursuit of "class action lawsuits," and with four different law firms representing the claimants (the plaintiffs) emanating from the Armenian Genocide era, the insurer (the defendant), in this case New York Life, still used every conceivable legal loophole spanning over a six-year period to evade payments. The final out of court and symbolic settlement of $20 million was reached after six years of negotiations.[26] Given the historical importance and high degree of relevance of this claim relative to the study presented in this book, we will present the details and the chronological evolution of this class action from its start in 1923 to its final settlement date of July 30, 2004.

Largely through the efforts of Vartkes Yeghiayan, a Los Angeles-based attorney, Martin Marootian, the heir of the insured Setrak Cheytanian, a New York Life policyholder who had died during the Armenian Genocide, retained a large national law firm, Robins, Kaplan, Miller and Ciresi, L.L.P., to claim policy proceeds. The law firm, in a nine-page letter, detailed the basis of the claim by Marootian and other persons similarly situated.[27] The history of Marootian's claim, like the cases of Holocaust victims, demonstrates the intransigent and evasive strategies utilized by the insurers to avoid payments. Marootian's unsuccessful claim process involved more than a dozen inquiries, requests, and letters that span eighty years. The futile attempts by Marootian, dragged for more than seventy years, from 1923 to 1997, are highlighted by the demands for documented proof of deaths, policy ownership and payments, and so on, in the claim filed against New York Life by the Robins, Kaplan, Miller and Ciresi Law Firm. The claim process was ignored until the filing of a repeat claim on October 8, 1998, after which the historical facts and background of the case were reviewed and the law firm requested that the claims be honored:

> By this letter, we demand the payment of benefits under the Cheytanian policy... with the present value of 3,000FF as of June 21, 1915. We further demand that New York Life publicly identify all policies issued in the Turkish Empire at any time between 1895 and 1918, upon which payments of premiums ceased before all premiums required to be paid under the policy were actually paid.[28]

For over a year after the claim was filed, the New York Life Insurance Company, consistent with its past strategy, remained silent and ignored Marootian's claim. This prompted Marootian's attorney on November 24, 1999 to file a new class action lawsuit. This time however, eleven additional claimants holding pre-genocide era New York Life Insurance policies were also included in the claim. The case became known as "Marootian et al. vs. the New York Life Insurance Company," and was filed in the United States District Court, Central District of California in Los Angeles.[29] New York Life's traditional policy of silence and neglect could no longer be sustained in the aftermath of the California's State Legislature unanimous passing of the Armenian Genocide Bill, SB 1915. The bill passed into law on September 20, 2000 and became known as the "Armenian Genocide Victims Insurance Act," which asserted California's public policy interest and recognized the rights of the heirs of Armenian Genocide victims to receive the life insurance policy benefits of their deceased forebears.[30] Perhaps most importantly, SB 1915 dictates that any court in California must retain jurisdiction over the claims subject to SB 1915, to ensure that the heirs and/or the victims of the Armenian Genocide have an opportunity to pursue their claim in a fair and reasonable forum. The SB 1915, however, fell short of compelling the insurers doing business in California to disclose, as is the case with the HVIRA, the names of all Armenians insured during the genocide era. Nevertheless, the SB 1915 came as a blow to the New York Life Insurance Company that had earlier called for the "dismissal" of the Marootian et al. case "with prejudice" on the basis of "improper forum selection," indicating the following:

- The plaintiffs have failed to present evidence that the forum selection clauses were incorporated in the policies through fraud.
- The forum selection clauses were not incorporated in the policies through undue influence or overweening bargaining power.
- France and England are more convenient forums since plaintiffs allege a worldwide class, many of the policies were reinsured by a European insurer, and many of the named plaintiffs and purported witnesses live thousands of miles from California.
- Enforcing the forum-selection clauses will not deprive plaintiffs of their day in court.[31]

Despite California's statutory limitation (SB 1915) allowing claims arising from the Armenian genocide era to be pursued in a California court system, New York Life kept its policy of prevarication by changing its strategy. It now decided to dismiss the case not on grounds of "improper venue" but rather on the newly invented pretext that the issue of the Armenian Genocide "adversely affects the nation's foreign relations," a matter the company claimed "is exclusively in the jurisdiction of the United States government and not the State of California." New York Life further insisted that the State of California is in no position to dictate foreign policy, especially on the grounds that "the U.S. Gov-

ernment did not recognize the Armenian Genocide in the first place."
The company's modified clauses used as arguments to deny the claims
included the following:

- California's Code of Civil Procedures section 354.4 is an unconstitutional invasion of the Federal Government foreign affairs powers.
- The Federal Government has declined to recognize the Armenian
  Genocide due to the adverse impact doing so would have on the
  nation's foreign relations.
- Application of Code of Civil Procedures 354.4 would violate the due
  process clause.[32]

In their final disposition in the United States District Court, on November 6, 2000, the attorneys of the New York Life Insurance Company concluded that "For all the reasons discussed above, this Court
is not the appropriate venue for the Plaintiffs' claims. Therefore, New
York Life respectfully requests that this Court dismiss this case, in its
entirety and with prejudice."[33] It is remarkable that New York Life's
dismissal of the case came despite an *amicus curiae* filed on October
16, 2000 in support of the plaintiffs for the claims to be pursued in a
California court system, which had persuasively argued as follows:

- Strong public policy and basic issues of fairness compel venue of this
  action in California.
- Over the past several years, there has been growing recognition in California and elsewhere that many insurance beneficiaries of Holocaust
  and Armenian Genocide victims have been systematically deprived
  of insurance proceeds morally and lawfully due to them.
- Unconscionable acts of predation by insurance companies against the
  heirs of such victims, such as demanding death certificates (where
  none could reasonably exist) and original insurance policies (items
  typically not preserved by the perpetrators of the atrocities) prior to
  recognizing or processing an insurance claim, demonstrate a rank of
  injustice which has long persisted.
- Responding to this injustice, the California Legislature unanimously
  enacted Code of Civil Procedure Section 354.4 in 1998 to address
  the Holocaust-related insurance, and on September 20, 2000 enacted
  Code of Civil Procedure Section 354.4 to deal with insurance issued
  to victims of the Armenian genocide.
- The Supreme Court [U.S.] held that a forum selection clause is unreasonable if (a) its inclusion in the contract was the result of "fraud,
  undue influence, or overweening bargaining power," (b) the selected
  forum is so "gravely difficult and inconvenient" that the complaining
  party will "for all practical purposes be deprived of his day in court,"

or (c) enforcement of the clause "would contravene a strong public policy of the forum in which the suit is brought....
- Finally, particularly given the advanced age of the claimants, to require them to travel to London or Paris to pursue their claims is, for all practical purposes, to deny them the opportunity to present their claims at all.
- The California Legislature has specifically recognized the "undue, unreasonable and unjust hardship" that imposition of these selection clauses would have on claimants. The Commissioner respectfully suggests that the motion to dismiss be denied.[34]

On November 28, 2001, Judge Christina A. Snyder, after weighing the claims and counterclaims, concluded that there were enough merits in the case to warrant a trial. In her concluding remarks, Judge Snyder stated:

> The Court finds that enforcement of the forum-selection clauses in the NEW YORK LIFE INSURANCE COMPANY life insurance polices which are the subject of this action would be fundamentally unfair. Furthermore, the Court finds that California Code of Civil Procedure Section 354.4 expresses a strong public policy of California against the enforcement of the subject forum-selection clauses, which may permissibly be taken into account in deciding the instant motion. On those grounds, and for the reason stated above, the Court finds the New York Life Insurance Company's motion to dismiss for improper venue must be and is hereby DENIED. IT IS SO ORDERED.[35]

With the court's denial to dismiss the case of Marootian's et al., New York Life's vice president, William Werfelman, in a dramatic reversal of the Company's traditional strategy of prevarication and intransigence, finally admitted that the policies were valid and the claims legitimate. In an apparent change of heart, he stated that the company was now willing "to offer $10 million to the victims of the genocide." The plaintiffs rejected the offer.[36]

While preparing for a trial on June 28, 2002, the attorneys of the New York Life Insurance Company served one of us with a subpoena, demanding that he hand over all the documents in his possession on pre-genocide era life insurance policies.[37] Specifically, the attorneys for the defendant requested eleven different documents that were or presumed to be in this author's possession.[38] The author complied with the subpoena and sent all the requested materials to the attorneys of the defendant.

While out of court negotiations on this matter were in progress, on January 28, 2004, New York Life doubled its "offer" to the plaintiffs to $20 million and a settlement was reached. California Sate Insurance Commissioner John Garamendi, who helped negotiate the agreement announced: "This settlement between the New York Life Insurance Co. and the plaintiffs will help bring justice to survivors of those killed during a deliberate, systematic and government-controlled genocide that began in April 1915."[39] On February 19, 2004, the U.S. District Judge Christina Snyder granted preliminary approval of the settlement for unpaid life policy benefits. According to the settlement, about $11 million will be set aside for potential claims by heirs of some 2,400 policyholders, $3 million will go to nine Armenian charitable organizations and $6 million will pay attorneys' fees and administrative costs. Judge Snyder set a July 30, 2004, court date to hear any objections from plaintiffs, who may opt out of the settlement. Indeed, on that same date Judge Snyder formally approved the $20 million settlement, a landmark legal settlement, the first ever, in connection with the Armenian Genocide that had started more ninety years ago.[40] A website was made available for the descendents of Armenian life policyholders seeking benefits from the New York Life Insurance Company.[41]

AXA S.A. (Union-Vie) Agrees to a Settlement

The case against the French insurance company AXA S.A. (formerly Union-Vie) was the second of its kind to be brought in a U.S. District Court in the Central District of California (Case No. CV–02–01750). The same group of attorneys that represented the plaintiffs against New York Life also represented Kyurkjian and Ouzounian et al. (the plaintiffs) against AXA S.A. (the defendant). After initial stonewalling and denials, AXA S.A. finally agreed, on November 18, 2005, to an out of court settlement. According to this settlement AXA agreed to pay $17.5 million, as follows: $11,350,000 "Claims Fund," to be paid to individual Settlement Class members; $3,000,000 "Community Fund," to be paid to charitable organizations based in France; $3,150,000, "Cost Fund," attorneys' fees and other court related expenses. In response to media inquiries, AXA S.A. denied that its decision to make payments to the heirs of the Armenian Genocide was "politically motivated" or served as recognition of Armenian Genocide. An announcement made in the name of the AXA S.A. executive management included the notice that "the payments represented the meeting of obligations from outstanding insurance policies from the time and had *no deeper significance* [emphasis added]."[42]

Over the years the New York Life Insurance Company and the Union-Vie (AXA, S.A.), by their own admissions, each paid less than 2 percent of their total debts on pre-genocide era life policy benefits to the heirs of the Armenian victims. A calculation of the ten million dollars unpaid in 1915 by each of the two companies, with a compounded annual interest of 5 percent, amounts to more than two billion dollars in today's dollars for each of the two companies.

Notes

1. Michael J. Bazyler, *The Battle for Restitution in America's Courts* (New York: New York University Press, 2003), p. xi.
2. Ibid., pp. 110–171.
3. Stuart Eizenstat, *Imperfect Justice: Looted Assets, Slave Labor, and the Unfinished Business of World War II* [BBS,www.publicaffairsbooks.com 2003].
4. International Commission on Holocaust Era Insurance Claims (ICHEIC) http://www.icheic.org (access date 07/17/2003).
5. Ibid.
6. Ibid.
7. Ibid.
8. Ibid.
9. Ibid.
10. Ibid.
11. Ibid. At the time of writing the list of potential life policyholders had reached more than 450,000 names, representing more than 500,000 insurance policies throughout Europe. Altogether ICHEIC has located life insurance policies from twenty-three countries (Austria, Belgium, Bulgaria, Czech Republic, Denmark, Finland, France, Germany, Greece, Hungary, Italy, Latvia, Libya, Lithuania, The Netherlands, Norway, Poland, Romania, Slovakia, Spain, Switzerland, Ukraine, and Yugoslavia). In a telephone conversation on July 25, 2003 with the Washington-based ICHEIC contact person, Mr. Dale Franklin, this author (HSK) was told that agreements were recently being concluded with Belgium, France, the Netherlands and Austria, using the German Foundation pact as a model. The French intransigence appeared to have been based on a French law that banned dissemination of the names of groups of people belonging to a certain religion or ethnic background. Ironically this post-war French law was designed to protect minority groups such as Jews in France from persecution. See also Gregg J. Rickman, *Conquest and Redemption: A History of Jewish Assets from the Holocaust* (New Brunswick, NJ: Transaction Publishers, 2007), pp. 244-252.
12. Eizenstat, op. cit., p. 268.
13. Ibid., p. 267. According to a *New York Times* report, "In more than four years of operation [ICEICH] has offered $38.2 million—or just short of the $40 million it had spent on expenses as of 18 months ago—to 3,006 claimants." (Treaster, "Holocaust List Is Unsealed by Insurers," April 29, 2003, Section A, p. 26). It is estimated that there are 2 million Holocaust survivors alive at present, many of whom live in Israel and Eastern Europe, who are entitled to compensation or restitution as a result of atrocities perpetrated against them by the Nazis and their collaborators. These acts included forced and slave labor, confiscation of assets, and looting of gold and art. Furthermore, there exist a large number of dormant bank accounts and unpaid life insurance policies, which may be recoverable by the rightful heirs. A question arises as to whether the successor companies that received payment after the war should be held liable for the payment of Holocaust claims. Holocaust survivors claim that European insurers did not search for the surviving beneficiaries and that in regard to any payments due, the claimants must

be paid by insurers who assumed the assets and liabilities of the old companies. Finally, East European countries signed treaties that led to the return of nationalized assets to the insurance companies, and European insurers enriched themselves by the non-payment of Holocaust-era insurance claims (http://www.unclaimedassets. com/israel.htm, [access date 7/25/2003]).

14.   Supreme Court of the United States. American Insurance Association et al. vs. Garamendi, Insurance Commissioner, State of California. 02/23/2003. Docket # 02–722. http://www.supremecourtus.gov (Access date 07/18/2003). (A large body of information on HVIRA can be obtained through Google.com search HVIRA.)

15.   Ibid., ibid.

16.   http://www.supremecourtus.gov American Insurance Association et al. vs. Garamendi, Insurance Commissioner, State of California. 02/23/2003. Docket # 02–722. Ginsburg, dissenting, pp. 1-3.

17.   www.appellate.net/docketreports/ pdf/docketreport6_2002.pdf – (access date 7/23/2003).

18.   Ibid., ibid.

19.   http://www.supremecourtus.gov American Insurance Association et al. vs. Garamendi, Insurance Commissioner, State of California. 02/23/2003. Docket # 02–722. Opinion of the Court, p. 11.

20.   Ibid., pp. 1-31. Justice David Souter, writing the majority opinion, stressed that "HVIRA's economic compulsion to make public disclosure of far more information about far more policies than ICHEIC rules require constitutes 'a different state system of economic pressure,' and in doing so undercuts the President's diplomatic discretion and the choice he has made exercising it." He went even further and opined that: "The basic fact is that California seeks to use an iron fist, where the President has consistently chosen kid gloves.... [But] our business is not to judge the wisdom of National Government's policy; dissatisfaction should be addressed to the President or, perhaps, Congress. In sum," he continued, "Congress has not acted on the matter addressed here…[and] congressional silence is not to be equated with congressional disapproval." And in the final paragraph, "The judgment of the Court of Appeals for the Ninth Circuit is reversed. So ordered." Justice Ginsburg, who wrote the dissenting opinion in the Supreme Court stressed that the voluntary nature of the disclosure of the names of insured victims by ICHEIC has been a "miserable failure."

21.   "Court Rejects Law on Holocaust Insurance." USA Today, June 23, 2003.

22.   Statement of Rep. Henry A Waxman, in the U. S. Congress, House of Representatives, on the Supreme Court Holocaust Decision June 26, 2003: "I'm deeply disappointed by the Supreme Court's decision. Although it is a devastating setback for Holocaust survivors and their advocates, Congress must redouble its efforts on this issue." Three months earlier, on March 27, 2003, Rep. Waxman had introduced a bill (H.R. 1210), The Holocaust Victims Insurance Relief Act (HVIRA), that was similar to California's HVIRA. In his June 26 press release, Waxman stated that "The H.R. 1210 was not constrained by the Supreme Court's objection to state conduct in foreign affairs," and that a National HVIRA was necessary in order "to put pressure on these companies to end their tactics of stonewalling and delay and ensure that survivors have the necessary information to file their rightful claims." Furthermore, the national HVIRA, according to Waxman, "…will require the insurance companies to live up to their moral and fiduciary obligations to help survivors identify outstanding policies. In most cases, company archives contain the only existing files related to the countless policies that were never paid out to

the victims of Nazi ghettos and death camps.... As a result, approximately 80% of the over 88,000 applications received by ICHEIC remain unresolved because the claimants cannot identify the company that issued their policy. Barely 2% of all claims submitted to ICHEIC have resulted in offers." (See also: www.house. gov/reform/min/maj/maj_holocasut.htm).

23. Joe Eskenazi, "Survivors rip court's overturn of state Holocaust law," in *Jewish Bulletin News of Northern California.* http://www.jewishsf.com/bk030627/sf03. shtml (Access date: 07/17/03).

24. Cited in the U.S. Supreme Court's dissenting opinion by Justice Ginsburg; American Insurance Association, et al., Petitioners v. John Garamendi, Insurance Commissioner, State of California, 2/23/2003, Docket #02-722; dissenting opinion, p. 11. Available online at http://www.supremecourtus.gov.

25. Gerald D. Feldman, *The Battle for Restitution in America's Courts* (Cambridge, UK: Cambridge University Press, 2003).

26. Robins, Kaplan, Miller & Ciresi, L.L.P. to New York Life Insurance Company, New York, New York. October 8, 1998. File No. 240223–0000. The plaintiffs are now represented by the following four law firms, with the exclusion of Robins et al: Quisenberry & Kabateck LLP, Los Angeles, CA; Shernoff, Bidart & Darras, Claremont, CA, Yeghiayan & Associates, Glendale, CA and Geragos.& Geragos, Los Angeles, CA. (see: www.ArmenianBar.org ; New York Life Insurance Case).

27. Ibid. This nine-page letter, addressed to New York Life General Counsel Michael J. McLaughlin, is perhaps the first public plea for post-genocide recovery of losses.

28. Ibid., Robins et al., p. 12. Note: New York Life issued three types of policies in Turkey: Ordinary Life, Twenty-payment Life, and Endowment. The Ordinary Life policies required the payment of premiums for life, and paid benefits at death only to designated beneficiaries. The Twenty-payment Life policies required the payments of premiums for a set number of years (e.g., twenty years), or only for so long as the policyholder lived during that period of time; benefits were paid at death regardless of whether the set term had expired. Like the Twenty-payment policies, the Endowment policies required payment for a set number of years. The Endowment policy matured on a set date even if the policyholder had not yet died.

29. The case is known as: "Martin Marootian, Karen Aghavian, Vera Arakelian, Yeranuhi Arakelian, Krikor Ermonian, Evieny Janbazian, Samuel Kadorian, Ruth Kaprelian, Mary Ann Kazanjian, Goharik Mangoyan, Zareh Momdjian, and Anik Tppjian, individually and on behalf of all others similarly situated, including thousands of senior citizens, disabled persons, and orphans, as well as on behalf of the general public and acting in the general interest (Plaintiffs), vs. New York Life Insurance Company (Defendant), No. CV –99–12073 CAS (MCX)" United States District Court, Central District of California.

30. California State Legislature, SB 1915, California Code of Civil Procedures section 354.4. The bill, which was co-authored by Senators Charles Poochigian and Jackie Speier, Senate Bill No. 1915, relates to the need for the immediate recognition of their plight and the urgency of the insurance payments for Armenian genocide victims and their heirs.

31. Stedman JR, Holmes JC, Hopkins RB (BARGER & WOLEN LLP). Attorneys for Defendant New York Life Insurance Company. U.S. District Court, Central District Californian, Case No: 99–12073 (MCx) November 6, 2000.

32. Ibid.

33. Ibid., 32.
34. Stein AG & Kahan LLP, Kaplan F: Attorneys of Amicus Curiae Harry Low, Insurance Commissioner of the State of California. United States District Court, Central District of California, Martin Marootian, et al., Plaintiffs, vs. New York Life Insurance Company, Defendant. Case No. 99–12073 (CAS (MCx). October 16, 2000.
35. United States District Court, Central District of California, Western Division. Martin Marootian et al., individually and on behalf of all others similarly situated, Plaintiffs, vs. New York Life Insurance Company, Defendant. Case No. CV–99–12073 CAS (MCx). Filed Clerk, U.S. District Court, November 30, 2001.
36. Kristen Kidd, "The Lives They Kept: Insurer and Debt of History," *Armenian International Magazine,* April 2002, pp. 24-27. New York Life offered $10 million based on an arbitrary formula that pays to the beneficiaries ten times the face value of the policies, plus $6.5 million to Armenian charitable organizations.
37. See: Hrayr S. Karagueuzian, "Unclaimed life insurance policies in the aftermath of the Armenian Genocide: Legal and historical perspectives," *Armenian Forum,* 2, 2000 (no. 22) pp. 1-55, and Hrayr S. Karagueuzian, "The Armenian Genocide and the unpaid life insurance policies: Legal and historical perspectives," in *Anatomy of Genocide: State-Sponsored Mass-Killings in the Twentieth Century,* Kimenyi A. and Scott O.L. (eds.) (Lewiston, NY: Edwin Mellen Press, 2001), pp 259-278.
38. Stedman, Holmes, Hopkins, II (BARGER & WOLEN LLP) to Hrayr S. Karagueuzian, June 28, 2002. The specific requests comprised eleven demands and included requests for all documents related to this author's written communications with the New York Life Insurance Company's archivist, and all other documents related to policy claims against the New York Life and the Union-Vie. The author complied with the subpoena.
39. *New York Times,* January 29, 2004; *New York Times,* February 20, 2004. (A list of the names provided by the New York Life Insurance Company appears on the website of Armenian Bar Association: http://www.armenianbar.org).
40. "Judge Approves $20 M Armenian Settlement," *New York Times,* July 31, 2004.
41. http://www.armenianbar.org (Access date 2/22/2006).
42. AXA S.A. and payments of life insurance policy benefits to the heir of the Armenian Genocide: see http://www.armeniapedia.org; http://www.armenianbar.org (Access date: 2/22/2006)

9

1915 Berlin Gold Deposit to Turkey's Account

The issue of restitution of the properties of the deported victims looted or collected by the Young Turks during and in the aftermath of the 1915 Armenian Genocide did not find expression in any historic junctures, including the Universal Declaration of Human Rights[1] and the Genocide Convention (both in 1948).[2] This historical aberrancy helped codify impunity and set a precedent. As David Matas, an expert on international law reminds us,

> Nothing emboldens a criminal so much as the knowledge he can get away with a crime. That was the message the failure to prosecute for the Armenian massacre gave to the Nazis. We ignore the lesson of the Holocaust at our peril.[3]

The ease with which the perpetrators of the Armenian Genocide escaped retributive justice seemed to have impressed the Nazi leadership as they were contemplating a similar initiative towards the Jews.

In the next chapter we will describe the anatomy of a nationwide massive institutionalized and organized bank robbery that was planned and executed systematically by the combined efforts of the ruling party boss and Interior Minister Talât Pasha, and the Finance Minister Djavid. All Imperial Ottoman bank branches complied with the strict government orders and delivered all of the bank assets, valuables and safe deposits, cash deposits and jewelry belonging to the deported Armenians. These patently illegal acts were justified by the so-called "Abandoned Properties Act." The clout and the machinery of two powerful ministries, Interior and Finance, were fully exploited in the execution of what appears to be the twentieth century's first state-sponsored massive robbery of its citizens. The confiscated assets from all Ottoman bank braches were systematically transferred to the Central Ottoman Bank in Constantinople. Upon the insistence of the bank's executives, Finance Minister Djavid provided receipts for the loot, which stated that the assets would be returned to the owners when they return to their homes. However, in September 1916 the

Ittihadist leaders secretly transferred five million Turkish gold pounds ($22 million in 1915) to Berlin's Reichsbank and deposited them, as we will see later, to the personal accounts of the triumvirate Talât, Enver, and Djemal.

In this chapter we will describe a gold deposit in Berlin's Reichsbank in 1915 that was unrelated to the 1916 gold deposit in the same bank by the Ittihadists. The similarities of the amounts of deposits and the bank created utter confusions amongst the Allies during the post-war period as they were in the process of confiscating and allocating German state assets. The sources and the faith of these two different deposits will be detailed in this and in the next chapter.

The Central Powers' assistance to Turkey was particularly transparent when, after the start of the "Great War" in 1914, the German and Austro-Hungarian empires deposited on behalf of their wartime ally, Turkey, the equivalent of 6.5 million Turkish gold pounds in Berlin's Reichsbank in 1915 as collateral for the issuance of Turkish paper currency. Withdrawals were made from the 6.5 million deposit, and when the victorious Allies confiscated this deposit in 1921 there were only 5 million Turkish gold pounds left, the same amount of money deposited by the Ittihadists in the Reichsbank in 1916. This, as we describe in some detail in this chapter, created confusion amongst the Allies who were contemplating the con-fiscation of German bank assets to recover their war-related damages, for which they accused Germany as the aggressor and the responsible party. The apparent "confusion" relating these two transactions was not quite that innocent. The British Foreign Office and U.S. State Department had a vested interest in concealing the origin of the 1916 "genocide gold" in order to win concessions from the ruling Nationalists for exploration of oilfields in Mesopotamia (today's Iraq) and in the Arabian Peninsula. This postwar political expediency helped obfuscate the truth of the victims' looted possessions for decades as U.S. State Department documents re-mained classified till the 1980s. With the declassification of U.S. archival documents we were able to piece together a relatively cogent story that unambiguously documents the origin, fate and purpose of these two ma-jor wartime gold transactions. In this chapter we will discuss the origin, purpose and fate of the 1915 deposit of five million Turkish gold pounds in Berlin's Reichsbank, and in the next we discuss the 1916 deposit of five million Turkish gold pounds in Berlin's Reichsbank by the Ittihadist leaders, the fate of which still remains elusive.

Both the German and the Austro-Hungarian governments contributed to the 1915 deposit as collateral to their wartime ally Turkey for the pur-pose of issuing Turkish paper currency, as described below.

The German Portion

In the aftermath of World War I, and in accordance with the provisions stipulated by Article 259 of the 1919 Versailles Treaty, the Reparation Commission (Kriegslastenkomission) of the victorious Allies prepared a detailed account of the 1915 German gold deposit in Berlin that was to be transferred to their accounts. The Managing Board of the Finance Service of the Reparation Commission prepared a report known as Annex 1424, which described in detail the sources and the purpose of the deposit. In accordance with an Agreement dated April 20, 1915, the German government granted the Turkish government an advance in gold amounting to 80 million marks. Under a further agreement, dated July 3, 1915, the Turkish government was to deliver this sum in full ownership to the Council of the Administration of the Ottoman Debt, as security for the first issue of currency notes to the same amount. In execution of these agreements the sum in question or at least part of it appears to have been deposited by the representatives of the Ottoman Public Debt at the Reichsbank in Berlin, and subsequently transferred to the Bleishroder Bank in Berlin.[4]

The Austro-Hungarian Portion

The Austro-Hungarian Empire extended a security loan in the form of a gold deposit in Berlin of a sum equivalent to 2 million Turkish gold pounds (total with German deposit of 5.2 million Turkish gold pounds) to the account of the Council of the Ottoman Debt for the issuance of Turkish currency notes. It was the combined Austro-Hungarian and German gold deposits (5 million) that was ultimately transferred on February 11, 1921 to the common accounts of the Allies, exclusive of the U.S.[5] The Council of the Administration of the Ottoman Public Debt" was created in 1881 and the purpose of this European financial establishment was to protect the interests of foreign bondholders of Turkish obligation (debts) by placing the deposits in the hands of the Council. The council of European bondholders was empowered to use the income of certain designated Turkish revenues to pay interests on foreign bonds and liquidate them over a long period. The members of the Council were mostly Europeans (French, British, German, Austrian, Italian, and Turkish), and after the war it was completely controlled by Germany.

Perpetual and corrupt bankrupt policies of Ottoman Turkey led to the creation of this Council to safeguard and more effectively control the financial interests of European bondholders. After 1918 the Allies tried to use the Debt Council to gain control of all of Turkey's finances but the Nationalists rejected the Treaty of Sèvres (1920), and the Lausanne Treaty (1923) regarded Turkish finances as an internal problem.[6]

According to the Versailles Treaty the Reparation Commission was empowered to oversee the transfer of this gold deposit to the accounts of the Allies:

> Germany agrees to deliver within one month from the date of the coming into force of the present Treaty to such authority as the principal Allied and Associated Powers may designate the sum of gold which was to be deposited in the Reichsbank in the name of the Council of the Administration of the Ottoman Debt a security for the First issue of Turkish Government currency note.[7]

After meticulous and thorough investigations of the German and Austro-Hungarian gold, the Finance Service Board reached the conclusion that the actual amount of the deposit that would ultimately be transferred to the accounts of the Allies, was less than the original deposit, and that at the time of the signing of the peace treaty "this deposit according to the information furnished by the Administration of the Ottoman Debt and the German Government amounted to 57,919,687.34 gold marks (about 5 million Turkish gold pounds), which seemed to imply that withdrawals had been made from the original deposit."[8] The discovery of a deficit from the original amount of deposit led to a stepped up investigation by the Reparation Commission to determine the causes and reasons of the deficit. As a result and on October 18, 1920, the Reparation Commission was requested to provide an explanatory report on the discrepancy between the original amount of 80 million gold marks as stated in the original contract, and the actual amount at hand at the Bleichroder Bank (57,919,687.34 gold marks) that was to be transferred to the Allies' account. The Ottoman Debt Council was specifically requested to provide information with regard to the deficit of 22,080,313 gold marks. On November 2, 1920, the Commission reported that withdrawals had been made from the original gold deposit in Berlin by the Administration of the Ottoman Public Debt.[9] As a result of these withdrawals, only a portion of the 80 million gold marks were actually left and were available to be delivered to the Allies. This deficit, after its discovery and determination of the reasons, was officially certified and accounted for by the Reparation Commission of the Allies:

> The German Government transferred on February 1921, the sum of 57,919,687.34 gold marks to the Banque de France. This amount is at present kept by the Banque de France as a deposit on behalf of the Reparation Commission for the common account of the Allied and Associated Powers. All documents certifying the delivery of the sum in gold transferred to the Reparation Commission as the authority designated by the Allied and Associate Powers in accordance with Article 259, Paragraph 1, of the Treaty of Versailles, i.e., copies of the receipts delivered by the Banque de France to the German representatives, dated February 11th 1921, and also the original of the letter sent by the Banque de France to the Finance Service on February 12th 1921,

informing it that the transfer had been effected by the German Government, and that the necessary checking and weighing of the coins had been carried out and at present are held in safe custody at the Banque de France. Acknowledgment of this transfer was made by the Finance Board of the Kriegslastenkomission.[10]

The investigation by the Allies of the origin and amount of the withdrawals continued even after the gold was transferred in February 1921. Their painstaking investigation of the deficit was motivated by self-interest, greed and political expediencies. Reduced to its original elements, this investigative behavior indicated that the Allies were bent on seizing all potential assets from the vanquished Central Powers. To meet such an endeavor, the Reparation Commission made the following revelations:

> On March 10, 1922 the attention of the Ottoman Public Debt, which in the meantime had been informed of the transfer of the Gold, was drawn to the discrepancy between the amount of the original deposit (80 million gold marks) and that of the deposit actually transferred (57,919,687.34 gold marks), and that the Administration was requested to furnish documentary evidence as to the withdrawals made by them from deposits in Berlin. The Ottoman Debt replied on March 28, 1922, that the deposit originally made at the Reichsbank amounted to 74,792,869.92 gold marks; the difference between this figure and the 80 million gold marks, mentioned in the Agreement of the April 20, 1915, had been directly paid over by the German Government to the Ottoman Government for various purposes. The withdrawals made by the Ottoman public Debt took place between September 1916 and November 1918, and reached a total of 16,873,182.58 gold marks [German portion only], which gave a residue of 57,919,182.34 gold marks, corresponding to the amount transferred by the German Government. Copies of the withdrawal orders by the Ottoman Public Debt to the Bleishroder Bank were attached to their letter.[11]

After an exhaustive and full accounting of all partial withdrawals prior to the final transfer of the gold to the general accounts of the Allies, the Finance Board of the Reparation Commission concluded:

> In view of these facts the Finance Board is of the opinion that the question should be considered as definitely settled as the declaration made by the Ottoman Debt fully explains the reason why the German Government could only transfer the sum of 57,919,687.34 gold marks, which was the amount of the Deposit at the Reichsbank in the name of the Ottoman Public Debt at the signature of the Peace Treaty. The duty of the Reparation Commission in regard to the transfer of the Deposit in question appears to be completely fulfilled. The Board do [sic] not accordingly propose to take any further action with regard to the execution of paragraph 1 of Article 259 for the Treaty of Versailles.[12]

The American Response

The State Department remained somewhat skeptical of the origin of the transferred gold, particularly when the U.S. Senate and various pro-Armenian organizations claimed that the gold seized by the Allies was looted and, as such, a partial allotment of the capital to Armenian orphans was in order. As a result of these allegations U.S. Secretary of State Evan Hughes requested from the U.S. High Commissioner in Constantinople, Rear Admiral Mark L. Bristol, to investigate and clarify the origin of the gold that was transferred on February 12, 1921 to the accounts of the Allies. Bristol thoroughly analyzed all pertinent official documents, and in a May 22, 1925 report to the U.S. lawmakers indicated that four official state documents had been examined: (1) Law of the Turkish government dated March 30, 1331 A.H. (1915) authorizing an issue of 6,583,094 Turkish pounds (paper); (2) A contract between the Turkish Minister of Finance and the Secretary of State of Foreign Affairs of German Empire for a loan of 80,000,000 marks to the imperial government dated April 20,1915; (3) A contract between the Turkish minister of finance and the minister of foreign affairs of Austria and Hungary for a loan of 47,025,00 kronen, dated May 1, 1915; and (4) A convention between the Imperial Ottoman government and the Council of the Administration of Ottoman Public Debt for the first issue of the paper money dated July 3, 1915.[13] Based on these documents, Commissioner Bristol reaffirmed that the Reparation Commission's findings on the issuance of 6.5 million Turkish currency notes was fully and completely covered by the combined German (4.3 million pounds) and Austro-Hungarian (2 million pounds) deposits. Furthermore, due to withdrawals, only 5.2 million pounds were actually transferred to the accounts of the Allies. Part of that investigative report reads as follows:

A perusal of these documents discloses that the imperial Ottoman Government authorized the first emission of paper money of 6,583,094 Turkish pounds on March 30, 1915; that on April 20 the Imperial Ottoman government concluded a contract with the German Empire for a loan of 8,000,000 marks, that on May 1 the Imperial Ottoman Government concluded a contract with the Austro-Hungarian Government for a loan of 47,025,000 kronen; and that on May 1, the Imperial Ottoman Government entered into a convention with the Council of the Administration of Ottoman Debt whereby the latter would issue the paper money against a deposit by the Turkish Government. The Administration of Ottoman Debt further definitely established the rate of exchange between the Turkish pound and mark and kronen at 18.45637 and 21.6978, respectively.... From the copies of the loan contracts between Turkey and Germany and Turkey and Austria-Hungary and the convention between Turkey and the Ottoman Public Debt Administration, it appears that the sums of 80,000,000 marks and 47,025,000 kronen were transferred to the credit of the Ottoman Public Debt Administration. Converting 80,000,000 marks at 18.45637 and 47,025,000 kronen at 21.6978, it appears that the equivalent in Turkish pounds would be 4,334,546.8 and 2,167,270.4 – a total of 6,501,817,139 Turkish pounds.[14]

The exhaustive U.S. State Department-initiated investigative report, completed on May 22, 1925, corroborates well with an earlier report prepared on May 22, 1923 by the Office of the Economic Advisor of the State Department, part of which reads:

The reference to the money taken from Berlin relates to the transfer of gold under Article 259 of the Treaty of Versailles and Article 210 of the Treaty of St. Germain under which there are held in Paris for the account of the principal Allied and Associated Powers, a sum of 57,919,680 gold marks, and a sum of 2,009,799 Turkish pounds.[15]

The United States, as a member of the victorious Allies, obviously had an interest in the gold, and probably considered itself entitled to a portion of it. Since the United States was technically not at war with Turkey, the precise determination of the origin of and title to, the gold became imperative. Was the Council of the Administration of Ottoman Public Debt a German or a Turkish government entity? That is to say, was the gold "Turkish," as alleged by some state department officials or was it "German," as conclusively ascertained by the Reparation Commission? Pursuant to this endeavor, the Office of the Solicitor of the U.S. State Department prepared, on June 12, 1923, a memorandum that raised the following question: "What interest may the United States claim in the Turkish gold turned over to the Reparation Commission by Germany and Austria under the applicable provisions of the Treaty of Versailles and Treaty of St. Germain."[16] The Solicitor researched the Ottoman Council Debt's structure and functioning system and reached the conclusion that the title of the gold belonged to Germany and Austria-Hungary and not to Turkey. Part of that memorandum reads as follows:

> The first question therefore to be considered is whether the title to this gold is in the Council of the Administration of the Ottoman Public Debt or in the Turkish Government. Before considering this question, it is important to understand the nature of the Council of the Administration of the Ottoman Public Debt. Because large loans had been made to Turkey by certain European powers and because of the wasteful and probably fraudulent administration of Turkish finances, it was proposed as early as 1879 that the interests of foreign bondholders of the Turkish debt should be placed in the hands of a committee or representatives of the governments of the foreign bondholders, which should administer certain of the revenues of Turkey with the view of protecting the interests of the bondholders and to give a basis of security in order that Turkey might negotiate other foreign bondholders in the future. By virtue of the Decree of Muharram of December 20, 1881, the Turkish Government allocated certain revenues to a committee of foreign representatives representing foreign bondholders. On this committee were representatives from England, France, Germany, Italy and Austria [the Dutch interests were in the care of the English representative].[17]

This memo clearly established that the Council was not a Turkish entity but rather a European one. A more concrete reminder of the total independence of the Council from any official and/or legal link to Turkey comes from the assertions made by the U.S. Senator William King of Utah in his letter to Secretary of State Kellogg: "The transfer by Germany of this deposit to the Council of the Administration of Ottoman Public Debt, which was a mere German agency, did not change the legal status of the deposit."[18]

The issue of the origin of the five million Turkish gold pounds transferred in 1921 to the common accounts of the Allies resurfaced again after the signing of Lausanne Treaty in 1923. This interest arose when U.S. Senator William King of Utah introduced a resolution, S319, alleging that despite earlier assertions to the contrary, the gold could have belonged to deported and massacred Armenians.[19]

The linking of gold taken over by Allies to the looted gold belonging to deported Armenians produced new and unexpected hurdles within the U.S. and British circles that were contemplating a lucrative trade partnership with the Kemalist regime in Turkey in order to win concessions for oil exploration. In response to these newly emerging stepped-up allegations, the State Department instructed the U.S. embassies in London, Berlin and Constantinople to conduct new independent and thorough investigations using all of their resources and financial clout to determine anew the origin and full accounting of 1921 gold seizure by the Allies.[20] This ramified investigation lasted for five months, from March 1925 to July 1925.

A comprehensive investigative report, prepared by High Commissioner Bristol, was particularly thorough and persuasive. The commissioner first and foremost investigated the allegations that the sum of five million Turkish gold pounds that had been transferred in 1921 to the accounts of the Allies was not the same as the 1916 deposit in Berlin's Reichsbank by Turkey. In his investigative endeavor, the aggressive and inquisitive commissioner hired two highly placed "informants" in Constantinople, whom he qualified as "reliable sources," and collected a vast amount of evidence by interviewing "eyewitnesses." He reached the conclusion that the 1921 German gold transferred to the accounts of the Allies had absolutely nothing to do with the 1916 deposit in Berlin's Reichsbank by the Ittihadists. In his conclusive remarks, the Commissioner reported to the U.S. Secretary of State:

> Conceding that the Turkish Government did actually deposit with the Reichsbank at Berlin the sum of 5,000,000 Turkish pounds…the High Commission does not believe that the presumption exists, or that the contention can be sustained, that this sum of money was related to, or in any way connected with, the 57,919.687 gold marks which were on deposit at the Bleishroder Bank and subsequently transferred to the Bank of France for the accounts of the Reparation Commission. Even if the facts, regarding the deposit of Turkish gold, with the Reichsbank [are true]…it would appear that at best two separate and distinct transactions have been confused.[21]

Bristol reasserted that the gold deposit in Berlin in 1915 was a completely different transaction and unrelated to the 1916 gold deposit in Berlin, and that "The transferred gold … could not have been in any way related to the 1916 Turkish gold deposit in Berlin."[22] However, although Bristol was unambiguous about the origin of the 1921 gold appropriated by the Allies, he appeared to be reluctant to acknowledge that the 1916 "Turkish gold" deposit actually belonged to deported Armenians. We will provide different orders of evidence in the following chapter that unequivocally demonstrate that the 1916 gold deposit in Berlin belonged to Armenian deportees, and will dwell in some detail on the U.S. and British motives to conceal and obfuscate the true nature of the 1916 gold deposit.

U.S. Motives for Concealing the Nature of the 1916 Gold Deposit

Through the carefully crafted use of words and language, U.S. High Commissioner Bristol skillfully protected Turkey from incriminating evidence and concealed Turkish wartime criminal conduct. Phrases such as "*conceding that* the deposit actually took place," "*alleged* Turkish gold deposit," and "*said to be* deposited"[23] highlight the Commissioner's vested interest in obscuring Turkish wartime criminal financial deeds. The motives can be found in the Commissioner's resolute quest to win a postwar policy of friendship toward Turkey. Marjorie Housepian Dobkin provides a lucid and in-depth account of U.S. policy and business deals with post-war Turkey in a 1972 monograph.[24] Her analysis shows that the exclusively business-minded policies of President Harding, and subsequently of President Coolidge, suceeded in "turning U.S. public opinion toward Turkey." The U.S. motivation, according to Dobkin, was driven by the deep "desire to beat the Allied Powers to what were thought of as the vast, untapped resources of that country, and chiefly the oil."[25] She reached the conclusion that it "[would not have been] possible to bring about the desired change in public opinion without denigrating what the Armenians had suffered."[26] Moreover, Bristol's personal closeness to Turks may well be based on the following motto articulated, in a nutshell, in Henri Berenge's letter to French Premier Georges Clemenceau: "He who owns the oil shall rule the world."[27]

British Motives for Concealing the Nature of the
1916 Gold Deposit

Great Britain was equally reluctant to expose the origin of the 1916 Turkish gold deposit in Berlin in order to not hinder lucrative post-war concessions in Turkey. A concrete reminder of the British motives to conceal the source of this genocide money can be found in the State Department documents that we unearthed.

Shortly before the start of the war, Turkey had paid 5,000,000 Turkish pounds to Great Britain for the construction of two battleships. The money for the two battleships, the *Reshadia* and the *Sultan Osman*, had been collected by "public subscription amid great fanfare" Housepian Dobkin reminds us in her lucid and well-documented study of the postwar Turkey's brute business deals with the West.[28] By the time the war had become imminent, the ships were ready to be released to the anxiously waiting Turkish sailors in the English shipyards for delivery to the Turkish navy. Then, on the eve of the transfer, Winston Churchill, in his position as Britain's First Lord of Admiralty, suddenly refused to permit the ships' release "On the ground that if Turkey was to side with Germany, they would be used against England."[29] Churchill's prophecy proved to be correct. While Turkey initially had a split allegiance to the opposing camps, the German faction, led by Enver, the minister of war, and Ittihad Party leader Talât, Turkey allied with Germany.[30] After the start of the war Great Britain not only kept the battleships for herself but also seized the five million Turkish gold pounds deposit for these two battleships. The issue of prewar financial contracts and agreements resurfaced during the postwar business negotiations. Eager to win concessions and business deals, both Turkey and Great Britain reached a mutually satisfactory agreement by producing the 1923 Lausanne Treaty that absolved Turkey and Great Britain of all financial liabilities incurred during the 1914-1923 period. This mutually agreed upon "pardoning" of sorts, encompassed all "measures of requisition, sequestration, disposal or confiscation." Article 58 of the Lausanne Treaty deals specifically with this issue and reads as follows:

> Turkey on one hand, and the Allied Powers, (excluding Greece) on the other hand, reciprocally renounce all pecuniary claims for the loss and damage suffered respectively by Turkey and the said Powers and the nationals (including juridical persons) between the 1st August, 1914 and the coming into force of the present Treaty [July 1923], as the result of acts of war or measures of requisition, sequestration, disposal or confiscation.... Turkey also agrees not to claim from the British Government or its nationals the repayments of the sums paid for the warships ordered in England by the Ottoman Government which were requisitioned by the British Government in 1914, and renounces all claims in the matter.[31]

The U.S. State Department, while pursuing a potential U.S. share of the 1921 gold seized by the Allies, was careful not to make Turkey liable for any pecuniary compensation. In fact the United States sided with Great Britain in its deals with Turkey. Here is what the Office of the Economic

Advisor of the U.S. State Department had to say with respect to the two battleships.

> A serious situation has also developed among the Allies with regard to their reparation. The French and the Italians have proposed one of the two courses; either, one, the British should place in the common pool of reparations the whole of the ten millions pounds made up from the money taken from Berlin and the money for the battleships, or, two, the British would retain the five million pounds for the battleships to cover their own claims and should place the other five million pounds at the disposal of the [other] Allies to cover their claims. The British, however, take the position that they will keep the money for the battleships themselves, and that they must also share with the others in the disposal of the five million pounds from the Berlin.[32]

The State Department finally reached the following conclusion with respect to the two battleships:

> The reference to the retention of the British of the 5,000,000 £ for the battleships to cover their own claims relates to the value of the payments made by Turkey for the construction of battleships in England which ships were seized by England in 1914. The amount involved is reported variously as 5,000,000 and 7,000,000. The question for consideration and determination is whether the United States desires to present any claim on behalf of its nationals who have suffered injury at the hands of the Turkish government to participate in the distribution of 10,000,000 or 12,000,000 £ which may be effected at Lausanne. My own opinion is that this Government should make no such request as the Untied States was never at war with Turkey and is not therefore in any position to demand a share of the reparations awarded under the Turkish treaty of peace with the allied governments..."[33]

When Great Britain renounced liabilities against Turkey that included not only financial debts, but also liabilities resulting from the "suffering of…nationals," she in essence also renounced Turkey's loot of its victims' riches as a liability in accord with Article 58 of the Lausanne Treaty. It can safely be deduced that Great Britain's motives to conceal the origin of the 1916 "Turkish gold" deposit in a Berlin bank was motivated by business and trade deals with Turkey.[34]

Notes

1. G.A. Res. 217, UN, GAOR, 3d Sess., pt. 1 (1948), Cited by Irwin Colter, "The Holocaust, Thefticide, and Restitution: A legal perspective," *Cardozo Law Review*, 20, 1998, p. 601.
2. Convention on the Prevention and Punishment of Genocide, 78 U.N.T.S. 227 (1948).
3. Davis Matas, "Prosecuting Crimes Against Humanity: The Lessons of World War I," *Fordham International Law Journal*, 86, (1989–90), p. 104.
4. RG 59 467.00R29/69, Annex 1424, Reparation Commission Finance Service to the General Secretary, May 3, 1922, p. 1.
5. Ibid., p. 2.
6. Donald C. Blaisdell, *European Financial Control in the Ottoman Empire: A Study of the Establishments, Activities, and Significance of the Administration of the Ottoman Public Debt* (New York: Columbia University Press, 1929).

7.   Supra, Note 4. OR: RG 59 467.00R29/69, Annex 1424, Reparation Commission
     Finance Service to the General Secretary, May 3, 1922, p. 1.
8.   Ibid., pp 1-2.
9.   Ibid., pp 2-3.
10. Ibid., pp. 3-4.
11. Ibid., p. 4.
12. Ibid., pp. 4-5.
13. RG 59 467.00 R29/68, Bristol to Secretary of State, May 22, 1925.
14. Ibid., pp. 4, 5. In this report the High Commissioner recognizes that the actual
     amount of the German gold transfer was not 80,000,000 gold marks but, rather,
     57,919, 680 gold marks because of several withdrawals, as detailed in Annex
     1424 prepared by the Finance Board of the Reparation Commission and discussed
     above.
15. RG 59 467.00R29/19, Office of the Economic Adviser, Department of State, May
     22, 1923. The Treaty of Versailles was signed between the Allies and Germany
     on June 28, 1919 and was followed by the Treaty of St. Germain that was signed
     between the Allies and Austria on September 20, 1919. See also Martin Gilbert,
     A History of the Twentieth Century, Volume One: 1900-1933 (New York: Avon
     Books, 1997), p. 556.
16. RG 59 467.00R29/16, Memorandum, Office of the Solicitor, Department of State,
     June 12, 1923.
17. Ibid., pp. 3, 4.
18. RG 59 467.00R29/59, Senator King to Secretary Kellog, March 13, 1925.
19. Congressional Records, Sixty-ninth Congress, Special Session of the Senate, Vol.
     67, No.12, March 17, 1925, pp. 301-303.
20. RG 59 467.00R29/69a, Secretary of State to Mark L. Bristol, American High
     Commissioner, Constantinople, 31 March, 1925; 467.00R29/69a, Secretary of
     State to Warren D. Robbins, Esq., American Charges d'Affaires *ad interim*, Berlin,
     July 1, 1925.
21. RG 59 467.00R29/68, Mark L. Bristol, U.S. High Commissioner in Constantinople
     to U.S. Secretary of State May 22, 1925, p. 6.
22. Ibid., p. 20.
23. Ibid., pp. 4, 8-9.
24. Marjorie Housepian Dobkin, *Smyrna, 1922: The Destruction of a City* (New York,
     NY: Newmark Press, 1972).
25. Marjorie Housepian Dobkin, What Genocide? What Holocaust? News from
     Turkey. in R.G. Hovannisian (ed.), *The Armenian Genocide in Perspective* (New
     Brunswick, NJ: Transaction Publishers, 1991), pp. 104-105.
26. Ibid., ibid. Dobkin's description of the U.S. foreign policy in the Middle East
     and the political structure in Turkey during the 1920–1923 formative stages of
     the Turkish Republic is lucid and highly informative. Here is an excerpt: "A close
     look at U.S. foreign policy toward Turkey in the years 1920-23 (and since) shows
     an unrelenting effort to maintain Turkey's friendship by maintaining a favorable
     image of that country in the U.S. press by every possible means.... During the war,
     the press, as has been pointed out, convinced the American public that the Turks
     had committed what was then considered the most barbarous and unforgivable act
     of extermination known to humankind.... In setting out to change this opinion,
     the Harding administration had a cast of characters well suited to the task. Charles
     Evans Hughes, the Secretary of State, had been an official of Standard Oil and
     was untroubled by conflict of interest. The official history of the Standard Oil
     Company of New Jersey covering those years boasts that the company flourished
     as never before when Hughes was in office." Also: "The High Commissioner,

Admiral Mark L. Bristol, was a positive gift to the Turks." A virulent anti-Semite, he equally abhorred Armenians and Greeks. "If you shake them up in a bag you wouldn't know which one will come up first," he wrote in his diary and in letters to his friends, referring to Armenians, Syrians, Jews, Greeks, and Turks, "but the Turk is the best of the lot." And, "The Armenians are a race like the Jews – they have little or no national spirit and poor moral character."

27. Ibid., p. 104. Dobkin provides another detail in the motives behind the U.S. policy shift and the unconditional alliance with Turkey: "What in the world happened to provoke such a shift? A shift, I need not add, that has remained to this day, granting [concessions] to Chester [U.S. High Commissioner]. Chester was on his way to Turkey to claim some right [rights that were first promised exclusively to the German Kaiser] to exploit the oil fields in Mosul, then belonging to Turkey and called 'the greatest oil find in history.'"

28. Ibid., p. 39.

29. Ibid., ibid.

30. Vahakn N. Dadrian, *German Responsibility in the Armenian Genocide: A Review of the Historical Evidence of German Complicity* (Watertown, MA: Blue Crane Books, 1996), p. 339; see also, Henry Morgenthau, *Ambassador Morgenthau's Story* (Plandome, NY: New Age Publisher, reprinted 1965 edition (originally published in 1919 by Doubleday Page & Co.), pp. 82-86.

31. Fred L. Israel, ed., *Major Peace Treaties of Modern History,* Volume IV. (New York: Chelsea House Publishers and McGraw Hill Book Co, 1967), p. 2329.

32. RG 59, 467.00R29/19, Department of State, Office of the Economic Adviser, May 22, 1923.

33. Ibid., pp. 3-4.

34. Lausanne Treaty, Article 58, in Fred L. Israel, op. cit., p. 31.

10

The 1916 Berlin Gold Deposit
by the Ittihadists

On March 17, 1925, just two months before High Commissioner Bristol's extensive investigative report became available to American lawmakers, the U.S. Senator William H. King introduced a resolution (Senate Resolution 319) in which he asserted that the 1916 five million Turkish pounds deposit in Berlin's Reichsbank was looted Armenian property collected by the Ittihadist leaders from the deported victims using illegal and arbitrary means of seizures and confiscation.[1] Part of his Resolution reads as follows:

> Whereas the United States Grain Corporation in the years 1919 and 1920 advanced to the Armenian Republic thirty-five thousand tons of wheat and wheat flour of the value of $13,000,000 which advancement was made necessary in part because the Turkish Government had arbitrarily seized and transferred to the Turkish treasury all bank accounts, both current and deposit, belonging to Armenians, by which Armenian gold in the sum of 5,000,000 Turkish pounds, amounting to $22,000,000 was transferred to the Turkish treasury, which gold was afterwards deposited by the Turkish Government in the Reichsbank at Berlin.[2]

Senator King then divulged his sources of information on the origin of the 1916 gold deposit in Berlin and provided details as to how such an enormous sum was looted from the victims and transferred to the Central Ottoman Bank in Constantinople. Here is an excerpt of Senator King's letter to the Secretary of State:

> ....In relation to the fund of 5,000,000 Turkish gold pounds which was deposited by Turkey in Reichsbank at Berlin in 1916...in a memorandum signed by the Right Honorable H.H. Asquith and the Right Honorable Stanley Baldwin, both of whom had been Prime Ministers of Great Britain, and in September 1924 addressed to the Right Honorable Ramsey MacDonald, then the Prime Minister of Great Britain, the following statement respecting this gold deposit was made: "...The sum of 5,000,000 (Turkish gold) deposited by the Turkish Government in Berlin, 1916, and taken over by the Allies after the Armistice, was in large part (perhaps wholly) Armenian money.

113

After the enforced deportation of the Armenians in 1915, their bank accounts, both current and deposit, were transferred by order of the State treasury at Constantinople. This fact enabled the Turks to send five million sterlings to the Reichsbank, Berlin, in exchange for a new issue of notes." The foregoing statement made by the most responsible officials in the British Government, one of whom is the present Prime Minister, that this deposit was of Armenian gold, which means that in equity that it belongs to the Armenians from whom it was arbitrarily seized by the Turks, is not to be ignored or gainsaid. An inference is of no validity in the face of the fact to the contrary.[3]

While Senator King was right on the origin of the 1916 gold deposit, he erred in regard to two important details. First, the looted gold was not taken over by the Allies after the armistice. As discussed in chapter 9, the gold taken over by the Allies was the 1915 German and Austro-Hungarian deposit and not the 5 million gold deposit by the Ittihadists. Second, the 1916 Berlin gold deposit was totally unrelated to the issuance of Turkish banknotes (paper currency). These two errors resulted from the fact that High Commissioner Bristol's thorough investigative report was not yet available to Senator King at the time he introduced Senate Resolution 319. According to Bristol's report Turkey was not obligated to make the gold deposit in exchange of banknotes, as stated in Bristol's report to the U.S. secretary of state:

The Department attention is [be] directed to the fact that, even if true, the transfer of this gold…was not made until 1916, and could not, therefore, have been employed by the Turkish Government or the Administration of Public Ottoman Debt in the first issue of the Turkish paper currency.[4]

Bristol's report then describes in minute detail the amount, composition and purpose of the 1915 gold deposit. The report corroborates very well with the accounts prepared by the Reparation Commission. Bristol's report unambiguously attests to the fact that the issuance of Turkish paper currency was fully covered by the 1915 combined German and Austro-Hungarian gold deposit and that there was no need for Turkey to deposit gold for exchange of banknotes until September 30, 1924:

….the Imperial Ottoman Government authorized the first emission of paper money of 6,583,094 Turkish pounds on March 30, 1915; that on April 20, the Imperial Ottoman Government concluded a contract with the German Empire for a loan of 80,000,000 marks; that on May 1 the Imperial Ottoman Government concluded a contract with the Austro-Hungarian Government for a loan of 47,025,000 kronen; and that on May, the Imperial Ottoman Government entered into a convention with the Council of Administration of the Ottoman Public Debt whereby the latter would issue the paper money against a deposit by the Turkish Government of an equivalent sum in gold.... The exact sum which was actually placed in circulation by the Ottoman Public Debt cannot be ascertained. On September 30, 1924, the Administration of the Ottoman Public Debt states that only 5,147,919 Turkish pounds of the first paper money issue was in circulation. From the loan copies of the contract it appears that the sums of 80,000,000 marks and 47,025,000 kronen, the equivalent in Turkish pounds would be a total of 6,501,139 Turkish pounds, the first emission of paper money did not actually exceed 6,501,817.2 Turkish pounds, the equivalent of the combined German and Austro-Hungarian loan.[5]

It appeared that the issuance of Turkish currency notes was fully covered by the German and Austro-Hungarian gold deposits up to September 30, 1924. Furthermore, since there were no supplementary Turkish notes issued during this time interval (1915–1924) requiring immediate additional Turkish security deposits, the High Commissioner's report concluded that the 1916 Turkish gold deposit could not in any way be linked to the 1915 German security deposit/loan. Having established the separate nature of the two transactions, Bristol's investigative report then went on to explain the nature of the discrepancies between the actual mount of the gold deposited in 1915 and the smaller amount (due to withdrawals) subsequently taken over by the Allies in 1921. Bristol's independent findings corroborated very well with the report prepared by the Finance Board of the Allies' Reparation Commission:

> With reference to the explanation of the Ottoman Public Debt as to the difference between the sum actually deposited....and the amount taken over by the Reparation Commission of February 11, 1921....the following appears to be a plausible if not correct explanation. Article 3 of the Convention contains the exclusive and irrevocable engagement of the Public Debt to repay the paper money bonds issued by the Turkish Government in gold.... The Administration of the Ottoman Public Debt has informed the High Commission that up to September 30, 1924, the sum of 1,371,220 Turkish pounds of the first paper money issue had been reimbursed.... The statement appearing in Annex 1424 indicates that the Ottoman Public Debt withdrew from the Bleishroder Bank between September 1916 and November 1918 a total sum of 16,873,182.58 gold marks, leaving a residue of 57,919,678.34 gold marks which corresponds to the amount transferred by the German Government in 1912. The total withdrawals of German marks by the Ottoman Public Debt Administration would have been sufficient to have reimbursed something over 900,000 Turkish pounds of the first paper money issue. It is known that the total reimbursement by the Public Debt amounted to 1,371,200 Turkish pounds and it appears reasonable to believe that the portion of this sum was reimbursed by the Public Debt for the withdrawal of the German marks. The remaining 400,000 Turkish pounds which were reimbursed were very probably made by withdrawal of kronen from the Banque Austro-Hungarian with whom it is understood the loan of 47,025,00 kronen, mentioned in enclosure #3, was deposited.[6]

The Commissioner's report discovered that in addition to the Austro-German security gold deposit, Germany provided the Council of the Administration of the Ottoman Debt with German Treasury bonds on behalf of Turkey, thus relieving Turkey from any obligation to secure the coverage of their paper currency. Here is a portion of the Commissioner's report:

> The High Commission desired to state for the further information of the Department [of State] that while the Imperial Government [of Turkey] actually made seven issues of paper money between July 1915 and September 1918, the first issue was the only one which was financed by a direct loan from the German and Austria-Hungary [*sic*] of marks and kronen. The second, third, fourth, fifth, sixth, and seventh issues of paper money made by the Imperial Ottoman Government were financed with German Treasury bonds which, in turn, were transferred to the Council of the Ottoman Public Debt Administration as guaranty for the banknotes issued.[7]

Commissioner Bristol concluded his lengthy report by categorically denying the allegation that the 1916 "Turkish gold" deposit was in any way related to repayment for the security deposit for the issuance of Turkish notes:

> Furthermore, in view of the fact that all subsequent issues of Turkish paper currency were financed from the loans of the German Government which were paid in German Treasury bonds, the charge that the deposited 5,000,000 Turkish gold pounds with Reichsbank in Berlin [in 1916] in exchange for a new issue of notes can hardly be substantiated.[8]

What, then, were the motives behind the speedy 1916 Turkish gold deposit in Berlin? The commissioner in his investigative report to the Secretary of State provided an insight into the motives and the circumstances of this sudden and unexpected deposit of a huge sum of gold by the Ittihadist rulers. The commissioner collected evidence through his highly placed "informants" and "eyewitnesses" and reached the conclusion that the major reason for the transfer of the gold was the fear of the top Ittihadist leaders that Constantinople would soon "fall" into the hands of the Allies.

> Furthermore, one of the informants volunteered the information that in 1916 when the fall and capture of Constantinople appeared imminent, the Turkish Government moved certain archives from Constantinople and forwarded the sum of 6,000,000 Turkish pounds gold to Berlin for safekeeping.[9]

One important question arises that needs to be addressed: why the inquisitive eyes and the aggressive searches by the Reparation Commission to eagerly locate German assets to offset the costs of war-related damages failed to discover the 1916 five million gold deposit in Berlin's Reichsbank. The Allies' Reparation Commission used every intrusive method to search and seize all German and Turkish State assets in German banks.[10] It can be inferred that these deposits were made under the real or assumed names of individuals with no state or government function.

Senator King's was not the only voice in America to call for a return of the 1916 genocide money to the victims' orphans; a call for a just disbursement of the looted money was also made by *Near East Relief,* a New

York-based private humanitarian and charitable organization whose board of trustees and executive committee included Rev. James L. Barton and the former U.S. Ambassador to Turkey Henry Morgenthau, Sr. In a letter addressed to the U.S. secretary of state the charitable organization reiterated that the 5 million Turkish pounds belonged to deported Armenians.[11] Rev. Barton, who was the head of the American Missionaries in Turkey during the deportations and massacres, had compiled an impressive corpus of evidence from the local missionaries who had witnessed firsthand the exaction, embezzlement and illegal confiscation of Armenian properties and bank accounts.[12] As we have seen in chapter Two, on the eve of their forced deportation many of the victims had actually entrusted the local missionaries with their life insurance policies, jewelry and cash. Henry Morgenthau, Sr., who was the U.S. ambassador to Turkey during the 1915 massacres and deportations, was also well aware of the details of the deportations and the illegal confiscations of Armenian riches through reports of the American consular corps in the Eastern provinces who witnessed first-hand these atrocities. The neutral position of the United States almost to the end of the war placed Ambassador Morgenthau and all subsequent U.S. representatives in Turkey in a unique and a privileged position to directly communicate with the top Ittihadist leaders. For example, Morgenthau frequently held private meetings with the powerful Minister of the Interior and later Grand Vizier, Talât Pasha, who often confided, with no hesitation, the merciless nature of his treatment of the Armenians. The ambassador was so deeply moved by these crimes that he left Turkey before the termination of his tenure and wrote his memoir, considered to be an authoritative and an unimpeachable account of the genocidal campaigns by the Ittihadists.[13]

The assertion that the 1916 gold belonged to deported Armenians is supported by a host of convergent orders of evidence. Since a major characteristic of the Armenian Genocide was "the maintenance of utmost secrecy of the scheme, to be safeguarded by camouflage and deflection"[14] it would be futile to expect the discovery of "state documents" attesting to the state's actual plunder of 5 to 6 million pounds from its forcefully deported citizens. More ominously, the forced deportations of 1915–1916 are now justified by the present Turkish government as "temporary measures" designed to remove the deportees from the war zones to "safer locations." In fact, the denial of the genocide began "officially" only in 1923, after the Lausanne Treaty, and it continues today making restitution an impossible task.[15] Fortunately however, the recovery of a historical fact is not and cannot be based on a single footnote. The late

American author and college professor Terrence Des Pres, in his writings on the Holocaust, convincingly argued that it is the convergence of four different orders of evidence, "official, institutional, private and material, that gives history its substance."[16] In the following sections we will present documentary narratives based on these four different orders of evidence making a compelling case that the five million Turkish pounds deposited in 1916 in Berlin's Reichsbank was "genocide money." The title of the genocide money deposit belonged, under assumed names, to the elite triumvirate: Interior Minister and later Grand Vizier Mehmet Talât Pasha, Minister of War Enver Pasha, and the Marine Minister and the Commander of IVth Army Djemal Pasha.

We now present four different orderts of evidence, official, institutional, private, and material, that trace the source of the 1916 gold deposit by the Ittihadist in Berlin's Reichsbank to the victims of the genocide.

Official Order of Evidence

The Ittihadist's strategy to confiscate the assets and bank accounts of the deported Armenians involved a three-step process. First, official ministerial memos were distributed to all European, American and local financial institutions, including insurance companies,[17] requesting lists of all Armenians holding accounts in their institutions. Second, by order of Interior Minister Talât, special "Liquidation Commissions" (*Tassfiye Komissyonu*) were to be set up in various provinces and cities in Turkey for the submission of the target lists. Third, by invoking the "Law of Abandoned Properties,"[18] all such capital and riches were taken over by the Ministry of Finance and transferred to the Central Ottoman Bank in Constantinople.[19] As part of this venture, in January 1916 and also as per Minister Talât's order, the Turkish minister of commerce and agriculture sent circular notes to all foreign insurance companies doing business in Turkey, asking them to submit lists of Armenians holding assets.[20] As we have seen, the foreign companies doing business in Turkey succeeded in not handing over the names and the assets of their clients to the Turkish government.

However, the situation regarding the local branches of the Central Ottoman banks was different. Under strong pressure and threats exerted by no less then Interior Minister Talât and Finance Minister Djavid (Cavid) Bey, and by local governors (e.g., Tahsin Bey, in the case of Erzerum), all Armenian bank accounts and riches were seized and transferred to the Turkish treasury in Constantinople. In a memorial presented in September 1924 to British prime minister Ramsey MacDonald by two former prime ministers, Stanley Baldwin and Herbert H. Asquith, the 1916 Turkish gold deposit was mentioned. Part of paragraph 4 of the memorial reads: "…the sum of LT 5,000,000 (Turkish gold) deposited by the Turkish Government at the Reichsbank in Berlin in 1916, was in large part (perhaps wholly) Armenian money." [21] The two former British Prime Ministers then provided a description on how these monies (gold) were stolen by the Turkish authorities and deposited in Constantinople: "After the forced deportation of the Armenians in 1915, their current and deposit accounts were transferred, by Government order, to the State Treasury." [22]

These statements bear much weight and significance because Great Britain was the first nation in the world to compile a comprehensive and detailed report on the massacres and deportations of the Armenians in 1915-1916. In fact, in February 1916 the British government commissioned James Bryce and Arnold Toynbee to compile evidence concerning the tragic events taking place in historic Armenia. The report, *The Treatment of Armenians in the Ottoman Empire, 1915-16*, was a monumental achievement and was printed in the British Parliamentary Blue Book series. [23] Based on primary sources, eyewitnesses, reports and narratives by local missionaries and foreign diplomatic corps, the report shows in great detail how the looting and confiscation of the wealth of the deported Armenians took place. These tragic facts however, did not seem to impress the British authorities who during the immediate postwar period were keenly pursuing a policy of appeasement towards Turkey to secure concessions from the rising Kemalist regime in order to explore the oil fields in Mesopotamia and the Arabian Peninsula.

Perhaps not unexpectedly, and in line with the British reluctance to expose Turkish wartime crimes during the 1923 Lausanne business agreements with Turkey, Great Britain produced an "official" rebuttal of the memorial signed by former prime ministers Baldwin and Asquith. The rebuttal contended that at the time of the signing of the memorial the two former prime ministers had no "official status." This British attitude is clearly exposed in a correspondence between the London-based U.S. Ambassador F.A. Sterling and Lancelot Oliphant of the British Foreign Office when the U.S. State Department was conducting its own independent investigation on the issue of the 1916 gold deposit in Berlin. The British official stressed the memorial's emphasis on the German and Austro-Hungarian origin of the 1921 gold transfer to the Allies but totally evaded discussing the origin of the 1916 gold. Here is part of Oliphant's reply to Ambassador Sterling:

> In September 1924, the Armenian (Lord Mayor's) Fund, published their memorial which they did without further consulting the Foreign Office, which was in no way responsible for the terms of the memorial, was surprised at their tenor, and in particular the statement that "Turkish gold" seized in Berlin by Allies after the armistice was in large part (perhaps wholly) Armenian money. The statement made by the Fund in their memorial about this "Turkish gold" is quite incorrect. The facts are that the gold sums in question consist of gold marks and gold kronen deposited in 1915 by the German and Austro-Hungarian governments as cover for the first issue of Turkish notes. The gold was not therefore deposited by Turkish Government, and cannot by any possibility have been derived from the property of deported Armenians.[24]

It was clear to Ambassador Sterling that the British Foreign Officer was purposely being evasive regarding the issue of the origin of the 1916 "Turkish gold" and was capitalizing on the gold taken by the Allies as being German and Austro-Hungarian and ignoring the origin of the 1916 gold deposit. Ambassador Sterling however, cognizant of the British evasive attitude, felt compelled to dismiss Oliphant's response to his report to the Secretary of State: "In view of the informal character of Mr. Oliphant's letter, I venture to suggest to the Department that it be not published but used only for guidance."[25]

Yet another important official recognition of the origin of the 1916 gold deposit comes from U.S. High Commissioner Bristol's investigative report. For the business-oriented commissioner, the desire to foster a close trade partnership with Turkey sufficed to completely ignore and conceal, and even acquiesce to, the Ittihadists policies of embezzlements, illegal seizures and confiscations. Nevertheless, Bristol asserted to the Secretary of State:

> After the enforced deportations of the Armenians in 1915, the Turkish Government passed the first "Abandoned Property" law. As a result of this measure, large stocks of merchandise, household effects, etc., in the customs houses, stores, and dwellings of Armenians are said to have been confiscated by the Abandoned Property Commission. [Liquidation Commission]. Two of the High Commission's informants in this city [Constantinople] stated categorically that in the provinces the branch banks of the Imperial Ottoman Bank and the Deutsche Bank were forced by the Commission to turn over the Armenian deposits under the Abandoned Property Law. Information is lacking as to the amount of money collected by the Abandoned Property Commission from the effects of the deported Armenians under this law, but the sum mentioned approximated 6,000,000 Turkish pounds.[26]

It is highly significant that both the British and the U.S. official documents independently asserted that more than five million Turkish pounds (gold) were looted by the Ittihadist elite from deported Armenians and from the Ottoman branch banks by invoking the so-called "Abandoned Property" law.[27]

Another important official assertion that the gold deposits in the Berlin Banks represented looted money with no official state stature or function comes from no less than the post-war Turkish foreign minister, Damad Ferid Pasha. In a letter to French prime minister George Clemenceau, dated June 30, 1919, this top Turkish diplomat requested that the French prime minister exert influence on recalcitrant Germany to extradite to Turkey the Ittihadist "criminals," who were guilty of extortion levied with injustice and fraud. Most relevant to the subject at hand was that the Turkish foreign minister requested that the German government provide the names of the banks in which these "criminals" had made deposits and the sums of those deposits:

> I beg. . .to request Your Excellency to be so good as to demand that the German Authorities will comply with the obligation imposed upon them by Articles 228 and 229 of the [Peace] Treaty and will agree to the extradition without restriction of all guilty persons who have refuge in Germany including Talât, Enver and Djemal...the three very guilty persons[28] .... It will be well at the same time for the German Government to furnish the names of the German Banks in which these criminals [Talât, Enver and Djemal] have deposited considerable sums of money produced by their exaction and embezzlement, as well as the amounts of these sums.[29]

Five days after the date on this letter, on July 5, 1919, the Turkish Military Tribunal in Constantinople, after five months of deliberations during which an enormous corpus of incriminating evidence based on the First Section of Article 45 of the Emperor's Civil Penal Code was presented in the court, Talât, Enver, Djemal and Dr. Nazim were sentenced to death in absentia. It is significant that in the opinion of the court these crimes amounted to no more than "common crimes" (*ceraimi adiye*) unrelated to acts of war.[30] The discovery of the letter-document sent by the top Turkish diplomat provides a clue as to why the inquisitive eyes of the Finance Service Management of the Reparation Commission failed to discover the large Turkish gold deposits in German banks. These deposits may well have been made under individual, most probably assumed, names, having no state or official stature (see below).

Institutional Order of Evidence

In the institutional order of evidence, the declaration of the former provincial governor of Erzerum, General Hasan Tahsin Bey (Uzer) to the Turkish media is compelling. During a public debate in which a number of prominent Turks were accusing each other of the theft and plunder of the riches of deported Armenians, General Tahsin's open letter to the Turkish newspaper *Djumhuriet* is significant. His declaration, made as a means of refuting accusations leveled against him, was discovered as an enclosure to a letter sent by the New York-based Near East Relief to the U.S. Secretary of State. In it, the former governor of Erzerum, perhaps the most populous Armenian Province and the site of the largest mass deportations,[31] stated:

In answer to accusation of robbery, Tahsin Bey by a letter published in Djumhuriet (of December 12, 1924) says among other things: "Before the decision for the deportation, the Armenians of Erzerum had trusted their gold and jewelry, against receipt, to the Ottoman Bank. After the deportation, the Minister of Finance [Cavid] claimed these deposits from the Ottoman Bank, arguing the law of "abandoned good [sic]." On the refusal of the Bank, long negotiations began between the General Management of the Bank and the Ministry of Finance, and finally, on the material guarantees given by the Ministry, it was decided that all the deposits of the Armenians in the Ottoman Bank of Erzerum should be remitted to the Ministry of Finance. Consequently, the accounted [sic] general Mr. Balladour, the manager of the Erzerum branch of the [Ottoman] Bank, and Cavid Bey brought them to Constantinople and handed them to the Ministry of Finance, against a receipt which is still in my possession and a photograph of which I am ready to publish. [32]

The former governor of Erzerum further vouched that the people in his town were not the only ones whose bank assets were seized and transferred to Constantinople: "The same operation took place in every district of Turkey, and the spoil produced considerable sums, from which the Turkish government had no trouble in taking the sum of 5,000,000 pounds for its financial operation."[33]

Relaying the true intent of the Temporary Law to the German Foreign Office, the Director of Deutsche Bank, Arthur von Gwinner, sarcastically stated that the true intent of the eleven articles of the Temporary Law of the Abandoned Properties might as well have been compressed into the following two: "First, all goods of Armenians are confiscated, and second, the government will cash in the credits of the deportees and will repay (or will not repay) their debts."[34]

The accumulated wealth of the confiscated assets of the deported Armenians from the various Ottoman branch banks reached the Finance Ministry in Constantinople. Cavid Bey, the deceptive finance minister and a trusted lieutenant of Talât Pasha, was now in charge of a staggering five million pounds. The fraudulent and dishonest financial transactions of Cavid Bey were known household items in German and Turkish circles. He was influential enough to speak on behalf of the ruling Ittihadist regime and make official declarations. He frequently visited Berlin and during one of his visits declared that the people at the German Foreign Office were "very accommodating" but that the circle of military officers was "not appreciative at all" of the Turkish contribution to the war effort and considered the alliance "completely superfluous."[35] Cavid Bey's uninhibited tendency to cheat and to falsify official financial records had earned him a notorious reputation. He was condemned in 1919 in absentia by a Turkish Military Tribunal to fifteen years of prison and hard labor.[36] A telling and vivid reminder of Cavid's inclination for fraudulent and deceptive activities while minister of finance comes from an insightful article published in the *New York Times* on July 13, 1919:

> Cavid...showed by his books that he had really tricked Germany and that if the allied and associated powers would only lend Turkey $500,000,000 gold he would then give them German paper worth $850,000,000, which, as the victors, they would have no trouble in collecting with a profit of $350,000,000. When they rejected his offer and experts began to audit his books he disappeared. According to the Ambassadors, Djavid [Cavid] was not a pronounced Germanophile, although a very bad financier.[37]

Grand theft and embezzlement of deported Armenian riches was also vividly portrayed by American Consul Jesse Jackson in Aleppo, Syria, who pointed out that the major role of the Ittihadists' genocidal scheme was "a gigantic plundering scheme and a final blow to extinguish the [Armenian] race."[38]

From these accounts it can safely be deduced that widespread, well-planned and organized looting and illegal confiscation of Armenian wealth took place during and in the immediate aftermath of the genocide. Interior Minister Talât was the top official ordering and overseeing the systematic looting of the Armenian riches; by applying the so-called "Abandoned Property" law he personally orchestrated the confiscation of Armenian financial assets deposited in Ottoman Imperial branch banks in the provinces and their transfer to the Ministry of Finance in Constantinople. Once in the central depository, Talât's lieutenant, Cavid, the fraudulent finance minister, would have no qualms in *accounting* for them (i.e., perpetrators never account for or pay the value of property stolen from the victims), *conversion* (i.e., failure to acknowledge the value of the property taken from the victim), and *embezzlement* (i.e., fraudulent appropriation for his own use of money and property entrusted to him).

Private Order of Evidence

The private order of evidence constitutes a source that is useful for recovery of past events. The private declarations of Interior Minister and later Grand Vizier Talât will be presented here. Through his many private conversations with Ambassador Morgenthau, the deceptive, merciless and greedy personality of Talât is revealed and is described in Morgenthau's lucid diaries. These traits are deduced from unsolicited and somewhat insouciant declarations that Talât repeatedly made to Morgenthau during his meetings. One day Talât said to the departing ambassador:

"I hear you are going home to spend lot of money and re-elect your President," said Talât – this being jocular reference to the fact that I was the Chairman of the Finance Committee of the Democratic National Committee. "That's very foolish; why don't you stay here and give it to Turkey? We need it more than your people do."[39]

Morgenthau had repeatedly attempted but failed to intervene on behalf of the dying and helpless Armenian women and children. One more time before his departure to the United States, the ambassador switched from his usual humanitarian appeal and instead brought to the attention of the recalcitrant interior minister the economic and financial consequences of annihilating an economically viable and productive segment of Turkey:

"If you are not influenced by humane considerations, think of the material loss. These people are your businessmen. They control many of your industries. They are very large tax-payers. What would become of you commercially without them?"[40] Talât snapped: "We care nothing about the commercial loss…. We have figured all that out and we know that it will not exceed five million pounds. We don't worry about that."[41]

Talât's precise knowledge of the total amount of the loot corroborates well with other independent estimates that also put the total amount of the loot of the bank assets of the deported victims to 5 million pounds.

Material Order of Evidence

Objective evidence of the theft of large sums of money from the victimized subjects can easily be ascertained by comparing the initial and final conditions of Armenian existence in their historic homeland: Did the Armenians have financial assets in Turkish banks before and up to 1915? Evidence points to the affirmative. Did they still have any capital left in the same banks in the aftermath of the war? Evidence points to the negative.

The survivors did not inherit a single penny from their parents' wealth. No compensation or restitution has ever been made. The centrally organized theft of the victims' wealth, "thefticide,"[42] caused unjust enrichment of Ittihadist leaders, such as Talât, Enver, and Djemal. The murderous intent of the deportation and the fraudulent nature of the confiscated Armenian wealth irritated right-minded Turks who during the 1918-1919 Turkish Military Tribunals in the aftermath of the genocidal war condemned the triumvirate to death. The Tribunal further described their modus operandi as "terrorism" designed to circumvent normal processes and escape liability and accounting.[43] In this respect the trials by a Turkish Military Tribunal represents a courageous and singular act of justice in Turkish history. As Dadrian has asserted, "Part of the task of this Tribunal (*cumlé vazifé*) was the investigation of the charges of massacres and illegal, personal profiteering (*taktil ve ihtikar*)."[44] The three words *taktil ve ihtikar* are close to the prophet Elijah's words in Old Testament scripture, "Have you murdered and also inherited?" (*ha-ratzachtah ve'gam yarashtah*).[45]

The Fate of the Armenian Gold Deposit in Berlin

The fate of the five million pounds of Turkish gold transferred in 1916 from Constantinople to Berlin remains an enigma. It is equally mysterious under whose name or names, assumed or otherwise, these large sums were deposited in German banks. The triumvirate reasoned that hiding the money and living under assumed names were necessary precautions to protect themselves, lest vengeful Armenians assassinate them[46] as, indeed, Talât hinted during one of his private meetings with Ambassador Morgenthau: "No Armenian can be our friend after what we have done to them."[47] Talât's prophecy proved true. He fled to Germany in October of 1918, just before the war ended, and in Berlin, on March 15, 1921, a lone gunman, Soghomon Tehlirian, the son of a victimized family, assassinated him.[48] According to an article in the *New York Times* published three days after Talât's assassination and under the heading "Death of the Grand Vizier," we learn that Talât "[h]ad plenty of money, which enabled him to rent a very large flat on the fashionable Hardenbergstrasse and surround himself with European and Turkish comfort." The article then went on to assert that Talât had an enormous personal fortune in a Berlin Bank: "There are stories that the Deutsche Bank has his fortune of more than 10,000,000 [ten million] marks in safekeeping."[49]

It was equally revealing in this article to learn that Talât lived under the assumed name of "Said Ali Bey."[50] The failure of the Reparation Commission to discover the 1916 "Turkish gold" in Berlin's Reichsbank could have been caused by the concealment of this fortune under the assumed names of private citizens. Here, the revelations made by the Turkish historian Dogan Avcioglu are pertinent: "…Among those who quickly enriched themselves in the process of the expropriation of the Armenians were [Ittihadist] party influential leaders…"[51]

The Present German Government and the Genocide Money

The documentary evidence presented in this book shows that the looted Armenian assets deposited in Constantinople's Central Ottoman Bank and then transferred in 1916 to the Reichsbank in Berlin remained untapped by the Reparation Commission of the Allies. This is a new finding that has not been recognized previously. There has never been a claim filed against a German Bank that protected the riches looted by the three leaders of a "terrorist regime," Talât, Enver, and Djemal. The prosecution of Soghomon Tehlirian, who assassinated Talât in 1921, in a Berlin district criminal court, and his acquittal by a German jury is significant.[52] Dr. Johannes Werthauer, a member of the defense team, rejected the prosecutor's plea that Talât was a "valued ally" and a guest in Germany. In his closing arguments the Dr. Werthauer remarked:

> We too have men prone to violence, men whom we have sent to Turkey so that they could drill the Turkish military into the art of violence...and it so happens that these men of violence were the ones who destroyed the Armenian people.... The order to deport an entire people is the vilest thought that can ever enter the mind of a militarist...the German people too are being accused of having allowed the issuance of such orders of deportation. Only by way of a total and unreserved repudiation of such principles and renunciation of such mean-spirited, criminal orders can we regain the respect to which, I believe, we are entitled.[53]

Dr. Niemeyer, professor of International Law at the University of Kiel, and another member of Tehlirian's defense team, exposed the direct role played by Germany in the extermination of the Armenians. In the context of the Turkish-German military alliance, the terms of the military alliance went far beyond the defined or understood duties and responsibilities:

> During the war in Turkey military authorities here at home, and [in Turkey], maintained silence and covered up the Armenian horrors, to an extent which bordered approval.... The generally accepted rules of international law are to be treated as binding integral parts of the law of the German Reich, as provide by Article 4 of the Constitution of the Empire.[54]

Dadrian collected massive evidence that documented the complicity and responsibility of Germany, with the direct involvement of Kaiser William II himself, in a war crime that nearly extirpated an ancient nation.[55] The observation in the preface of Dadrian's monograph, made by Roger W. Smith, professor of government at the College of William and Mary, is revealing:

> Indeed, there is already sufficient evidence for Germany to acknowledge such guilt, not as the actual perpetrator of the genocide, but as an accessory of that crime of genocide. Again and again, officials fretted about possible German financial liability in the wake of revelations inculpating German officials on the matter of personally ordering Armenian deportations. With the advent of the era of Chancellor Adenaur (1949-1963), there emerged a new Germany and a new democracy that may well be acclaimed as s new rampart of Western civilization. As such, [Dadrian's monograph] should afford an opportunity to the heirs of the Adenauerian legacy to redeem themselves once more as they did with respect to the victims of the Jewish Holocaust.

They have a chance to demonstrate for all to see that justice delayed is not necessarily justice denied.[56]

After the 1921 trial of Tehlirian in Berlin, the issue of the Armenian Genocide, let alone the legal rights of the victims for the recovery of their stolen properties, remained on the sidelines. It is estimated that the current value of the stolen Armenian wealth reaches staggering trillions of dollars.[57]

The Post-Ittihadist Governments and Their Motives for Denial of the Genocide

With the exception of a short period after the Turkish defeat at the end of World War I and the ensuing armistice, successive Turkish governments have adamantly denied, and continue to deny to this day, that there was ever a policy of intentional destruction of the Armenians. The denial of the Armenian Genocide is motivated not only by the desire to conceal the grand theft of the riches of their victims, but also to shroud in secrecy the fact that high ranking Turkish officials in the post-Iittihadist regime were actually not only active members of the Ittihad party during the massacres but also participated in various capacities in the planning and execution of the crime, and most particularly, in covering it up.

The identities of the organizers of the genocide became progressively known during the few months of the aborted Turkish Military Tribunals in Constantinople that started in December 1918 and was prematurely terminated in May 1919. Much has been learned about the major figures of the genocide through a thorough examination of Turkish official documents and analyses of testimonies of eyewitnesses during these court martial deliberations. Based on the wealth of this first order evidence, the British High Commissioner in Constantinople, Admiral John de Robeck sent, on February 18, 1920, the following expository report to London in which he identified a major figure in the planning, and execution of the genocide: "Dr. Şakir was a member of the small secret Committee known as *Tashkilati Mahsusa* [Special Organization] formed by the Central Committee of the Committee of Union and Progress [CUP, the Ittihad] to organize the extermination of the Armenian race."[58] Six months later, on August 29, another report was prepared, this time by the British intelligence service in Constantinople, and it confirmed de Robeck's earlier assertion: "*Tashkilati Mahsusa* was created by the CUP in 1914 for the extermination of the Armenians and was controlled by the infamous Behaeddin Şakir."[59]

An insightful account was also provided by the Turkish publicist Ahmed Emin Yalman, who had held many intimate conversations with the Ittihadist leaders when he was detained with them in a Malta prison. He learned that "two influential" Ittihadists helped create the Special Organization. While the identity of Dr. Şakir as one of them is all too familiar, the other, according to Dadrian, was Dr. Mehmet Nazim.[60] Yalman had no trouble describing the Ittihadists' anti-Armenian measures as a "policy of general extermination" designed to eliminate "the danger" to Turkey of "a dense Armenian population in the eastern Provinces."[61] The two physicians, fearful of widespread potential epidemics resulting from the thousands of decomposing corpses piled up in the streets of the eastern provinces where large scale massacres had taken place, had with the help of Interior Minster Talât and Chief of Internal Security Ismail Canbolat, set up the Supreme Hygiene Council, whose task was to destroy the bodies of the victims. The two Ittihadist physicians delegated another physician, Dr. Tevfik Rüştü (Aras), who, conveniently, was the brother-in-law of Dr. Nazim. According to a secret document presented as evidence during the Military Tribunals by Mustapha Raad, police director-general, Dr. Rüştü was sent to the eastern provinces where the massacres had taken place with tons of lime. Dr. Rüştü successfully put in place the necessary machinery for the quick disposal of the corpses by transforming wells into mass graves. He ordered and oversaw the throwing of the bodies in the wells, which were then filled with lime and sealed with earth. Dr. Rüştü accomplished his task within the six month period allowed to him by the Ittihadist leaders.[62]

According to the Turkish historian Dogan Avçioglu, Dr. Rüştü was a partisan Ittihadist, who raised funds for the Ittihadists' clandestine activities during the Armistice and was arrested on February 2, 1919 by the Tevfik Paşa Cabinet along with other Ittihadist leaders.[63] It is of a great historical consequence that Dr. Rüştü, the mastermind of the mass graves, later became a long-serving minister of foreign affairs in the new Turkish Republic, from 1925 to 1938, under Mustafa Kemal's presidency. He then was appointed as the Turkish ambassador to Great Britain from 1939 to 1942, and then president of the Administration of the Banking Council (*I'ş Bankasi*) from 1952 to1959. He died in 1972 at the age of ninety. [64]

Dr. Tevfik Rüştü, however, was not the only Ittihadist who participated in and later concealed evidence of his crimes, and then assumed high ranking government position in the newly founded Turkish Republic. Many others who had been under suspicion of war crimes, and were arrested and detained in the Malta prison by the British, later found their way to high-government positions in post-war Turkey. For example, Şükrü Kaya, the head of the Office of the Settlement of Tribes and Immigrants, responded to the German consul in Aleppo, Dr. Walter Rössler, who was attempting to secure the release of Armenians working for the Germans: "You don't seem to understand what we want. We want an Armenia without Armenians." [65] After the war, Şükrü was arrested and detained by the British in the Malta prison, but on September 1921 he escaped and made his way to Ankara where he joined the nationalists. Şükrü Kaya later became foreign and interior minister in the Kemalist government.[66]

The actions of Abdülhalik Renda, provincial governor of Aleppo, were described by the commander of the Third Army, General Vahip Paşa, during the Mazhar Commission's investigations in this way: "Among other things, Abdülhalik burned thousands of people alive in the Muş Province."[67] For this reason Abdülhalik was included in the core group of prisoners that bore the highest responsibility for the massacres. He remained in the Malta prison and was not part of the early exchange of prisoners between Great Britain and Turkey and was not released until the last batch of the hard core criminals were exchanged on 31 October, 1921. Abdülhalik then rose to become finance minister, education minister and then defense minister; he even became president of the Turkish Republic, at least for one day, after the death of the Mustafa Kemal.[68]

The Turkish historian Taner Akçam identified the names of many more prominent Ittihadists who participated in the enterprise of destruction and who later occupied ministerial positions in Mustafa Kemal's cabinet, including the ministries of Public Work, Foreign and Internal Affairs, Trade, Defense and Justice. Every stratum of the Turkish government at one time or another was infiltrated and controlled by former Ittihadists accused of "gross injustice" (i.e., massacre) that made acknowledgment of "past" crimes by postwar successive Turkish governments a near impossible task.[69]

It is clear that all post-Ittihadist governments, up to and including the current government, had legitimate motives to cover up the mass murder and conceal the evidence of the grand thefts committed by the Ittihadists and subsequent misappropriation of Armenian wealth by Kemal's government. While the current government makes a case of not being part of the past crimes, it falls short of condemning past Turkish governments' control by Ittihadist hard core criminals.

Notes

1.   Congressional Record, Sixty-Ninth Congress, Special Session of the Senate, Washington, Tuesday, March 17, 1925. Vol. 67, No.12, p. 305; RG 59 467.000R29/57, Senator Borah to the Secretary of State, 5 February 1925. In this letter the text of the Senate Resolution introduced by Senator King was attached.
2.   Ibid., p. 302.
3.   RG 59 467.00R29/59, Senator King to Secretary Frank B. Kellog, 13 March, 1925.
4.   RG 59 467.00R29/68, Mark L. Bristol, U.S. High Commissioner in Constantinople to U.S. Secretary of State, May 22, 1925, p. 4.
5.   Ibid., pp. 4-6. The report provides clear and accurate numerical accounts of the chronology of various gold and currency issuance transactions that took place between Turkey and Germany in years 1915-1916.
6.   Ibid., pp. 6, 7.
7.   Ibid., p. 7.
8.   Ibid., p. 8.
9.   Ibid., pp. 3-4.
10. Martin Gilbert, A History of the Twentieth Century, Volume One: 1900-1933, p. 678. For example, the determined hunt by the Allies to locate and seize as much German wealth and assets as possible was particularly transparent in the case of France. The French were adamant to secure reparations for all their war-related damage from Germany even if it meant physically operating the main German industrial plants and extracting German raw materials by force. In a defiant statement, for example, the commander of the French occupation forces in Germany, General Dugoute, announced that the "French army should remain in Ruhr, if necessary for a thousand years" (Gilbert, idem. p. 678).
11. RG 59, 467.00R29/64, Near East Executive Committee to U.S. Secretary of State Frank B. Kellog, May 1, 1925.
12. Turkish Atrocities: Statements of American Missionaries on the Destruction of Christian Communities in Ottoman Turkey, 1915–1917, compiled by James L. Barton (Ann Arbor, MI: Gomidas Institute, 1998).
13. Henry Morgenthau, Ambassador Morgenthau's Story (Ann Arbor, MI: Gomidas Institute, 2000; reprinted edition; originally published in 1919 by Doubleday, Page and Company).
14. Vahakn N. Dadrian, Warrant for Genocide: Key Elements of the Turko-Armenian Conflict (New Brunswick, NJ: Transaction Publishers, 1999), p. 1; Vahakn N. Dadrian, "The Naim–Andonian documents of the World War I destruction of the Ottoman Armenians: The anatomy of a genocide," International Journal Middle Eastern Studies, 18, 1986, pp. 311–360. The documents and the cipher telegrams cited in the Naim-Andonian documents were authenticated and verified beyond a shadow of doubt; they constitute valuable primary source information that describe major state crimes committed secretly by extra-legal means without the consent of the Parliament.
15. Richard G. Hovannisian (ed.), Remembrance and Denial: The Case of the Armenian Genocide (Detroit, MI: Wayne State University Press, 1998).
16. Terrence Des Pres, Writing Into the World: Essays 1973-1987 (New York: Viking Penguin, A Division of Penguin Books, 1991), p. 251.
17. Hrayr S. Karagueuzian, "Unclaimed life insurance policies in the aftermath of the Armenian Genocide," Armenian Forum (The Gomidas Institute), 2:2, 2000, pp. 1-55.

18. Shavarsh Toriguian, *The Armenian Question and the International Law*, 2nd Edition (La Verne, CA: University of La Verne Press, 1988), pp. 85-88.
19. Vahakn N. Dadrian, "Genocide as a problem of national and international law: The World War I Armenian case, and the contemporary legal ramifications," *Yale Journal of International Law*, 14:2, 1989, pp. 221–334.
20. RG 84, File, 850.6. Counselor Moustafa Cheref to New York Life Insurance Company, January 11, 1916. On May 16, 1915, a law was issued on administrative instructions regarding movable and immovable properties abandoned by the deported Armenians. The law made provision for the formation of special committees who would prepare lists and report all "abandoned" property and place it in safe custody in the name of the deportee. Most of the movable properties were looted, while the immovable ones were sold at one hundredth of the price by members of the commission to friends and other Turks, and the money was either pocketed or sent to the Finance Ministry in Constantinople. This law, known as the "Abandoned Property Law" (*emvali metrouke*) was turned down by the provisions of the Sèvres Treaty in 1920 but was reinstalled by the Lausanne Treaty in 1923 by Mustafa Kemal. See: Shavarsh Toriguian, *The Armenian Question and the International Law*, 2nd edition (La Verne, CA: University of La Verne Press,1988), pp. 85-88.
21. RG 59 467.00R29/59, King to Kellog, 13 March, 1925; *Congressional Records*, Sixty-Ninth Congress, Special Session of the Senate, Vol. 67, No.12, 17 March, 1925, pp. 301-303.
22. Bristol to Secretary of State, ibid., (n. 4) p. 4.
23. James Bryce and Arnold Toynbee, *The Treatment of Armenians in the Ottoman Empire, 1915-16: Documents Presented to Viscount Grey of Falloden by Viscount Bryce*, Uncensored Edition, edited and with an introduction by Ara Sarafian (Princeton, NJ: reprinted by Gomidas, 2000).
24. Lancelot Oliphant to F.A. Sterling, April 22, 1925, RG 59 467.00R 27/63 (enclosure).
25. Sterling F.A. to Secretary of State, April 24, 1925, RG 59, 467.00 R27/63, p. 2.
26. Bristol to Kellog, May 22, 1925, ibid., (n. 4), p. 3.
27. Shavarsh Toriguian, op. cit., pp. 85-88.
28. FO 371/4174/98910 War Cabinet WCP 11 02. Damad Ferid to Clemenceau, June 30, 1919.
29. Ibid., ibid.
30. Vahakn N. Dadrian, *The History of Armenian Genocide, Ethnic Conflict from the Balkans to Anatolia to Caucasus*. (Oxford & Providence, RI: Bergham Books, 1995), pp. 317-343; see also Dadrian, "Genocide as problem of national and international law: The World War I Armenian case and its contemporary legal ramification," *Yale Journal of International Law*, 14:2, 1989, pp. 302-303
31. *United States Official Documents on the Armenian Genocide. Vol. I: The Lower Euphrates*, compiled and introduced by Ara Sarafian (Watertown, MA: Armenian Review, 1993). See also Vol. II, 1994.
32. RG 59, 467.00R29/64 Near East Relief to Secretary of State, May 1, 1925. Enclosure: Memo of the *Comité Central Des Refugiées Armeniens* (Central Committee of Armenian Refugees).
33. Ibid., Enclosure.
34. Ibid., (n. 19), p. 267.
35. Vahakn N. Dadrian, *German Responsibility in the Armenian Genocide: A Review of the Historical Evidence of German Complicity* (Watertown, MA: Blue Crane Books, 1996), p. 129.

36. Takvimi Vekáyi, July 5, 1919. Cited in Vartkes Yeghiayan, *The Armenian Genocide and the Trial of the Young Turks* (La Verne CA: American Armenian International College Press, 1990), pp. 106-114.
37. *New York Times*, July 13, 1919, p. 2. More on Cavid's criminal behavior comes from Somerset Calthrope, the British High Commissioner in Constantinople. In his report to Lord Balfour, British Foreign Minster, Calthrope stated: "Djavid Bey was undoubtedly deeply implicated in the crimes of which he is accused, and his moral responsibility is enormous." FO 371/4173/68097, Calthrope to Balfour 20 April, 1919. Cited in Gary Jonathan Bass, *"Stay the Hand of Vengeance; The Politics of War Crimes Tribunals* (Princeton, NJ: Princeton University Press, 2000), p. 130.
38. RG 59 807.4014/148 (enclosure in Ambassador Morgenthau's August 30, 1915 report). See also the statement of the Swiss historian Zurlinden: "What really happened was an expropriation carried out on the greatest scale against 1.5 million citizens," in Dadrian, op. cit., p. 270. This point was confirmed by the Turkish historian Dogan Avcioğlu: "Among those who quickly enriched themselves in the process of expropriation of the Armenians were the [Ittihad] party influentials..." in ibid., p. 271. An insight into the purchase power of 1916 equivalent of some $22-24 million dollars stolen from the victims' bank accounts and safe deposits can be gained by comparing this amount to the amount of money used to purchase the Danish West Indies (present U.S. Virgin Islands) by the U.S. Government. On January 16, 1917, President Woodrow Wilson signed a treaty for formal transfer of the islands with a U.S. payment to Denmark of $25,000,000 in gold coin. The purchase was finalized and the Islands became U.S. territory on March 31, 1917. (http://www.state.gov/r/pa/ho/time/wwi/107293.htm)
39. Morgenthau, *Morgenthau's Story*, p. 259.
40. Ibid., p. 224.
41. Ibid., p. 225.
42. Irwin Cotler; "The Holocaust, thefticide, and restitution: A legal perspective," *Cardozo Law Review*, Vol. 20, 1998, pp. 601-623.
43. Takvimi Vekâyi, July 5, 1919; #3573. Cited in Vartkes Yeghiayan, *The Armenian Genocide and the Trials of the Young Turks* (Laverne, CA: American Armenian International College Press, 1990), pp 106-114; see also Vahakn N. Dadrian, "A textual analysis of the key indictment of the Turkish Military investigating the Armenian genocide," *Journal of Political and Military Sociology*, 22:1, Summer 1994, pp. 133-171. It is important to note that Article 142 of the 1920 Sèvres Treaty, to which Turkey was a signatory, qualified the Ittihadists' rule as a "terrorist regime."
44. Vahakn N. Dadrian, ibid., (n. 35), pp. 321, 329.
45. I Kings 21:19 (editor's translation).
46. Jacques Derogy, *Opération Nemesis, Les Vengeurs Arméniens*, (Paris: Librairie Arthemes, Fayard, 1986).
47. Morganthau, *Morgenthau's Story*, p. 225.
48. New York Times, 18 March, 1921, p 3.
49. Ibid., ibid.
50. Ibid., ibid.
51. Vahakn N. Dadrian, ibid., (n. 19), p. 271.
52. George R. Montgomery, "Why Talât's Assassin was acquitted," *New York Times, Current History*, July 1921, pp. 551-555.
53. Ibid., 30, p. 288.
54. The Trial of Talât Pasha at: http://armenianhouse.org/wegner/docs–en/talaat–1.html#.

55. Dadrian, ibid., (n. 30), pp. 287-289.
56. Roger W. Smith, "Preface," in Vahakn N. Dadrian, *German Responsibility in the Armenian Genocide: A Review of the Historical Evidence of German Complicity*, (Watertown, MA: Blue Crane Books, 1996), p. xvi.
57. Dikran Kouymjian, "Confiscation and Destruction: A manifestation of the Genocidal Process," *Armenian Forum*, 3, 1998, pp. 1-12.
58. FO 371/5089/E949, February 18, 1920.
59. FO 371/5171/E12228, August 29, 1920, p. 7.
60. Vahakn N. Dadrian, "The role of the Turkish physicians in the World War I Genocide of the Ottoman Armenians," *Holocaust and Genocide Studies*, Vol. 2, 1986, pp. 169-192.
61. Ahmed Emin Yalman, *Turkey in the World War* (New Haven, CT: Yale University Press, 1930), p. 220.
62. Taner Akçam, *"A Shameful Act: The Armenian Genocide and the Question of Turkish Responsibility"* (New York: Metropolitan Books, 2006), p. 363.
63. Dadrian (n. 60), The role of the Turkish physicians.
64. Taner Akçam, op. cit., pp. 363-364.
65. Ibid., p. 362.
66. Ibid., ibid.
67. Ibid., p. 363.
68. Ibid., ibid.
69. Ibid., pp. 362-366.

Summary and Conclusions

"... A bold plan was formulated in my mind. This consisted of obtaining the ratification [of the U.N. Genocide Convention] by Turkey among the first twenty founding nations.... I know, however, that in this consideration both sides will have to avoid speaking about one thing, although it would be constantly in their minds: the Armenians." —Raphael Lemkin, Totally Unofficial

In academic discussions, rarely do the definitions and uses of specific terms carry the intense weight as does the word "genocide" in general, and the term Armenian Genocide in particular. Various scholars have produced a large body of literature in which there is a wide range of definitions of genocide, its uses and abuses, and its sometimes frivolous uses (similar uses and misuses have been made of the word "holocaust"). In addition to its significance for scientific classification and research, the definition of the deed of genocide encompasses significant legal, moral, and political issues. The term was coined and defined in 1944 by Raphael Lemkin, a Jewish lawyer from Poland who had lost all of his family in the Holocaust. Lemkin, however, was also aware of and strongly impressed by the horrors of the Armenian Genocide. The term was subsequently codified legally in the aftermath of the horrors and destruction of the Holocaust, and in 1948 the United Nations enacted the Convention on the Prevention and Punishment of the Crime of Genocide (that came into force in 1951), which defined genocide as a crime under international law, not only in times of war but in times of peace as well.

The continued denial of the Armenian Genocide by Turkey, which is based on selfish political and economic considerations, and its denial or non-recognition by the United States and Great Britain, allies and two of the victorious countries in World War I, is a main factor in the non-restitution of Armenian property. Such denial constitutes both direct and indirect assistance for successive Turkish governments. With the exception of a short period after its defeat at the end of World War I and the ensuing armistice, they have denied – and continue to deny to this day – that there was ever a policy of intentional destruction of the Armenians; they have been partially successful in their denials and have

135

escaped judgment for their crimes. The Turks have invested considerable effort in erasing the memory of the Armenians and Armenian history in the Ottoman Empire, as though they had never existed. Vast sums of money have been and continue to be spent to deny or invalidate any guilt. Armenian sites, including churches, have been neglected, looted, destroyed, or requisitioned for other uses, and Armenian place names have been changed.

Nevertheless, there is no question as to the truth of the event. A wide variety of sources from the period comprise proof that a comprehensive mass extermination of the Armenian civilian population in various parts of Turkey (and certainly not only in the battle zones) was carried out, and was done so on the order of the Turkish authorities in Constantinople. While specific facts and details can be legitimately debated, and some of the Armenian claims about the genocide can be questioned, the historical sources create an unequivocal and unshakable picture. The Armenians refer to it as the "forgotten genocide," which took place under three successive regimes – of the Sultanate, of the Ittihadists, and of the forces of Mustapha Kemal (Ataturk). The Turks refer only to an "alleged genocide" and accuse the Armenians of treachery and subversion. Again, we can argue with some of the facts, details, or circumstances, but there can be no doubt about the fact of the genocide itself. It appears that massive efforts of denial and contemporary political interests are part of the attempt of the Turkish leaders and their supporters to undermine the certitude of the claim that what had occurred was, indeed, a genocide. These efforts have succeeded in creating disagreement among researchers, seeming historical controversies, and claims of lack of proof. In addition, they created intentional neglect and repression of the subject, and confusion over the events surrounding it.

The Czech writer Milan Kundera once wrote that man's struggle against power is the struggle of memory against oblivion. In this sense, all of the conditions that justify remembrance of the Holocaust are valid for the Armenian Genocide as well. The continued denial of the genocide by Turkey is as terrible as if Germany had denied its crimes in World War II. The degree of denial by Turkey – that is, absolute denial – is far greater than, for example, Japan's policy of distortion, denial and disguise regarding its massive crimes against the Chinese in the 1930s and 1940s, although Japan apologized, at least in vague terms, in 1995. It is also greater, for example, than such policies as not fully recognizing the mass killings of Native Americans in North America, ignoring the effects of centuries of black slavery, or the merely semi-recognition of the virtual genocide committed in Australia against the aborigines after the arrival of the European settlers.

This state of denial of the Armenian Genocide fosters non-restitution of stolen Armenian wealth. One keeps wondering if denial will continue to remain an effective instrument to perpetuate the immense enrichment realized by consecutive Turkish governments since 1915. The recent successful out-of-court settlements of the class action lawsuits brought against the New York Life Insurance Company and the AXA S.A. (formerly the French Union-Vie) by surviving heirs of the victims constitutes testimony to the present day validity of this unique class of cases. Dozens of other American and European companies had also sold thousands of policies to Armenians in Turkey in the years preceding the genocide. The Equitable Assurance Company of New York, La Fédèrale of Switzerland, Star of London, and the Victoria Insurance Company of United Kingdom were among the more active ones. The names of those insured with these and other companies remain concealed by the insurers to the present day. The disclosure of these names and due compensation of policy benefits to the heirs of the victims could help in a small way to catalyze the path for at least some overdue justice of a victimized people. Justice would not only strengthen the rule of law and soften the bitterness and sufferings of the genocide victims' families, but would also act as a deterrent to future acts of crimes against humanity.

While the insurers' intransigence was and remains a formidable obstacle to the collection of policy benefits, the Ittihadist leaders' attempts to confiscate policy benefits as state property and the outright denial of the genocide by successive Turkish governments provided the insurers with a means of sorts to escape their contractual responsibility. The Ittihadist leaders' attempts in 1916 to collect for themselves the life insurance policy benefits of the deported Armenians may have provided a precedent for the Nazis' thefts of the Jewish assets through illegal appropriation of the deportees' possessions and life insurance policy benefits throughout Germany. However, although the Ittihadists were unable to collect the benefits of the policies, they were most effective in confiscating all of the victims' bank accounts and valuables and depositing the proceeds of the loot in their own personal accounts in German banks.

The contention that the Armenian genocide set a precedent emanates from the historical perspective indicating that the Nazis were influenced by their knowledge of the Armenian Genocide and their appreciation of the fact that the perpetrators of the atrocity escaped punishment. In fact, historians have convincingly argued that Hitler himself and his cohorts were aware of the fate of the Armenians and were greatly encouraged by the world's apathetic reaction to their deaths. Quoting from the German publication Obersalzburg, Vahakn Dadrian, who meticulously researched the Armenian Genocide, including in records in German archives, stated that "Hitler must have known exactly" about the Armenian genocide because one of his closest collaborators during the early stages of Nazi movement was Germany's former consul at Erzerum, Dr. Max Erwin von Scheubner Richter.[1] This consul provided gruesome eye witness accounts of the 1915 massacres that could easily have been communicated to Hitler during many of his private meetings with the Führer before the start of the World War II. Erzerum, a major town in the historic Armenia, witnessed the largest number of forced deportations of its population, and unspeakable acts of lethal violence, deportations, arson, theft and plunder were committed under the watch of the Consul von Scheubner Richter. Dadrian asserted that Hitler had planned and modeled his lethal attacks on the Jews on the strategies and plans used against the Armenians by the Young Turks and the Kemalists:

> Wartime deportations; extirpation through exhaustive labor; death marches; incitement of other people for the purpose of enlisting their help in the destruction of the victim population; "natural decimation" through attrition by way of artificially induced hardships involving exposure to harsh climatic conditions, starvation and epidemics; shameless acts of enrichment through the appropriation of the possessions of the deportees; and the creation of concentration camps.[2]

While the potential impact of the impunity of the Armenian genocide on that of the Holocaust has been largely ignored, Davis Matas, the Canadian international law expert elaborated on the insidious impact of such impunity on the Holocaust:

> Because the perpetrators of the Armenians genocide were not prosecuted, the Nazi-organized Holocaust against the Jews became possible. There is direct linkage between the failure to prosecute the crimes against humanity before World War II and their commission during World War I. This failure did not occur because there was no offense or because there was no jurisdiction. Both existed, and still the prosecutions did not occur. This reluctance to act, in spite of the offense and in spite of the jurisdiction, made the Nazis more brazen and the Holocaust more likely.[3]

Matas went on to conclude his insightful remarks by stating:

> Nothing emboldens a criminal so much as the knowledge he can get away with a crime. That was the message the failure to prosecute for the Armenian massacre gave to the Nazis. We ignore the lesson of the Holocaust at our peril.[4]

The independent assertion made by Israel Charney, Director of Holocaust and Genocide Studies in Jerusalem, Israel, that the Armenian Genocide was a "dress rehearsal" for the Holocaust is vindicated by the conclusions reached by the Canadian legal scholar.[5] One is equally pressed here to mention the thoughtful narrative of Terrence Des Pres on the occasion of President Ronald Reagan's May 5, 1985 visit to Bitburg, Germany to honor German troops who died in World War II, among them forty-nine members of the SS, Hitler's killer elite:

> Reagan's symbolic gesture is of course less acute than attempts to cancel the Armenian agony. What needs emphasis is that these separate cases – Turkey's denial and Reagan's dismissal of two of the century's worst crimes – are not only related, not only connected intimately, but are identical as signs of the narrative of power, in which knowledge serves the state and truth is what world leaders say it is.[6]

It is important to make clear, however, that in comparing the Armenian Genocide and the Jewish Holocaust we do not infer that they are identical events, but rather that although each has unique features, they have similar characteristics; both belong to the category of genocide. The genocides of the Armenians and the Jews clearly have major convergent features that include the inescapable crimes of economic exploitation of the targeted victim groups. Both Armenians and Jews were ethnic and religious minority groups under dominant monolithic parties that subjugated them, the Ittihad (CUP) and Nazi parties, respectively. The political impotence and statutory powerlessness of the two minority groups, combined with their economic ascendancy, resulted in the escalation of hatred towards the two groups and led ultimately to the commission of lethal violence. It is argued that this intense hatred paved the way for each of the perpetrators to carry out its radical solution (the Nazis called it the Final Solution) to the Turkish-Armenian discord and the German-Jewish tensions. But, again, although the two cases were similar – Talât Pasha's assertion that "The Armenians enriched themselves at the expense of the Turks" and the Nazis' pronouncements that "the Jews controlled Germany's economy" are cases in point – they were not identical, as there was no real, practical, Jewish problem in Germany. The fact that neither the Jews nor the Armenians had parent states to counter these allegations and deter the planned mass murders further amplified the vulnerability of both groups as targets for victimization.[7]

On November 9, 1938, the Nazis unleashed a wave of pogroms against Germany's Jews and within a few hours had damaged thousands of synagogues and Jewish businesses and homes. These vandalisms, which later became known as the *Kristallnacht,* the Night of the Broken Glass, left dozens of Jews dead and $50 million worth of damaged Jewish property. The destruction was mixed with theft and plunder. Many of the Jewish homes and businesses destroyed in these state-sponsored pogroms were covered by insurance policies, but the insurance companies paid one-half of the Jewish insurance policies proceeds to the Reich and expropriated the other half for themselves.[8] A vivid reminder of insurance company-Nazi leadership complicity is the declaration made by Hermann Goering, second in command to Hitler, in the aftermath of the *Kristallnacht,* that on the orders of the Nazis let loose the people's rage against the Jews:

> It is insane to clean out and burn a Jewish warehouse then have a German insurance company make good the loss. I am not going to tolerate a situation in which the Insurance Companies are the ones who suffer. Under the authority invested in me, I shall issue a decree, and I am, of course requesting the support of the competent Government Agencies, so that everything shall be processed through the right channels, and the Insurance Companies will not be the ones who suffer.[9]

With this declaration, the Jews of Germany would pay the cost of the damages of the violence directed against them.

The Armenian experience with life insurance policies differed from that of the Jews in two respects: First, the Nazis were successful in collecting half of the policy benefits of their victims, while, the Ittihadists' attempt to do the same failed, as the American and European insurers used a variety of bureaucratic maneuvers to conceal the names and identities of those insured and successfully evaded payments to the Turks. Second, Germany acknowledged the Holocaust and the non-relatedness of the mass murder of the insured Jews to acts of war; this recognition pressed the insurers to show slow but nevertheless positive signs of cooperation for a just settlement of the policies. In stark contrast to German recognition of its atrocities, Turkey's ongoing denial of the Armenian Genocide and wartime crimes against humanity helped and continues to help the insurers escape accountability.

Most surprisingly, perhaps, the documents analyzed in this book show that the insurers knew that the Turkish government was directly responsible for the murder of Armenian citizens without due judicial process. This hitherto unknown revelation offers a new primary source of documentary materials unrecognized in previous Armenian genocide studies. It is of considerable significance because death of an insured resulting directly from "acts of war" or due to "judicial condemnation" can negate policy benefits – and result in substantial "profits" to the insurers. However, this did not happen, at least initially, with the two giant insurers of the time, New York Life and Union-Vie; these two insurers honored a small number of the claims made against them, which attests to the criminal nature of the mass murders, independent of war. However, as the number of the claims started to increase, the insurers changed their policy of honoring the claims of the victims' heirs. Indeed they reverted to expediency and corporate greed and used every possible legal loophole in their means to evade payments. These deceptive strategies included demands for non-existent (and non-obtainable) death certificates, legal addresses of the deportees, lapses of premium payments and, finally, qualification of the insured victims as enemy subjects. Most ironically, requests by these insurers from their respective governments that Turkey reimburse them for the very few payments they had made to the heirs of the victims exposed the corporate greed. In the recent claims made against New York Life in Los Angeles, California, this giant insurer insisted that the claims were being pursued in an "improper venue" and that payments to the genocide victims would unduly "interfere with U.S. foreign policy." Furthermore, it further argued that the United States "had not recognized the genocide" and that payments could "upset the U.S.-Turkish relationships" and "weaken international efforts against terrorism." While the New York Life insisted that the U.S. did not recognize the Armenian Genocide, the irony is that the settlement reached between the plaintiffs and the New York Life was devoid of the word genocide and no allusion whatsoever was made that the massive dormant claims were the result of genocide. Nevertheless, one major fact remains unshaken: the insurers never used the "acts of war" clause to describe the death of their insured. Certainly such a definition could have allowed the insurers to deny payments. However it is clear that the criminal nature of the murders must have been so patent and so blatant that even the insurers hesitated to invoke war-related clauses to escape payments.

There is great importance and significance in recognition by the United States and Great Britain of the Armenian Genocide. It is both a moral imperative and has historical meaning and, moreover, it may have a practical impact by helping the Armenians see partial justice and at least some restitution. Without the recognition of these two countries it will be very difficult, and actually almost impossible, for any Armenian to get back even some of the wealth stolen from them.

Today much work needs to be done to compile a list of all the Armenians who held life policies with U.S. and European companies in the pre-genocide era. At present there is also no comprehensive assessment of the material wealth stolen from them. The wealth is enormous by any account and includes thousands of illegally confiscated homes, bank accounts and valuables (jewelry, objets d'art, etc.), shops, factories, churches, monasteries, schools and various cultural centers and buildings.[10]

We have to be aware that as time passes it will become increasingly difficult to restitute the Armenians for even some of their former wealth. Partial restitution of Jewish wealth was made in the 1990's, fifty years after the Holocaust, whereas almost a century has passed since the Armenian Genocide and no restitution has ever been made. In both cases the subject of the economic aspects of the genocides has recently gained more attention. The restitution of part of the Jewish wealth was achieved through a combination of several events and factors: West Germany recognized its crimes immediately after the war and signed a Reparations Agreement with Israel in 1952; the world largely recognized the Holocaust, which has become part of its collective memory; the Soviet Union and the Eastern Bloc have collapsed; and, finally, the U.S. administration and the White House, and President Clinton personally, have directly and actively worked towards such restitution. There was also fertile collaboration during the negotiations between the U.S. delegation and delegations of the western European countries, France, Germany and Austria (but not with the government of Switzerland). In the Armenian case the governments of the United States and England, whose companies were involved in looting the Armenian wealth, do not recognize the genocide.

The recent twin settlements of a class action lawsuit against New York Life and AXA S.A. (formerly the French Union-Vie) established an important contemporary precedent, however symbolic, for compensation and restitution of lost Armenian wealth. It is unfortunate however, that the Armenian Genocide remains unacknowledged by Turkey and many other countries, including the United States. The scrapping of the 1920 Sèvres treaty and the introduction of the infamous Treaty of Amity and Commerce in Lausanne between the United States and Turkey in 1923 not only ignored the Armenian calamity, but also codified impunity. The Lausanne Treaty constituted a "victory" for Turkey's "Turkification" agenda and an economic opportunity for the West. As articulated by the author Marjorie Housepian Dobkin, for the West "there were many issues of importance at Lausanne but oil usurped the center of the stage."[11] Technically the United States was not a party to the Lausanne Treaty, but a separate 1923 treaty signed between the United States and Turkey in Lausanne also ignored the matter of Armenian losses, thus allowing insurers and perpetrators alike to escape their obligations to the victims. This escapist behavior is in line with the traditional symbiotic negation-profit syndrome: there is profit in negation and negation in profit. In this case, as in many others, but to exceptional degree, we can see the behavior of politicians and states that prefer interests over morality. In the tension between politics and morality, the calculations of politics are very often the stronger ones.

The recent publication of the names of many (it is not clear if the list is complete) pre-genocide era insured Armenians by the New York Life after decades of concealment was made possible only after decades of protracted, passionate and frustrating litigation. This victory, however symbolic, opens a new chapter to end the suffering and bitterness of the thousands of victims' heirs who still await their recognition and justice. The heirs of the victims insured with other European companies may never be known because the policyholders are either dead and/or their heirs may never know that their parents and grandparents had purchased policies. Whether the actions of the New York Life and AXA will set a precedent for successful settlements with other U.S. and European companies remains to be seen. That the insurers' policy of concealment of the names of their insured Armenians is greatly facilitated by Turkey's denial of the Armenian Genocide is unquestionable. Writing about and discussing the Armenian Genocide in Turkey is punishable by law.[12]

One cannot imagine Germany doing anything like this today, and the Nuremberg Trials of Nazi war criminals seem to be the reason, at least in part. Concealment of the names of policy holders by the insurers and the denial of the Armenian Genocide by Turkey remain the two major obstacles for a just and fair resolution of this unique class of claims. The concealment of genocide-era life insurance policies in the United States was greatly facilitated by the existence of high-level insurer-government relationships. For example, New York Life's successful evasion of policy benefit payments was facilitated by the Lausanne Treaty, which ignored the existence of Armenians. This infamous treaty was signed in 1923 when Calvin Coolidge was president of the United States. Coolidge later refused to run for a second term as president, and chose to become a member of New York Life Insurance Company's board of directors instead.[13] Another important U.S. government figure well connected with the New York Life was Charles Evans Hughes, who was governor of New York from 1907-1910 and the U.S. Secretary of State from 1921-1925; he served twice in the United States Supreme Court, first as an associate justice from 1910-1916 and then as Chief Justice from 1930-1940. During his tenure in the Supreme Court he dissented from the prevailing opinion that a life insurance company is not involved in interstate commerce. His ardent support and loyalty to the life insurance business was apparent in his December 9, 1926 speech at the twentieth anniversary convention of the Association of Life Insurance presidents in New York in which he severely criticized government supervision of a company's business: "It would be equally disastrous if State supervision were incompetent, capricious and constituted interference rather than a help."[14] Hughes' unconditional loyalty to New York Life's interest was warmly embraced by a New York Life board member, Lawrence F. Abbott, who in his commissioned book on the history of the firm wrote: "Charles Evans Hughes probably knows more about the essential principles and administrative problems of life insurance than any other public man or private citizen not actively and daily engaged in the business."[15]

It can therefore be inferred that it was with the tacit assistance of President Coolidge and Secretary of State Hughes that New York Life succeeded in having all of its genocide era documents in the State Department "classified," thus preempting public scrutiny and claims. It is no secret that by 1930 New York Life had amassed an unprecedented fortune, as acknowledged by Abbott who noted that in less than eighty years the company had "grown from a fifty thousand dollar experiment into a billion, six hundred million dollar institution – an increase of more than thirty thousand fold, or three million percent.[16]

New York Life's president, Darwin P. Kingsley, in his 1930 speech reiterated the Company's immense gains and then proudly proclaimed that

> Even we who are engaged most aggressively in Life Insurance probably fail to grasp adequately what it is doing and what it is likely to do…. The whole country gasped a bit recently when the announcement was made that our outstanding promises to pay now total $100,000,000,000…. [t]he really amazing thing is not the size of the figures but the extent of the public service which these figures represent and the prophetic significance of that service. Life Insurance really represents a peaceful social revolution. It is democracy in a new form and in a new field; it is cooperation in a truly democratic way between units which represent all the real values of the world.[17]

The Armenian victims had bought life policies as a measure of precaution and protection for their families in the midst of a hostile environment that witnessed repeated intolerance, exploitation, and, ultimately, lethal violence from 1865 to 1925. A life insurance policy was perhaps a small way to provide material security to the survivors. The irony, however, is that plans for future generations espoused by the victims was also the dominant motto upheld by the New York Life's agents in their zealous pursuit of selling life insurance policies. In the words of New York Life's President Kingsley:

> He who appreciates the true function of life insurance and believes in its civilizing influence has nothing of the "*apres moi le deluge*" attitude towards life. His motivat-

ing thought is not "after me let the deluge come," but "after me come my son and my son's son." And so he plans for future generations.[18]

And yet the insurers ran away from their obligations, choosing a path that fostered and continues to foster denial of the Armenian Genocide. The recent settlements of the class action lawsuit against New York Life and AXA, S.A., however symbolic, open a new chapter in a class of cases where a large-scale denial of life policy contracts occurred over decades. Unilateral negation by the insurers however, neither invalidated nor deprived the contracts of their legal validity. "Law," as noted by Sir Frederick Pollock, the British contemporary expert on international law, "does not cease to exist because it is broken or even because for a time may be broken on a large scale."[19]

In Chapter 21 of the First Book of Kings, we read the story of Naboth, who had a vineyard, located in the fertile Jezreel Valley beside the palace of King Ahab. Ahab wanted Naboth's vineyard garden because it was close beside his house, but Naboth refused to give him "the inheritance of his fathers." Ahab's wife Jezebel derided him, and contrived to have Naboth stoned to death for supposedly having cursed God and the king. When Ahab heard that Naboth was dead, he went down to Naboth's vineyard, to take possession of it. But God sent the prophet Elijah the Tishbite "to meet Ahab in the vineyard and to speak to him saying 'Have you murdered and also taken possession?'" Elijah then told Ahab that he and his offspring would be punished severely because of his sin against Naboth, a fate that indeed came to pass.

It seems to us that this powerful story is in many ways quite applicable to the subject of this book. The Turkish state and individuals of its leadership, albeit of the past, murdered the Armenians, and both they and subsequent Turkish governments seized or appropriated their possessions. There is, however, no Elijah prophesying punishment, or even demanding recognition of the evil committed. The case of the Armenian Genocide demonstrates that contrary to the justice evinced in the biblical story, the evildoers have not been punished, and that justice has been neither seen nor done. Furthermore, the perpetrators, then, and the perpetrators' successors, now, continue to succeed in their ongoing denial that the crimes were committed, not because people or states deny the barefaced untruth, but because of material and pragmatic interests. Should they succeed, future generations may never know anything about the atrocity, for it will have been forgotten.

The Armenian Genocide is an extreme case of an egregious evil that has not been recognized by the heirs of the perpetrators and by many countries. The denial is possible because most countries behave in the same way or in ways which are very similar. Rather then upholding moral values, they prefer to look after and promote their own material interests. In the course of time we have learned that the attitudes and the conduct of the third party, who is neither the perpetrator nor the victim, is crucial to the occurrence of acts of genocide on the one hand, and to its denial on the other. This is of immense importance in the struggle to prevent acts of genocide in the future.

To paraphrase the title of Stuart E. Eizenstat's book *Imperfect Justice*, which deals with the restitution of Jewish properties looted and stolen during the Second World War, we can say that in the Armenian case, the situation is, as yet, one of a perfect injustice.

Notes

1.   Vahakn Dadrian, "The Historical and legal interconnections between the Armenian Genocide and the Jewish Holocaust: From impunity to retributive justice," *Yale Journal International Law* 23 (2), Summer 1998, p. 535.
2.   Vahakn N. Dadrian, The History of Armenian Genocide. Ethnic Conflict from the Balkans to Anatolia to the Caucasus (Cambridge, MA: Blue Crane, 1994), p. 259. The intense hatred expressed by the German military towards the Armenians and Jews is exemplified in the statement made a prominent German officer General Major Fritz Bronsart von Schellendorff, who served in wartime Turkey during World War I. "… the Armenian is just like the Jew, a parasite outside the confines of his homeland, sucking off the marrow of the people of the host country" (Dadrian p. 259).
3.   Davis Matas, "Prosecuting Crimes Against Humanity: The Lessons of World War I." Fordham Int'l L. J. 86, 104 (1989-1990), Cited in: Vahakn N. Dadrian, "The Historical and Legal Interconnections Between the Armenian Genocide and the Jewish Holocaust: From Impunity to Retributive Justice," *Yale Journal International Law* 23 (2), Summer 1998, p. 555.
4.   Davis Matas, in Dadrian, "The Historical and Legal Interconnections," p. 555.
5.   Israel W. Charney, "Introduction," p. ix in a monograph by Dadrian V.N., "Documentation of the Armenian Genocide in German and Austrian Sources." Reprinted from *The Widening Circle of Genocide. Genocide: A Critical Biographic Review*, vol. 3, Israel C.W. ed. (New Brunswick, NJ: Transaction Publishers, 1994). See also, Robert F. Melson, *Revolution and Genocide: On the Origins of the Armenian Genocide and the Holocaust* (Chicago: University of Chicago Press, 1992). Melson conceptualizes the processes of genocide by the comparative method drawing parallels between the Armenian and the Jewish Holocausts by arguing that both genocides evolve around "revolution contingent upon a set of factors, including twisted ideologies and ill-considered fantasies rotating around a murderous hinge and targeting a highly vulnerable population, while taking advantage of the opportunities afforded by a war."
6.   Terrence Des Pres, *Writing into the World* (New York: Viking Press, 1991), p. 261.
7.   Supra 1, Dadrian, "The Historical and Legal Interconnections," p. 555.
8.   Gerald D. Feldman, The Battle for Restitution in America's Courts, Cambridge, UK, Cambridge University Press, 2003. According to a declaration made by

Rabbi Abraham Cooper, Associate Dean of the Simon Wiesenthal Center: "There is documentary evidence that the insurance companies paid only one-half of the Jewish insurance proceeds to the Reich and kept the other half for themselves." Cited in the U.S. Supreme Court's dissenting opinion by Justice Ginsburg; American Insurance Association, et al., Petitioners v. John Garamendi, Insurance Commissioner, State of California, 02/23/2003, Docket #02-722; dissenting opinion, p.11, available online at http://www.supremecourtus.gov.

9.   "Stenographic Report on a part of the conference on the Jewish question under the presidency of Filed Marshall Goering at the Reich Ministry for Air on 12 November 1938-11 o'clock," RG 260, Office of the Military Government of the United States in Germany, Finance Division, Box 181, p. 1, NARA. Cited in Gregg J. Rickman; *Conquest and Redemption: A History of Jewish Assets from the Holocaust* (New Brunswick, NJ: Transaction Publishers, 2007), p. 16.

10.   Dikran Kouymjian, "Confiscation and Destruction: A Manifestation of the Genocide Process," *Armenian Forum* 1:3, Autumn, 1998, pp. 1-12.

11.   Marjorie Housepian Dobkin, *"Smyrna 1922: The Destruction of a City,* 2nd edition (New York: Newmark Press, 1998), p. 223.

12.   *New York Times*, June 14, 1998, A8. See also R.G. Hovannisian (ed.), *Remembrance and Denial: The Case of the Armenian Genocide* (Detroit, MI, Wayne State University Press, 1998) and Roger W. Smith, Eric Markusen, and Robert J. Lifton, "Professional Ethics and the Denial of the Armenian Genocide," *Holocaust and Genocide Studies*, 9:1, Spring 1995, pp. 1-22. The recent ban of a scholarly symposium in Turkey, planned for May 25–27, 2005, on the theme of "Ottoman Armenians during the Decline of the Empire: Issues of Scientific Responsibility and Democracy" is a concrete reminder of Turkey's penchant to conceal the facts. The conference organizers had invited non-Armenian Turkish scholars whose work produced facts that were not in accord with the official Turkish line. Justice Minister Cemil Çiçek, speaking on the floor of the parliament, called the Turkish organizers of the conference "traitors" and accused them of "stabbing the Turkish nation in the back." In a press conference held by Professor Edhem Eldem, of the symposium's host, Bogazici University (Bosphorus) lamented "that the one that would lose the most as a consequence of this ban will unfortunately be Turkey." Perseverance and hard work by the Turkish scholars paid off and the conference finally took place in September 2005. See: Sebnem Arsu, "Seminar on 1915 Massacre of Armenians to Go Ahead," *New York Times*, September 24, 2005, p. 3.

13.   Lawrence Fraser Abbott, *The Story of NYLIC: A History of the Origin and Development of the New York Life Insurance Company from 1845–1929* (Newark, NJ: A.S. Browne, Inc., 1930), p. 167.

14.   Supra, p. 313. In a 1923 resolution brought before the U.S. Senate, Senator King accused Hughes of total subservience to American business and alleged that Hughes placed "at the disposal of the American Business interests in the Near East the United States Naval Squadron," which was dispatched there to protect American interests and foster "business" for American firms. See: The Lausanne Treaty and the Chestor Oil," *Arm Rev*, 73, 1982, pp. 89–90.

15.   Supra, p. 312.

16.   Supra, introductory remarks in Abbott's book.

17.   Ibid., p. 327.

18.   Ibid., p. 289.

19.   Supra 1, Dadrian, p. 559.

Appendix 1

M.-W.

New York, March 20, 1915.

Hon. William J. Bryan,
    Secretary of State,
        Washington, D. C.

Dear Sir:-

Confirming my conversation of yesterday with your
Mr. Rose, Foreign Trade Adviser, I beg to say:

New York Life Insurance Company, a corporation
of and domiciled in New York, has been transacting the
business of life insurance in the Turkish Empire for some
twenty years past, so that it now has outstanding contracts
of insurance with subjects of that Empire aggregating in
the neighborhood of $10,281,134.

After the breaking out of the European War, and
in August last, the Company discontinued making new contracts of insurance in the Turkish Empire, and in October,
1914, determined permanently to withdraw from Turkey, and
pursuant to this determination there and then duly cancelled
its contract with all soliciting agents in the Empire.

Subsequently, and on the 4th of December, 1914,

Hon. William J. Bryan - (2)

the Turkish Empire passed a law imposing such exacting conditions for the right of foreign insurance companies to do
business in Turkey, that the Company would not have complied
therewith for the privilege of doing business in the Empire
even if it had not already withdrawn therefrom.   Among the
conditions imposed by this law was the requirement to deposit
in a bank designated by the Minister of Commerce a cash
caution of from 5,000 L to 15,000 L.

Having withdrawn from the Turkish Empire for
the purpose of new insurance, this Company desires to
fulfill all its existing insurance contracts precisely
as made without unnecessary delay or inconvenience to its
policyholders.   For this purpose, and this only, it wishes
to maintain an office in the Turkish Empire without subjecting itself to the requirements or penalties of the insurance
law.

Obviously such an office will be for the conven-
ience of its Turkish insured.   Otherwise its policyholders
in Turkey must deal with the Company either at its Home
Office in New York, or at some office in Europe outside
of the Turkish Empire.   This necessarily will involve
inconvenience, expense and delay. For example, if the
Company is not permitted to maintain a liquidating office

Hon. William J. Bryan, - (3)

in the Empire, the beneficiary of a Turkish insured who
wishes to make proofs of death must send into a foreign
country for blanks for proofs of death and submit to all
the inconvenience and delay incident to dealing at such
long range.   All this the Company hopes to obviate by
maintaining a liquidating office within the Empire.

Therefore may we not ask for the good offices
in our behalf of the American Ambassador to the Ottoman
Empire to the end that the Company may obtain permission
to maintain a local office or offices in the Turkish
Empire for the liquidation of outstanding contracts with
its Turkish insured, without subjecting itself to the new
Turkish insurance law?

Yours faithfully,

General Counsel.

Appendix 2

NEW-YORK LIFE INSURANCE COMPANY,

346 BROADWAY, NEW YORK.

VICE-PRESIDENT'S OFFICE.

November 20, 1922.

To the Honorable,
      The Secretary of State,
            Washington, D.C.

Sir,-

In connection with the negotiations which we understand are about to be conducted with representatives of the
Turkish Government for the establishment of peace with the
nations with which Turkey has been at war, and in which
negotiations we understand this Government may participate, we
beg to lay before you certain claims of the New York Life Insurance Company.

The New York Life Insurance Company, as part of its general
foreign business, had written insurance upon the lives of many
persons who were residents within and subjects of the Ottoman
Empire as it existed before the War. As required by the insurance laws of the State of New York, and in accordance with established insurance practice, the Company maintained a reserve
against such insurance based on the standard tables of life
expectancy. Much of this insurance was written upon the lives
of subject peoples, such as the Armenians and others who have,
during the years since the outbreak of the European War, been

153

-2-

The Honorable, The Secretary of State,

subjected to massacre and illegal killing and fatal exposure by or with the acquiescence of the Turkish authorities. In consequence of such illegal action and wilful failure of the Turkish Government to protect the lives of those within its jurisdiction, the New York Life Insurance Company has incurred very heavy and extraordinary losses through the lives of its insured having been prematurely terminated by such violent death.

Insofar as records are now available, and these are but partial, this Company has actually paid out, or had claims filed against it, as insurance on the lives of persons killed within the Ottoman Empire by massacre or in consequence of deportation, substantially the following sums:

    On French franc policies, frs. 1,772,538.
    On Sterling policies,   £   45,214.
    On dollar policies, $ 7,938.

After deducting the reserves against these policies, there remains:

    Francs,   1,348,775.
    Pounds,   26,873.
    Dollars,   6,141.

These sums, at current rates of exchange, amount to approximately $230,000, and measure the loss so far suffered by this Company, for which we believe the Turkish Government is, and should be held, responsible. The ultimate loss will doubtless prove to be greater than has been developed by the claims so far filed. We respectfully urge that the Department of State present and

The Honorable, The Secretary of State, -3-

support a claim for reimbursement by the Turkish Government of these losses suffered by the New York Life Insurance Company.

The New York Life Insurance Company is not the only insurance company similarly situated. An important French Insurance Company, known as La Compagnie l'Union is in a somewhat similar situation. This Company has already filed a claim with the French Government, a copy of which we enclose herewith, and which deals more fully with some of the technical aspects of the situation. We believe it likely that the French Government will, in connection with the pending negotiations, seek to have this claim of La Compagnie l'Union recognized by the Turkish Government, and we respectfully suggest that the similar situation of the New York Life Insurance Company be laid before the appropriate American officials abroad, to the end that they may, if the Department approves, collaborate with the French officials who will be dealing with this problem to the end that the Turkish Government may be brought to recognize in principle their responsibility in this class of cases and that recognition of this principle may be subsequently availed of to secure satisfaction of the losses incurred by the New York Life Insurance Company in consequence of the actions of the Turkish Government which are here complained of.

We may also point out that we have been advised that the Turkish Government proposes, or is considering, the confiscation

The Honorable, The Secretary of State, -4-

of claims for insurance upon the lives of those Armenians
and others who have been massacred, with a view to collecting itself the insurance upon the lives of its victims.
This possibility, as well as the general situation here referred to was laid before the Department by the New York Life
Insurance Company's letter of February 26, 1919, to the then
Secretary of State.

We are, dear Sir,

Respectfully yours,

Vice-President.

Index

For Product Safety Concerns and Information please contact our EU
representative GPSR@taylorandfrancis.com Taylor & Francis Verlag GmbH,
Kaufingerstraße 24, 80331 München, Germany

Batch number: 08158437

Printed by Printforce, the Netherlands